LABOUR OF
LOVE

LABOUR OF
LOVE

THE "PARTLY-POLITICAL" DIARY OF
A CABINET MINISTER'S WIFE

BY

JANET JONES

Politico's

First published in Great Britain 1999
Published by Politico's Publishing
8 Artillery Row
Westminster
London
SW1P 1RZ

Tel 020 7931 0090
Fax 020 7828 8111
Email politicos@artillery-row.demon.co.uk
Website http://www.politicos.co.uk

First Published in Hardback 1999

A catalogue record of this book is available from the British Library.

ISBN 1902301072

Printed and bound in Great Britain by St. Edmundsbury Press.
Cover Design by Advantage

For

Felicity Anne Campion

(née Kadera)

August 27th 1951 to March 18th 1998

who would have been as amused

PREFACE

I am a teacher in South London and an unpublished writer of other books ... there are a lot of us about.

However, there is only one government of the day and, in this case, only one change of government in eighteen years and only one radical reform of the House of Lords in hundreds of years. I happen to have married a man who is working amongst all that. And I have kept a diary.

I am not proud of this book: despite my independence, my education, my disapproval of myself, it rides on the back of my husband's working life. Without that, nobody would be interested and you would not be reading this. But I have swallowed my pride. My husband would tell you that I am not interested in his work. I would say that I may not like the work or want to do it myself, but that is not the same as not being interested.

I went out for the evening for the first time in two months in February 1997. I was asked what it was like for Ivor as he and his colleagues were preparing for power; what it was like for me being at the centre of things. There was an impression that he and—by association—I are at The Centre of Things. That there is a centre of things. I don't think there is. As George Eliot wrote of Mr Vincy: he 'had as little of his own way as if he had been a prime minister: the force of circumstances was easily too much for him...'

Janet Jones
South London, 1999

1996

Wednesday, 13th March

I am reading in the morning because I have a year's unpaid leave from Lambeth College. Ivor rings: 'Have you heard the news from Scotland?'

'No.'

28 children in Primary One have been shot by a man with four guns.

I cannot think of anything to say. I watch the news.

Ivor took our little boy of six to school this morning. He is wearing a bright red sweatshirt, identical to the Dunblane children's.

I ring my Oldest Friend. She saw her three children in dark-blue sweatshirts off to school in Scotland this morning. She is feeling sick, and cannot eat her lunch. In the end she says ' ...You can only pray to God.' In the 40 years I have known her, since I was four and she was five and a fortnight, I have never heard her say anything like that.

I walk the dog and think about Dunblane.

I go to school early to pick up William and I stroke him when he has a drink of milk and a chocolate biscuit:

'Get your hands off me!'

Thursday, 14th March

There are prayers for Dunblane at school: 'The teachers reminded us of it.'

Sunday, 17th March

Ivor is being asked to perform in a Christmas concert in the Lords in December. He wonders if he and a few other Labour peers can sing 'The

Stately Homes of England'. He thinks 'Iolanthe' is safer.

It doesn't much matter. They are going to abolish the hereditary rights of peers to a seat in the House of Lords, so none of it will make sense for much longer.

Monday, 25th March
We had pork for lunch on Sunday. The BSE crisis looms large. Then we went to Kew Gardens

Tuesday, 26th March
Ivor says of BSE: 'This could bring the government down.'

We had supper on Saturday with Colleen and Merlyn Rees. They are Ivor's oldest friends from all his years in British politics. Merlyn has been Home Secretary once and Secretary of State for Northern Ireland. The New Labour Government will have no experience.

'No new government has experience,' says Merlyn.

Thursday, 28th March
I drove to Junction 15 on the M4 and met my brother, Jones The Business, at eight in the morning. We drove on to our family bungalow in Devonshire. We have spent as much time there as possible since 1958. Some of it needs rescuing. The old wall is down and the new wall is up, the new windows are in, the roof is half on and the new bathroom is built. The electrician said that when he came out with the plumber, the plumber said: 'Who would want to live here!', while he, the electrician, said: 'What a perfect place to live!'

The daffodils were coming into flower. And on a walk we met a lamb with its umbilical cord hanging and a bloodstained coat. It wobbled. Across the valley we could hear the men working on the roof: sounds of iron on slate.

Friday, 12th April
Ivor picks up Lady Cynthia Asquith's Diaries (1914-1918) which I have been reading.
'Dreadful ... dreadful book ... party, party, party while millions were dying.'

The Tories lose the by-election, turning their 10,000 majority into a New Labour 14,000 majority. The longer this government runs, the worse its results will become. If they manage to go another year, until next spring, they'll be drummed out of town. Then New Labour will have to deal with a population with high expectations of them. They may be drummed out themselves in 2002 unless they can meet those expectations. Yet the Tories may fall apart with internal rifts in the meantime, just as Old Labour did. The public won't vote for them.

William is throwing off a virus, not before giving it to my brother, Jones The Business. He wonders if he has got rid of it now his uncle has got it. Ivor is in Swansea for the night.

I am looking forward to the beginning of term next week: whole days to myself to get on with my book. In fact, on Tuesday I am going to spend the day with Priscilla finalising it. Priscilla and I have only known each other since we were 14. She has been in and around London publishing all her working life.

In the meantime, this diary is the best vehicle I can think of for me to continue to write through the next few years: it lends itself to the fractured nature of my life: family life, earning a living, writing, Ivor's work, running a home, some social life—with a small 's'—and on and on. With a diary, I can work at odd times, picking up an hour here or there, without the need for sustained concentration. In the long run this could be interesting.

There are so many changes afoot: the local one of the demolition of the hereditary peerage within the House of Lords; the demise of 18 years of Conservative Government; the arrival of the New Labour Government; the congealing of Europe; the break-up of the USSR; the rising power and influence in the East; the USA's struggle to be an international policeperson; moving on in Science and Art and Thought...

William has come in. Could he kill a dinosaur? Could I kill a dinosaur? Could Daddy? Could he kill me? Could he kill the dog? I didn't think the dog would let him kill her. But if she did?

The telephone rings. The garage, who I gave up on ten days ago, are ready to take in my car. (My car was hit by a coach when it was parked outside the house all by itself and is dented.) The garage can't have my car now. I've arranged for it to go to another garage—who can't take it until I've had the OK from the insurance company.

It is difficult to sustain Great Thoughts against the killing of dinosaurs and the denting of cars. A good example of why a diary is a good idea at this time.

Tuesday, 16th April

I caught the train to Royston and spent the day with Priscilla working on *The Magic Blob*. This is my last book which is written for children. She had picked up the small-but-important mistakes and the lopsidedness of the chapter lengths. If we could become a little team...

Ivor is worried about his speech tonight on beef.

Friday, 19th April

I finished *The Magic Blob* yesterday. I had thought it would take a fortnight but it took seven hours' hard work. So I posted it off to Priscilla, today. Then she gives me a disc and I hope my younger stepson can tell me how to get it printed out.

The Israelis are bombing the Lebanese.

On Monday I can get to grips with *The Everywhere Chair*. That is my next book. Also for children.

Wednesday, 24th April

Sara and Len, neighbours and colleagues, ring. Can they bring their daughter Florence round? They are off to St Thomas's Hospital to have the baby. They arrive and Sara is hunched in the back of the car. Len is distracted but tells me Florence has had no breakfast. I dress myself and give Florence breakfast and she cleans her teeth and I re-do her hair. Ivor walks the dog. William does his piano. Florence starts drawing. I get William's After-School-Club picnic. Florence has no coat so I find her a jacket of William's. We all set off for school.

'Will the baby be out now?' asks Florence.

'No, babies take a long time to come out. Sometimes they stop and have a rest.

'Does it hurt?' asks William.

'No, they have painkillers and St Thomas's has the best painkillers in the world.'

We drop Ivor off on the north end of Lambeth Bridge. Reach school. Wave William off. Take Florence into the Nursery and explain what is happening. Buy cigars. Go home. Put laundry in. Start work.

10.30 a.m. Len rings. They had a little boy at 9.30. All well.

Work.

Put out laundry. Put in more laundry.

Work.

Have lunch. Bread mouldy. Watch the news. The Tory Right have been told by Major they are in 'cloud cuckoo land'. The government have been told by the Commission that they must present written proposals to solve the beef problem.

Work.

Write this.

Tell Ivor of the new baby. He says 'Sniff the pork... just have a sniff at it.'

Go and get William who's lost another tooth. Give him his supper. Helen and Homer come. Helen works in the Treasury. Homer is her and my brother, Jones The Business's son and my nephew. William's cousin.

Childhood friend rings. They have a new baby too and it doesn't sleep.

Ivor rings. I go and pick him up. He has been allowing me to use his car while mine is in the garage.

Go and get Chinese takeaway for supper. Never sniffed the pork.

Thursday, 25th April

Pick up spanking smart car from the garage: 'Nothing the matter with the car at all ... you'll get another ten years out of it.'

Pick camellia for the new baby's household.

Gather William and his banana and pick up Florence and take them both to school.

Marge, Ivor's friend from New York, rings. When and where is Ivor giving her and her friend lunch? I have no idea.

Mother, Jones The Pictures, rings. They are going to stay with Jones The Business, and Helen (of the Treasury), and Homer.

I ring Ivor. Fix to take dog to vet. He's had a letter from Blair: will he chair the committee on the reform of the House of Lords? Ivor rings me back. Have I sniffed the pork? No, but I will make sure we have some supper. Will I also get us a hotel in Florida? We are planning a visit to my older stepson in the US and would like to fit in Florida too. I ring Florida. I get us a hotel. And a car.

I ring vet. Nearly a whole morning has gone and I have done no work. I have my lunch with the news. The IRA have tried to blow up Hammersmith Bridge. Go to Sainsbury's for two suppers for two.

Ring my cousin, nearly-finished-training-at-St-Thomas's, to see if she can babysit for our friend Richard's birthday party and the State dinner. She has to ring the pub where she is working to see where she is on the rota.

Ivor comes home. We play Snap.

I throw out the pork without sniffing it. We have duck breasts, salad and homemade bread. I drink too much Hungarian white wine.

I talk to Ivor about my idea for this diary. He says, 'You'll have to get the politics right. Come and listen to the debates. It'll be more about Lambeth

College.' I say that may not be a bad parallel. I teach at Lambeth College. I first taught at Vauxhall College and was employed by the Inner London Education Authority. Then ILEA was demolished by a government. Vauxhall College and I were moved into the care of the local authority: Lambeth. Then all the colleges within Lambeth became one college: Lambeth College. Then we were taken out of the control of the local authority and put under the Further Education Funding Council: FEFC. It nearly speaks for itself.

Ivor's committee to reform the House of Lords is to meet in private and report directly to Blair. The other members are Derry Irvine, Ray Plant, Donald Dewar, Jack Straw, Mo Mowlam and Ann Taylor. Ivor said Ted Graham, Labour's Chief Whip in the Lords, is very hurt. He'd written to Blair to say he'd like him on it; he knows a great deal about the nuts and bolts of the Lords. Why will the others be there? Derry will be Lord Chancellor, Ray is a constitutionalist, Donald Chief Whip, Jack Straw is Shadow Home Secretary, Mo? ... Mo?—whose sister's caretaking job I inherited in 1974 and who dropped in and out as she passed through London—I think Mo will be Home Secretary. Ivor doesn't think it's as subtle as that: 'It will all have been decided in a hurry'. And Ann Taylor will be Leader of the House.

Tuesday, 30th April

Our friend Richard's 60th birthday party: Thirty six of us in a Coin Street basement. It was my cousin's turn on the pub rota so Monica, William's London Godmother, babysat.

Wednesday, 1st May

Priscilla's disc arrives so I can start making copies of my book and then send them off to publishers. I'm excited, which is sad as I'm bound to be rejected and disappointed.

Saturday, 4th May.

Cousin is babysitting tonight. Ivor has his ritual struggle with the white tie and tails from the successful London tailor, Moss Bros.

'At this moment,' I say, 'there are several hundred men all over London cursing and fumbling.'

'I doubt that', says Ivor, 'they'll all have been ready hours ago.'

I disagree: these occasions smell of male sweat, discomfort and, in the case of everybody who does not rely on Moss Bros, mothballs.

We are driven to the Palace. Ivor's shirt and collar creak and shift, like a ship moored against a dock. There are dog hairs gracing my frock. The man who opens the car door for me, wearing a uniform you would expect to see in a theatre or on a screen, does not try to look up my skirt. This is not always the case. We then go and mill around with everybody else who isn't in the Royal Party and look at the pictures. The Rembrandt is my favourite outside the self-portrait in Vienna. Then we all have our hands shaken by the Royal Party (the guest of honour is the French President, Chirac) and go into dinner.

I find my place between the Ivory Coast Ambassador and Viscount Cranborne who is Leader of the House of Lords and Lord Privy Seal. Ivor is his Opposition version. No two tail coats are the same shade of black. One or two look as if they had been consigned to the dressing-up cupboard and pulled out again in this emergency. Indeed as if they had been donated by one generation and rescued by another.

There is no doubt about the smell undisguised by the heavy wafts of scent from the sweetpeas that decorate the tables. The tables are stunning ... flowers ... silver ... gold ... crystal ... linen ... sometimes there is a little note telling us about the china. I pick up the china and look at it. I am sure Viscount Cranborne finds this vulgar but of course is too proper to appear to notice. What's the point of beautiful things if they are not to be looked at? There is wine and speeches and toasts and national anthems. The wine is brilliant and the food is not, but neither are helped by the smells which disturb the palate. No chef would choose to have sweetpeas and mothballs under diners' noses.

Tuesday, 7th May

The alarm goes at 5.15 a.m. By 6.00 I'm at Heathrow. By 8.00 I'm round Bristol and we stop for the dog and me to pee. I'm at the house before 9.30. I start clearing up. The electrician, the plumber, the carpetmen and the builder all arrive. I clean and clean. Eventually all depart. I start back to London and stop at 10 p.m. at Leigh Delamere to find they have started serving breakfast. I drive over Lambeth Bridge at midnight.

Thursday, 9th May

Still feeling stiff. At least the end is in sight. Even the furniture and the washing machine are getting organised. Of course there is plenty of cleaning left to do and nobody has begun to think about anything outside the house.

The first draft of *The Everywhere Chair* is three-quarters written. It's gone fast given the endless interruptions.

Friday, 7th June

Writing now, I realise that I did not take this diary to the USA. We had a family holiday in Pennsylvania and Florida. The only thing that went wrong was that I was nearly banned from the flight out. The tickets were bought in the name 'Richard' but I have my own name on my passport so the name on my ticket and the name on my passport did not match. The official we came up against at Heathrow was as difficult as he could be. In the end he sent me off to another queue, at the end of which I had to have my ticket reissued. This all took time and increased stress—I remember a Swiss official pointing out the same thing in Geneva. There was no question of them not letting me on the flight.

Yesterday I got two publishers' rejections of my book. The day before that I'd had another. One rejection to come.

I am just getting back to *The Everywhere Chair* when the phone rings again. It is my boss's boss from Lambeth College to say she has no work for me in September. Nobody else has any English teaching for me. She suggests I put in for the Lambeth College job advertised in the TES last Friday.

The terms on which I took my year's unpaid leave were clear: I had the right to come back to a job; the college had the right to change the nature of that job. There was no question of my having to re-apply. I do not bother to say any of this to this woman. It is seems that some of the others took hold of my work while I was away and are now refusing to let it go. She will not stand up to them; the easy thing for her to do is to make one difficult phone call—to me.

This is very serious. From the financial point of view first; I'm committed to debts taken on the assumption that I'd have my job back; and the new work is all in Norwood, miles from home and school. I am hurt. Those people who I tried to protect and to share my work with, have cut me out when my back was turned. So much for my 20 years of getting better and better at my job.

Monday, 10th June

I spend one and a half hours picking up two rejected *The Magic Blob*s. The traffic and the sun are heavy. Then I settle to two hours' work.

I ring another woman at work (boss's boss's boss ... there are two more above her) and am told I can have an ALS job, (that is one of the jobs advertised in the TES) but I must have an informal interview. Cheek.

ALS stands for Assisted Learning Support. That means teaching groups or individuals who are not literate or numerate enough to do the work they are supposed to be doing. This can be 50% of our students.

While William is at French Club I go to Smith's and find a present for the new baby next door and I survey the children's books: Just William, Arthur Ransome, F. Hodgson Burnett, E. Nesbit, Pooh, Alice, then the contemporary established authors: Roald Dahl, Jill Murphy and two new unknowns they are trying to make a go of. What a world of exclusivity I am failing to join.

When we get home I cook William's supper, feed the dog and the gerbils and finish the laundry. Then we visit the new baby next door.

While William is eating his supper I get two calls from immediate colleagues at work to show solidarity and I make one call to the union. The union is unequivocal that I should not have any interview. Going to one suggests that I do not have a job.

Cousin comes to baby-sit and plays cowboys and indians while I change and check the contact number at the Italian Embassy. We arrive last and are rushed straight into dinner. I like the tapestries on the walls. The retired British diplomat on my left talks about Tehran ... the Koran ... Muslim Fundamentalists' cruelty to women. The Austrian on my right describes watching Russians shoot Dutch conscripts when he was nine. His parents sent him to collect the identity discs, which were thrown in the fire with the bodies; he burnt his fingers but it meant that his parents could get messages out to the next of kin. He was caught once, with his little brother and they were both beaten. It was also his job to milk the cow they kept hidden. He did this regularly until he was shot in the back. His half-Jewish stepfather managed to escape from Dachau to a salt mine by slitting the throat of an SS officer and walking back to Austria in his uniform. My dinner companion is now 87.

I only hear this after we have talked about Brian Urquhart at the UN. He is surprised that I have read Brian's book, which is a serious book; wives are not supposed to be serious at dinner tables.

When we get home there have been two more sympathetic calls from colleagues. Ivor tells me he was asked: 'Is your wife a painter or a writer?'. He also tells me this is not a compliment: 'It's those clothes.'

Sunday, 16th June

A nasty week is over. Several days of work lost. Hours on the telephone. Going to see my boss's boss's boss's boss ... The Power behind The Throne of The Boss. I have a job for September and I have not had an interview. The union did their stuff and my immediate colleagues did theirs. The Power did her stuff and I did mine. Not only do I have a job, but I also have a choice of which job. I can either have my old one back, running the English 'A' Levels in Norwood, or I can move into ALS anywhere I like. If I take my old job, I will have to do all my work in Norwood, miles from anywhere (when I was working there I used to irritate people by saying I was going back to London when I finished for the day). If I do ALS I can base myself at Vauxhall, which is five minutes from home if the traffic is bad and six minutes from William's school. ALS, however, is known to kill you from the neck up. On the other hand, taking back my old work in Norwood would leave one or two noses well out of joint and a very unhappy English 'team' for me to try and work with.

I'll have to go for being brain-dead in Vauxhall.

Monday 17th June

I rang The Power and said Vauxhall, please. The dog is walked, the laundry is done and here I am: lovely study, lovely desk, lovely time, lovely peace, lovely home ... but I need money.

Ivor has seen Angus Ogilvy; the Prince of Wales wants real live Labour people round him, real advice and he doesn't know anybody. And then Angus Ogilvy drove Ivor back to the House.

Ivor fears a New Labour Government will be no different from Lambeth College, worse indeed. He has had a call out to see Blair for weeks now. (I got to see The Power in under 24 hours.)

'How can I consult him?' wonders Ivor.

I say he will have to make decisions on his own. What else can he do?

Ivor says do I mind if he says something, but I need to do something about my hair. I make the point that I am not a Painted Lady.

Priscilla has four agents' addresses and numbers for me to try. I'll do that as soon as I get my fourth rejection and my fourth *The Magic Blob* back.

I went to a private view. There were two pictures I'd like to have taken home: a grey and clumsy West Country scene and some precision-painted asparagus. Nearly a photograph turned on to a computer screen, except that would not be delicate enough. The greens were good. The first was Art, the second was a Technical Triumph. Very few can do both.

Tuesday, 18th June

They defeated the Government in the Lords last night by 34 votes, on the introduction of Nursery Vouchers. A nonsense scheme. £1,000 worth of education a year to those who can already afford, it and are already spending it, and £1,000 worth to those who couldn't afford to make up the difference to buy anything. There was much plotting and trotting to and fro to achieve this: pretending to go home and then rushing back from hiding to vote. It's called an ambush.

'Kids' stuff,' says Ivor. Well, yes actually.

Thursday, 20th June

It has only this morning occurred to me that if I sell this diary and if it then sold well—which is possible—I would have far more chance of selling *The Magic Blob* and *The Everywhere Chair*.

I had to go to Lambeth College yesterday. More stories of who has and hasn't got a job; who has been given a job on a nod and a wink and who hasn't.

Last week I was party to taking 38 six-year-olds to St James's Park. We looked at the trees, described them, felt them, measured them (by holding hands round them or putting our fingers round the saplings) but nobody actually knew what any of them were so I'm not sure how much we learnt. We had a picnic on the grass, causing much excitement among the pigeons; we played in the play area; we walked over to Buckingham Palace and were asked to count the windows. It was a distraction from everything else in existence.

The Government has been found to have acted illegally by denying benefit to asylum seekers. A man has been dragged screaming from a Methodist chapel for deportation. He has been here illegally for 17 years and has a British wife and child.

The British have been told their beef will be considered for export if they stop blocking EU business, start culling BSE vulnerable cattle and set up proper checks on the safety of the herds and the processing of the meat and other beef products. A lot of people suffer while the rest of us sit and watch a government die on its feet. Like the cows.

I watch a spot of Ascot on BBC1: 45,000 people watching half a dozen horses. Ivor has started getting invitations to these things: Ascot, Wimbledon, Glyndebourne, as the prospect of a Labour Government gets closer. He doesn't accept them. His politics don't work in enclosures, courts or boxes, nor in Society. His works in meetings, debates, speeches and on the telephone.

Sunday, 23rd June

By ten past eight we are swimming in the training pool at the Queen Mother's Sports' Centre. We have the whole pool to ourselves. Monica, William's London Godmother, comes in from the big pool to tell us about her Eurotunnel job.

We have six cousins to lunch and then follow them into Stockwell to admire gardens and have an old-fashioned garden tea: enamel teapots, china cups (no cup matches its saucer), homemade gooey cakes, even a few panama hats. Come home smelling and seeing roses and jasmine and lawns.

From my window I can see St George's Crosses tied to aerials on cars, lorries, motorbikes, all because England beat Spain at football and are playing in the semi-finals against I-don't-know-who on Wednesday evening. They still talk of the World Cup in 1966. This is the European competition. Our sights are sinking.

Four of us took 20 six-year-olds to Westminster Abbey last week. We were smiled at by the lunchtime crowds as we crocodiled our way down Victoria Street. We passed a motorbike squashed under a lorry but nobody said anything. We were met by the School Governor who is also an Abbey guide who showed us where the monks slept, played, washed their hands and hung their towels. She pointed out where 26 of them were buried during the Black Death. We saw where they had their meetings and their route through St Faith's Chapel into the Abbey itself. She showed us where the monks sat and asked us to imagine that we were the only people there. She showed us where the monarchs were crowned, the chair they sat in and Edward the Confessor's tomb. We finished at the memorial to Angela Burdett-Coutts, who founded the children's school.

A stranger gave Jamie Lee £1 to buy an ice cream which caused consternation among the adults and joy to Jamie.

Friday, 28th June

The turmoil over my job is calming. I met my new boss's boss in Brixton and tried to get some of the nitty-gritty details clear. As far as I can make out I shall have little to do for the first four or five weeks. After that I will be marking about 400 assessments and teaching the many who can't do them. At least I will be back on the payroll.

The house looms, alarmingly unprepared for the summer. We need furniture, a cooker, a washing machine, curtains, rods to hang the curtains on, mats, fireguard. It's endless and next to impossible to do from London.

Monday, 8th July

Busy.

Thursday was the worst. I left London at 4.50 a.m. with the car loaded with furniture, curtains, lampshades and the dog. We reached the house at 8.20. We left about five and I got home about ten feeling ill with exhaustion.

Gwen, my grandmother's oldest friend, came for the weekend and Ivor caught the 7 a.m. train to Swansea, to be driven back tomorrow for the Mandela dinner, and back to Swansea the next morning and back again the next day.

William was ill and the school rang me up on Friday to go and fetch him.

For most of last week Ivor was leaving before 9 and not getting home until midnight. He is very tired. At which point my mother, Jones The Pictures, rings to say my father, Jones The Books, is in the Royal Free Hospital with his asthma; they may discharge him in a few hours.

Tuesday, 9th July

Jones The Books came out yesterday evening.

Ivor is due back this evening. Sara is bringing Florence and the less new baby to tea. My cousin is babysitting. We have the Mandela dinner: 'The Queen is a very gracious lady. I am sure she will make a country boy at rest.'

When Ivor was asked to a discreet dinner to meet the Queen's men— because she was anxious about the lack of contact with the Opposition and was uncertain how much she might be diminished by a new regime—he was told she is a devout woman, says her prayers and tries to do her best every day and then goes to bed. And she does the same thing the next day, and the next, and the next. He was able to say that the Queen will not be affected at all. Though as the hereditary peers lose their voting rights they will not be part of the Palace of Westminster and the Queen's men will focus more on their lands and their businesses and their horses.

Nelson Mandela shook my hand, looked me in the eye and said: 'Hello, how are you?'

I became smiling jelly. Ivor then said,

'Mr. President, I am VERY pleased to see you here.'

'I am very pleased to be here,' he replied. He wore a black silk shirt, with tiny white edging and no tie. His top button was done up. The rest of us were stuffy and without style. There was the usual smell of mothballs everywhere.

I was sitting between Sir Robin and Sir Robin. They muddled themselves up and one Sir Robin sat in the other Sir Robin's place. This matters, because the placement is rigorous and one Sir Robin is more important than the other Sir Robin as far as establishment protocol is concerned. The Less Important Sir Robin, who belonged on my right, turned out to be Sir Robin (now Lord) Renwick, ex-ambassador to South Africa. He sat next to me for two hours without asking a single question. He told me things. He behaved as if I had no mind, knowledge or thought of my own. This continued until I had volunteered enough opinions that he changed tack, nearly managing to disguise what he was doing, and offered more thoughtful pearls: the mistake Nelson Mandela had made by not following his (The Less Important Sir Robin's) advice and meeting Chief Buthelezi the moment he came out of prison; the problems of moving investment into South Africa ... the need for that investment if the whole of Africa is not to be destabilised. I tried not to be a swine to his pearls and started to talk of Nelson Mandela's book. Oh, The Less Important Sir Robin told me, that was not The Real Thing because The Real Thing had been destroyed in prison. I did not think so. I said I thought it had been hidden first and smuggled out later. I was told not.

The More Important Sir Robin, on my left, was Sir Robin Butler, Secretary to the Cabinet. I had last seen him in a documentary about the Brockwell Lido (I think) swimming hard. I mentioned it. 'My daughter said it couldn't do me any harm.' He said. His next 'holiday' is a working trip to Africa; he thought he would read Nelson Mandela's book while he was there; what was it called?

The other person I shall continue to remember who was at the table was Trevor McDonald, the newscaster. His pleasure, as Nelson Mandela was escorted into dinner by the Queen, followed by other ex-prisoners and the Royal Party, reminded me all over again how big is the sea-change that has taken place.

These sea changes can be too big for some of us to grasp: at a similar dinner for Zimbabwe and President Mugabe I heard a local guest disapproving:

'What do you think of them? I don't think much of them, not much education. When I asked the one I was next to what university he went to, he wasn't very clear .'

'When you are in prison,' I informed this Horror, 'you cannot go to university. And', I decided not to spare her, 'I believe the President was not even allowed out of prison to go to his baby's funeral.'

I finished off by guessing that, nonetheless, the President had more degrees by correspondence than the Horror and I put together.

After dinner I found myself with Tommy Strathclyde. He is the Government Chief Whip in the House of Lords. Ted Graham is his

Opposition version.

Tommy Strathclyde has a brand new daughter, his second. I asked if he thought daughters should inherit. No. He has a nephew. If you bring in daughters you will have a whole lot of problems. Perhaps he has an elder sister who might turn up and be difficult.

He is much concerned that he might be disestablished by a New Labour Government.

'But you'll still have your family, your land and your business. You just won't have a vote.' said I.

He was not much comforted. He looked glum:

'... a whole new set of problems nobody's thought of ...'

'I think they have,' I said. 'You can't in your heart think it's right,' I tried. But he does think it is right.

The Cecils came over. These Cecils are Viscount Cranborne, Leader of the House of Lords and Lord Privy Seal, and Viscountess Cranborne. They all think it is right. New Labour is the rise of the bourgeoisie. The old aristocracy are on their way out of the House of Lords and when, for a moment, they think it might actually happen, they don't like Ivor at all. Then they stop believing it will happen ... Ivor's a decent chap really ... not one of us but an honorary one of us. He is not one of them. He is a self-made man. And his sons and daughter are having to make their own ways.

Over the next year or so we may see another bloodless revolution. Just as the National Trust has bought or been given lands for the nation to enjoy, so the country's second chamber will be taken from individual families for the self-made for their working lifetimes—self-made through church, politics, art, science and government service. All routes to all achievement that you can think of except inheritance. Of course you can always inherit advantages of home and education and opportunity ... but not that seat in the second chamber.

I also met Trevor Baylis, the man who invented the wind-up radio, which is opening up contact for the less-developed world where there are no batteries or power supply. He was concerned that two buttons had burst off his shirt front. Then the Queen's equerry appeared and told him—in tones a mixture of the confidential, obsequious and officious— 'The Queen would like to have a few words with you.'

He got more concerned about his shirt front, took a step back, threw his arms out, beamed and addressed us all:

'Did you hear that?'

He got a burst of laughter from us. He asked me to keep an eye on his menu and guest-list which he had been guarding and then changed his mind:

'No, no. I've got to take them, to carry them in front of this shirt.' And he left us.

'It makes the monarchy worthwhile,' said Ivor. I don't think the monarchy should be a treat for children at a party. Why not do it properly and have a conjuror?

When we get home and I tell Ivor about my conversation with Tommy Strathclyde, Ivor tells me Tommy's peerage is only two or three generations old: 'then, that's often the way.'

Wednesday, 10th July

Distinctly jaded.

Check Nelson Mandela's book. Nearly all of it was written in prison and smuggled out. I then re-read chunks of it.

Thursday, 11th July

There is no space booked for me when Nelson Mandela addresses both Houses of Parliament in Westminster Hall this morning. I had not realised I would want to go and have left it too late. I shall see if it is on television.

Friday, 12th July

It was. I wish I had been there. He told us off: a benevolent headmaster with a schoolful of children who had been mean-minded and not played fair. The British could have done so much more over the last 80 years. He praised William Wilberforce for standing alone, but thereafter there are poor bits of history. Macmillan may have smelt the winds of change but that was not enough. His anger rang out.

Tuesday, 6th August

We are at the house. Hence the silence. I have cleaned. Tidied. Cleaned. Made things work. People have been to stay. Ivor has been and is temporarily gone. They have all had weather varying from good to respectable. Today is foul and William is at the farms. The wind is gusting and galing.

We have had walks, climbs, swims. We have dug out the front stones. Creosoted the gates. We have a living, working, comfortable house.

Wednesday, 7th August

A beautiful morning. I am sitting drinking tea in the sun at seven. Dog dogging. Woodpeckers, who have nested here, woodpeckering.

I shall linseed oil the back door if the weather holds up.

Wednesday, 18th September

That was how the summer passed. People to stay. The farm. Riding. The river. Swimming. Then we came back.

William is back at school and I have gone back to work after my year's unpaid leave. I am assured I am back on the payroll but the work I have done in two and a half weeks could total ten hours. Very difficult for a professional teacher who is used to being busy. I am working out how to appear busy. It does not justify paying me and I do not see how this can go on. And as for Senior Management (as opposed to Very Senior Management)—they have been spending their days, two or three at a time, sitting in the doorway saying WELCOME and wearing their best clothes. They must be the most expensive receptionists in London.

The number of students to be seen in the building is minimal.

The autumn wind is rising today and Ivor has gone back to the house. He says it's warm.

My father, Jones The Books, collapsed with his asthma last week: two days of fighting for each breath.

It is odd without the dog. She is at the house with Ivor.

Monday, 7th October

My nice little job is beginning to settle into a routine. 'It can't last' said my colleague Norman who, along with many other responsibilities, has taken it upon himself to be the Voice of Doom.

There are upheavals at school for William, threatening an end to several happy years: fighting in the class, biting, five disruptive children, an unsettled group and neither teaching nor learning. We go and see the headteacher and begin to find out where else we could send him to school. The headteacher tells us she has an educational psychologist starting with the class today, for three weeks ... she says her methods have 'never failed'. The desks will face the front. The children will be attended to when they are attentive and ignored when they are not. Let us hope it does not fail this time because he cannot stay in the chaos for a whole year.

The other school I go to see is hopeless. It is the only private school that takes boys and girls, does not dress the children in other-worldly clothes and we could take William to in the mornings - just. It is in Clapham and I walk through the door and cannot work out what is wrong at first ... it is eerie ... there is something missing. Then it hits me and I decide at once that my (not Ivor's) scruples about using the private sector are nothing compared to my scruples when faced by apartheid. Because that is the effect of it. Among the 300 children I see not one black face. And this is in Clapham, South London in 1996. I'm not impressed by the fact that only the girls dance and only the boys play football ... or that when I ask about the disciplinary system used in the school I'm looked at as if I've spat on the floor... but that is nothing compared to the larger nature of the place.

The Hamilton/Greer saga continues, promoted by the *Guardian*. Did Al Fayed pay out to Hamilton in little brown envelopes? What gifts did Hamilton accept?

New Labour were up in Blackpool, beaming in unctuous innocence as the Government squirmed, when the Labour Baroness Turner popped up to support her old friend Greer.

'She's too straight, too loyal for her own good' said Ivor.

He had to ring her in her hotel room in Blackpool. She said she would do whatever was in the best interests of The Party. He suggested she step aside from her front-bench job now and that they 'have a chat' when it's all died down. Ivor then dictates a statement to Donald Dewar.

Early next morning Blair rang...were they too ruthless?

'What else could you do?' Ivor is rhetorical. Should he speak to her? 'No.' Ivor thinks not, she is raw, 'Wait 'til you're back in London and it's all died down.'

'He wanted a bit of an inquest,' said Ivor as he went back to his bath.

The Sunday papers revealed such a torrent of trouble for John Major yesterday that Ivor spent a lot of time saying 'Poor Bugger'. There was one headline, referring to the Government's determination to make an independent impression within the EU, that I liked: 'John Major stands firm: he misses dinner.'

Tuesday, 8th October

When he was in Blackpool Ivor had dinner with the EU's man in London. He was told: you should let it be known what you want to do. People are saying you do not want to stay in the Lords and see through the end of the hereditary peerage but that you want to go to Washington or the UN. And yesterday Michael Wheeler-Booth (who is Clerk of the Parliaments and believes he is being hurried out of his job by Cranborne) gave him lunch in the Garrick and warned him that Cranborne was plotting against him, had the knives out for him and was buttonholing 'senior members of the Labour Party' and telling them: Ivor's not interested in the Lords, he wants to go back to the UN.

'He can't bully you,' said Michael Wheeler-Booth, 'he doesn't like it ... he wants Charles Williams to do your job.'

Now Cranborne is a Cecil of a Cecil of a Cecil of I don't know how many Cecils (a friend of Elizabeth I originally, I think) and he and his father, by some special dispensation, have votes in the House.

Charles Williams used to work for A Newspaper Magnate.

Perhaps Cranborne dreams that opposite Charles Williams he could stand straight and tall and squeaky clean and could lead the return of the aristocrats (or the retention of the aristocrats) ... we would all be there with our placards crying 'Cecils forever' 'Hereditary Peers Rule OK!' 'The Privileged have Principles!'

I enquired how Ivor was going to protect his back from these knives.

'How can he stab me?'

Back in the House, Denis Carter came to see Ivor.

'Several of us...'

'How many?'

'About twelve...'

'Who?'

'Margaret Jay... Tessa Blackstone... think that Ted Graham ought to be replaced.' Ted Graham is the Opposition Chief Whip. He could not take up his scholarship to the grammar school because his mother could not afford the expense. His father was a meat porter paid in beer. He did not go to university. He is well over sixty. He is not Very New Labour. Who do they think should replace him? Denis Carter. Strange, that.

Friday, 16th October

Peter Temple-Morris, a Tory Pro-European, is at the head of a group of 30 Tory MPs who have said, privately to the Labour Party, that they will vote with the Labour Government after the next election. They are not Coming Out now because they do not want to be publicly disloyal in the run-up to the election.

Ivor held an Opposition front-bench meeting yesterday. After it was over,

Tessa Blackstone said it was time to get rid of Ted. Derry Irvine, who was listening, said after she had gone: 'What cheek.'

The only other person who has been to see Ivor over this is Stanley Clinton-Davis.

Two do not make twelve.

Derry and Ivor then talked about who should do which job after the election. Ivor said politicians should go to Washington and New York as Grade One diplomats (no wonder he's started rumours about himself if he has been talking like this!).

'Tessa could do the UN. She's not up to Washington.'

'That'd get her out of the way,' said Derry.

They agreed Ted ought to have a year as Government Chief Whip.

School remains a problem. The Problem Child, now distinguished from the disruptive children, when ignored—according to the new regime—spends his time writing FUCK on the board over and over again. If he is put out of the room, he bangs his head against the wall so the sound echoes through the classroom and down the corridor. In a battle of wills a six-year-old can only lose in the end.

Thursday, 7th November
Continue to worry about school. At the AGM last night, from a school of about 300 children, there were ten parents. Two of them were Ivor and me. A third was so drunk he was shouted at by a fourth.

We went to the fireworks at Leeds Castle at the weekend ... and to the fireworks in Jones The Pictures' and Jones The Books' garden on Tuesday.

On Monday we took about 38 children to the Tate Gallery. This revealed that the class teacher is the weakest link in the chain of problems at school; she could not find a picture she said she had already visited in preparation for taking the children to see it. She knew nothing about the pictures she could find and she did not know how to talk to the children. This despite the fact that The Problem Child had been left behind in the school because his mother had not come to bring him along as she had said she would. When I last saw him he was writing 'I had sex' on a piece of paper on the floor outside the secretary's office.

Also November
The class teacher sent one child home with misspelt spellings to learn.

One day she went away and never came back. Too late for The Problem Child who had been permanently excluded.

Spring Term 1997

Thursday, 16th January 1997

Ivor went into St Thomas's on 6th December to have a tangerine-sized polyp removed from his colon. He came out on 17th December.

On Christmas Day the dog ate William's chocolate Father Christmas.

We went down to the house as soon as we could. The temperature went down to -8C, with the wind chill taking it down to -27. The river froze. It has not been so cold there since 1963. We managed to be warm in the house and, unlike all our neighbours, our water supply did not freeze.

I failed to get any work done on *The Everywhere Chair*.

Then we came back to London.

We have had the plumbers in the house here for two days, trying to sort out the central heating. It gets hot at the top of the house and stays cold at the bottom. After two days and some mess and a lot of money the heating remains hot at the top and cold at the bottom.

The Shadow Cabinet sent Ivor a Get Well card. The women signed with their first names only, the men signed with their surnames too—as if they were all Gordons or Donalds or Tonys. The Labour Peers did the same thing. The Shadow Cabinet thumped the table when Blair said how pleased he was to see Ivor well and returned to the Shadow Tasks.

The row between Jack Straw and everybody else (JS refusing to disagree with Home Office proposals to allow the police a free rein to bug, even solicitors with clients and doctors with patients) continues because JS is afraid to be seen as being Soft on Crime. When he announced to the Shadow Cabinet New Labour's policy on flogging ('we're against it') there was a spontaneous, table-wide burst of laughter. JS was 'plum red'.

'Ooooooo Jack,' said someone, 'you're getting Soft on Crime!'

Blair told Ivor he didn't care what happened so long as there wasn't a row in public. Ivor told Blair that was rather his view but there was no way the Labour Lords' voting contingent (average age 71) would toe a line and not oppose free-range bugging. Indeed, James Callaghan was letting it be known that he was writing his speech to be delivered in outrage. The Party does not want that kind of public division. Not a good idea. It's the Tories who row in public these days.

I am sitting writing this at work. Maybe I'll be able to start getting some of my own work done here. I'll have to learn to work with people drifting around. There are three members of staff in here and no students.

Friday, 17th January

The school is being inspected and there are more than 40 parents at the meeting with Ofsted ... never there before and only there to complain.

I have come into work early today to find that I was not the first so I have not got the quiet I would like. We have three staff and one student in the room.

The Lords voted last night not to include smaller guns in the gun-tightening exercises.

There has been a row about landmines. Princess Diana has been in Angola with the Red Cross drawing attention to the damage done by landmines and proposing they are banned. Earl Howe put his head up and said she is a 'loose cannon' ... banning landmines is Labour policy, not Tory policy. Photographs of Earl Howe are here and there. I recognise him but I cannot think from where. I then read the potted biographies which surround some of the photographs ... he was at school with a man who, when we were born, lived next door but three. Then this man grew up and went to Oxford, and was one of a trio of would be 18th century gentlemen: he became a scholar, one went into the Church and the third was Fred Curzon. I think Fred was working in the Mayfair branch of Barclays when I was caretaking in Mayfair. Then, I think, he went to South Africa with Barclays in the mid-seventies and I expect I asked him about that ... suggesting, probably not very subtly, that apartheid might bother him. That was the last time I saw him until the photographs of Earl Howe appeared ... That was what became of Fred Curzon when his father died in 1981.

Monday, 3rd February

Nick Hinton has had a heart attack and died in Bosnia. He was 54. When we were neighbours in local politics he ran The Save the Children Fund. About ten years ago we met them all on the edge of Vincent Square. Josie was in her pushchair, Deborah was pushing and Nick was carrying a roll of carpet. They looked as if they were just beginning, as they should have been. I have written to Deborah.

Ivor's car has failed its MOT. It sits, a lump, of metal, in disgrace in the street. My more modest—and much sturdier—vehicle is now central to family transport. I am even lending it to Ivor on Wednesday. This is nice of me. He will complain that it is dirty. My retort—that at least it works—might not deter him.

Tuesday, 4th February

Betty Boothroyd made her joke about Pre-election Tension. It did not have a spontaneous flavour. But there is excitement about not if but when ... 27th March? 1st May? Not much to choose between them. Not even six weeks.

A saga has been brewing over the fridge. I went down to the kitchen and something was wrong. I sniffed. There was a tinge in the air that shouldn't be there. I nosed out the source of the tinge: the fridge. It was not working. I checked the socket and changed the fuse. Nothing. I rang the manufacturers:

'It sounds like the compressor,' said the Voice.

'What would a new compressor cost?'

'Between two and three hundred pounds.'

'And what is your call-out charge?'

'£48.50 for the first eighteen minutes.'

l wonder how many people call them out.

We spent the whole of Saturday carrying fridges and commuting between South London Electrical Appliance Shops and breaking a cupboard off the wall to get the dead fridge out and the live fridge in (which cost less than a compressor without the call-out charge).

In the midst of the fridge turmoil half the lights in the house fused and I was up the ladder in the fuse box and threading bits of wire through fuses. Once the dead fridge was out of the kitchen, my plan to dump it in the street was vetoed by Ivor. It now stands in our backyard, dominating the space.

I mentioned this volume to Ivor the other day who had forgotten that I had ever mentioned it before. I said I must have done because I had written about mentioning it. He said he would read it. He thought a bit of The Edwardian Lady would go down well. I said a touch of Alan Clark would be needed to spice that up. He said there were things I could not say. I said of course he could cut the odd thing which he said was big of me. I told him I couldn't try to get it published until he had retired from politics. He was glad to hear it.

Yesterday was the Peers' party.

'Did Blair come?'

'Yes. And said all the right things. And left.'

'Did Cherie come?'

'Yes. And said a few things to a few people.'

Friday, 7th February

The central heating sounds calmer. We are sleeping better.

Ivor has rung Lambeth about the fridge. They are sending him a form.

Tuesday, 11th February

There is a nasty to and fro in Lambeth College. Three jobs and four people and all four people have been offered one of the three jobs. Some were offered them before others and that is how Senior Management are disentangling their mess: by keeping their words to those offered first and breaking their words to those offered last. Four people's feelings have been hurt and Not-so-Senior Management have been made to look foolish and More Senior-Management has been caught telling fibs (do they think we never talk to each other? ... or are daft?) and Very Senior Management has been proved, once again, to be The Power. She has also been the subject of special praise from the inspectors who have been inspecting Lambeth College: 'The Governors expressed their satisfaction ... The Governors echoed the warm praise of the Inspectors ...'

Thursday, 13th February

I asked what had happened to Ivor's committee for the Reform of the House of Lords.

'I saw the report today.'

'What does it say?'

'It's only one side—I've got everything I want except a Royal commission.'

According to the newspapers, the Liberals agree with all the proposals, the main point of which is to undertake the reform in two stages:

1. Disband the hereditary peers: stop them voting, sitting, claiming expenses, handing their votes on to their sons. The detail is not

yet there: would they be allowed in the building?

2. Decide how to replace them, what to call the Second Chamber, whether or not to put an age limit on membership.

The interesting thing is the time lapse between Stage One and Stage Two. It could be one year or ten years. New Labour have committed themselves to Stage One early on in the New Government. Stage Two remains open-ended.

According to Ivor, the main problem will be running the Lords through the early parts of The New Government. He won't easily be able to persuade the hereditary peers to disband themselves (in the bad old joke, turkeys don't vote for Christmas) unless they can see that the alternative—dozens of sudden New Labour Peers in order to outnumber them—is ridiculous and unnecessary. Apart from that, there will be the rest of New Labour's legislation to be got through the Lords. They have committed themselves to Welsh and Scottish Assemblies for example—and an unreformed Lords could delay it.

There is an ugly rumour that Ivor will lose his August holiday in the rush to get the new laws passed. New Labour could yet prove to be A Pain. I have no desire to see our lives overridden by Public Affairs.

We are down at the house in the rain. Ivor has to take the train to London this afternoon. It is solitary here for Mother, Son and Dog alone.

Saturday, 22nd February

The postman got stuck on the track in the mud. To the side of the track to be precise - he made the mistake of turning by going down the hill. Of course he couldn't get back up, again. He was rescued by our neighbour Roger and his all-purpose vehicle.

Ivor rang: 'Your father's in *The Times* today. Have you seen it?'

'I've got it but I haven't opened it.'

I open it after taking lunch off the burn and singe it had got into while we were talking.

Libby Purves has written a piece arguing against privatising Oxford or any other university. She talks about how she had advantages and treatment not found in most universities and names Hugo Dyson, Lord David Cecil and Jones The Books as people who taught her despite her being at an all-women's college. (An all-women's college was a leftover from the Dark Ages and soon people won't know what they were.) They taught her on her own. She says it is important that these dons have to argue with 'chippy, working class' minds. What she forgets is more and more dons started off with chippy, working class minds themselves.

The reason I enjoy this piece is that I remember them all. Margaret and Hugo Dyson came and spent Christmas with us when we were children. Hugo's gassed, First-World-War lungs would be gasping. Lord David Cecil used to Be Amusing with Rachel in our drawing-room and I would creep down after they had gone into the dining-room and lick out the empty glasses and smell the scents and cigar and Libby Purves too—at one of Jones The Pictures, and Jones The Books, parties—standing with her foot up against the wall and a glass of sherry in her hand.

My parents once made the mistake of having one of their 'Undergraduate Parties', as they were called, the morning after the clocks changed. Half the guests came at the old time, half came at the new time, the party took twice as long and twice as much sherry was consumed.

Today has got even more exciting. William found William-the-Boar mating. Then we had hail and storm-force winds. Then the hunt came down the valley. I have not seen them here for at least 30 years. I heard the horn, saw a red coat and then realised there was a pack of hounds and it was the hunt. It was a shadow of what it used to be. The average age was over 60. The first red coat I saw was the only red coat. There were six followers. A dying echo of the 18th century. Much like the hereditary peerage. There'll be nobody hunting here before long. I stood on our hedge with my hands on my hips. They kept the dogs together so they didn't climb the walls. I was trying to be polite ('Good morning ... good morning') but make the point that I did not want them on our land. They found nothing even though they went up the valley to the earths. We walked up later to see what had been done. The dogs had been digging and it looked as if somebody had blocked up one set of earths a while ago in order to chase the foxes into another. It is a dangerous area to hunt: the ground is rough with loose boulders and hidden holes. Granny's friends used to skip the meet when it came this way.

Monday, 24th February
Back in London.

The fridge greets us from the backyard. Ivor says he got the form from Lambeth to remove it and has filled it in and returned it.

More alarming is the thundering—a combination of guns and hooves—coming from the basement. The gerbils must be quivering in their cage. The central heating has gone into battle; the pipes are a conduit for explosions and assaults. Ivor had mentioned that the plumbers had been in over the holiday to finalise their work on the system, but I had not appreciated that the result might be so bombastic. Neither, to be fair, had Ivor. We turn everything off ... electricity, gas, water ... and there is silence. Ivor contacts the plumbers.

I have had time to look at the mail and find an invitation to the reunion of the Oxford High School class of 1970. Over fifty of us have been traced. And nearly all of us live in London/Surrey/Kent/Oxfordshire. Four have got as far as Scotland, one to France, two to the USA. And half have changed their names. Those that do not fall silent after telling how old their children are, tend to be civil servants, doctors, teachers, lawyers but there is also a violin-mender, a film producer, a farmer, a novelist and playwright. We are a batch of Middle England's forty-something survivors. None of the boys from the group of us who started in 1955 have been found. There were only three or four.

Tuesday, 25th February

Classmate from 1955 rings up. We have not spoken to each other for 27 years. She has the idea that a few of us, who spent a lot of time together through our adolescence should have dinner. This would mean that two of our num-ber, who got as far as Scotland, would come south to join three of us who are already here. We formed The Spinsters Union thirty five years ago. We have all broken faith with it in one way or another.

Classmate rings up again. The Scottish contingent is not keen on coming south. No problem, says Classmate, the three of us will fly to Aberdeen. In the meantime, she and I will have dinner at her club.

Wednesday, 26th February

Ivor is depressed by an exchange he has with Derry Irvine. Derry knows what he will be doing in a New Labour Government. Nobody else does. Derry does not know what anybody else will be doing. 'Tony's not talking to any-body,' he says. He also says he thinks the Leader of the House of Lords should be a politician, not an academic. This unnerves Ivor as it suggests there is gos-sip to the effect that somebody other than he will be Leader of the House of Lords.

'Blair is talking to Roy Jenkins' he says glumly. 'There will be a row if he is appointed.'

Thursday, 27th February

The Wirral by-election.

Friday, 28th February

'A Kick in the Wirrals' is *The Sun's* way of telling us what happened yesterday. A comfortable Tory majority has become a comfortable New Labour majority: 'It happens to us all,' says Ivor.

Saturday, 1st March

William's birthday party. The children play around the dead fridge in the backyard.

Monday, 3rd March

Ivor says if he does not get a job in the New Labour Government he will make some money. He said the same thing when Old Labour lost in 1979 and when Margaret Thatcher sacked him from Brussels in 1985.

Tuesday, 4th March

I am sitting in the Staff Common Room where a colleague enjoys a joke: is this a piss of paper or a shit of paper? He teaches English to Speakers of Other Languages.

Someone from Blair's office is seeing Ivor today with the draft New Labour Manifesto. This is to check that they won't upset the Lords with anything it says.

Wednesday, 5th March

The Man from Blair's Office cancelled. Too busy dealing with the Pensions row.

Classmate from 1955 was the same as she was when she was four. You can say that about a successful lawyer in her forties. She gave me a good evening at Black's, which I am sure I should have heard of, but hadn't. There were a lot of people smoking in jerseys.

The plumbers came again. If you turn the heating on it roars and shouts and the water is much too hot. We don't seem to be making much progress.

The dog is having digestive problems—to put it delicately. I am feeding her salazopyrin and hoping.

Thursday, 6th March

The Man from Blair's Office had time to bring Ivor the New Labour Manifesto. Ivor read the constitutional stuff, the foreign affairs stuff and the EC stuff. His main concern was to make it clear that hereditary peers will lose their votes and their seats in the House. He also added a more general phrase to describe the select committee that will sit to decide on the second chamber.

We went to a piano recital in St John's Smith Square for the first time in our lives despite having lived near it for more than 40 years between us. I don't like Brahms.

Friday, 7th March

Now we cannot turn the central heating off. Since we have been having glimpses of spring weather, this is not encouraging.

Dog not right. I double the dose of salazopyrin. And clean the carpet.

Sunday, 9th March

Today's *Sunday Times* has a piece telling us that Everyone who is Anyone is keeping a diary these days, in the hope that one day it will keep them. There is then a list of these individuals which does not include me. It also gives ten pieces of advice for Everyone to follow. I am able to follow two of them: keeping a diary—not recollecting in tranquility—and keeping my mouth shut. The rest of the advice—not sparing yourself, feuding, being a man—for example, I am either unable to follow or would not wish to follow.

Monday, 10th March

I am lame. We spent yesterday afternoon up and down the stepladder, dealing with the overgrowth of roses and jasmine and honeysuckle in the backyard. (It has not yet covered the fridge.) This should not make me lame. However, I am. I went to work with a stick. And I felt some fellow-feeling for Douglas Hogg who has broken his foot and been filmed and photographed, crutches and all, as a symbol of a government limping to a close, accident prone and ridiculous.

The Labour peers are plotting another ambush. Ivor comes home full of the irritations of some people's unhelpfulness: there is a £500-a-head lawyers' dinner tonight, with Cherie and Tony. It is at the River Café, owned by Richard Rogers' wife. Richard Rogers and Ann Mallalieu will come and vote. Derry Irvine? No. Derry will not. He is committed to a Very Important Dinner. He must know RR and AM are at the same one.

'He thinks we're playing silly games. '

'Has he ever been in politics before?'

'No.'

'So he's got a lot to learn?'

'Yes.'

Ted Short, when rung up and asked to vote, said no and slammed the phone down.

Richard Attenborough offered to vote but was told no thank you because if the Tory Whips catch sight of him they will guess what is happening and call in their voters.

As it turns out the Tory Whips do get wind of something—all they have to do is look in the car park and see how many and who are parked—and the Tories keep talking in the Chamber while the Whips keep telephoning in their office. Despite this, the Government loses. The Labour theory is that Tories cannot be bothered to disturb themselves from their firesides, television sets and dinner tables to come in and vote for a dying government that they do not approve of. At least four pieces of legislation are now so delayed that they won't get through before the election. At the end of the evening, Ivor sees Ann Mallalieu on her way out of the House. She is off to the dinner and hopes she'll be in time for the coffee.

'It must be the most expensive cup of coffee you have ever had,' says Ivor.

Tuesday, 11th March

I am less lame. My fears of premature arthritis fade.

Dog Under Control.

Ivor hears from Lambeth. Will he put the fridge out in the street for 6 a.m. on the 13th?

Wednesday, 12th March

Ivor wrote to Blair about a month ago, suggesting they discuss who does which job in the Lords if they win the election. After the Shadow Cabinet, Ted Graham approached Jonathan Powell:

'What about Ivor seeing Tony?'

'He's much too busy fighting an election to think about that.'

'I suppose,' says Ivor, 'it'll all be done on the back of an envelope on the Saturday afternoon.'

That would be Saturday May the third if the election is on May the first, as is expected.

Neil Kinnock had everyone in place before he fought his election (Ivor had said he did not want to go and govern Hong Kong). John Smith did not get near enough to an election to place anybody.

'It'll be chaos,' says Ivor.

If Blair wants to work on the same principle as a firefighter, that is a matter for him. Ivor prefers to have done some work beforehand to prevent fire breaking out wherever possible.

Dog less Under Control.

Thursday, 13th March

When I come home from work, the fridge has gone. However, the dog is very much less under control.

William and I take the dog to the vet. The vet tells me I should feed the dog boiled rice and white fish.

Ivor is trying to find out when his Easter holiday might be. He speaks to Emma Nicholson who has spoken to the police who say the House is going up on Maundy Thursday, to sit again on Easter Tuesday. The police know more than most people: they have to look after the building

The Government has lost another two points in the polls. I say they will continue to lose points and the longer they leave the election, the worse they will do.

'Melt down', says Ivor. 'I agree.' He also says that Blair said in yesterday's Shadow Cabinet, that Major had wanted to go in March but was 'leant on'. So much rumour and gossip.

We light a candle for Dunblane at seven o'clock and put it in our window.

Friday, 14th March

The plumbers turn up. He's been very busy. Could he come and put in the new hot water valve which, he maintains, is the Final Solution. Of course he can. He says he will be back in the middle of next week.

Ivor comes home with Ted's new theory: Blair's not talking to them because he is talking to somebody else. And he is going to sack them come the New Labour Government.

Saturday, 15th March

I get a letter from the Parking Committee for London—they will give me my hearing at 1.15 on the 21st of this month in their office on the Haymarket. I begin to gird my loins.

Sunday, 16th March

The dog is under control once more although the smell of boiling rice and white fish lingers in the house all day. Worst at the top, where our bedroom is.

Walk in Kensington Gardens. Feed the birds on the pond. On the way home, Ivor buys newspapers which tell him the date of the election will be announced tomorrow or Tuesday or Wednesday and it will be the 1st of May.

On and off, through a family Sunday—roasting lamb for lunch, building a cardboard farm, baking a lemon cake, mending a worn rug—we go round and round what could happen in six weeks time.

On the weekend of 3rd/4th May, these are the possibilities:

1. More Conservative Government, in which case:

a. Ivor goes on with the job he has now (Leader of the Opposition in the House of Lords) until their internal election in November, when he is or is not re-elected, or
b. Ivor gives up the job he has now and goes back to the Bar. He says his first case would probably be a buggery in Birmingham.

2. A New Labour Government, in which case:

a. Ivor is offered a job in the Cabinet, or
b. Ivor is offered a job not in the Cabinet, or
c. Ivor is offered nothing. He is left looking for that buggery in Birmingham.

3. Other possibilities include:

a. a hung parliament,
b. a coalition,
c. death.

Ivor wants 2a. So do I. Especially given the chance of 2b, WHICH I DO NOT WANT AT ALL.

That is what we talk about most. 'He might want to send me to Washington.' An Ambassador to the USA. I see no charm in that whatsoever. If I went too, it would cut William's and my lives in pieces: my job, his school, his friends, my friends, family, roots—you cannot put a life in a suitcase. But if I did not go too, our lives would be sliced up in another way: a one-parent family doing its best in London and a non-parent father unable to do his best in the USA. The dog is too old to go anywhere. She would have to be put down. Ivor would prefer that job to no job—I have no difficulty understanding that. I would not prefer him to have that job to no job—Ivor has no difficulty in understanding that.

'There's no point in worrying about something that may not happen,' he says several times through the day, to himself as much as to me.

'It wouldn't have been the same with John,' is also said. John Smith and Ivor could talk to each other.

Monday, 17th March

I tell Ivor he should spend his time over the election getting new suits: if he's given a job he'll need them in his new job, if he's sacked, he'll need them in court. In either case, he won't have time to get them after 1st May.

The traffic is jammed up, so I set off early to get William to school and myself to Lambeth College. On the route back, we find a car and a motorbike squashed together in the middle of the road. We get over Lambeth Bridge in slow motion to find Millbank closed because of burst pipes and Horseferry Road closed too. I look up Horseferry Road to see if I can see what is going on. I see a body under a car. William does not see. He is late for school and I am nearly late at Lambeth College

The election is confirmed for 1st May. Major's loudspeaker breaks down in Luton.

Maurice Peston, who sits on the Opposition front bench in the Lords, tells Ivor 'his contacts' tell him that his job is safe. Maurice's son, Robert, is political correspondent of the *Financial Times*.

The Sun comes out for Blair. This is double-edged. *The Sun* is not known for its radical and reforming thrust or for its moderate and liberal view of the world. 20% of the population read it. It demands a reading age of 11.

We now know we will get a fortnight's family holiday.

Tuesday, 18th March

The Parking Committee for London ring me up: Lambeth are withdrawing and will not contest my appeal on Friday. I've won! Most unusual. Let's hope Westminster will do the same thing. I wonder if that will take two years as well.

Flurry in the Lords: the House is rising for Easter on Friday (note doubling-up of the metaphors of politics and religion) and the Government is either dropping its legislation or rushing it through as part of a wheel and deal with the opposition. Jack Straw has managed to upset the Labour peers again. Ted has sent A Scorcher to Donald Dewar who has apologised to him and Ivor. At the start of the longest election campaign for 70 years, it would not be a good idea for the Labour peers to start badmouthing New Labour.

I wonder what job Jack Straw will have come 3/4 May. That could be an indicator of how Blair is going to do his job - and of what kind of person he is.

Thursday, 20th March

At the Shadow Cabinet Meeting yesterday, the last of this parliament and perhaps the last Labour one of 18 years, the last of this century and the last of this millennium, Blair was trying 'to keep the lid on' excitement and over-confidence and give instructions: They will be watching Us not Them ... it all Depends on Us ... do not make Any Mistakes ... The Most Dangerous Assault is Tax and Spend ... Gordon has prepared a piece of paper for everyone to keep by their sides when they answer questions ... when you are giving an interview back in the constituency You Will Be Monitored.

Friday, 21st March

The Tory Whips in the Lords have got a sweep running on the New Labour majority. Most of them are betting on 70 - 100.

The Downey Report (nicknamed the Sleaze Report) into whether or not politicians were bribed to put down parliamentary questions is being delayed. Major behaved like a trapped rat when confronted with the fact in the Commons.

Parliament rises today.

I go and meet Ivor for lunch in the House as soon as I can get out of Lambeth College. I had kept the afternoon clear because I had thought I would be appealing in the Haymarket. The television monitors have PRO-ROGATION showing on them. And after lunch we go down to the House of Commons and I sniff the air of the place. 20th century British government is over. Whether we have New Labour or More Conservatives, the next government will take us into the next century and the next millennium. The air is not fresh. It is over-full with breath and sweat. The smell of animals working. We are on our own. I read the entry by the Clerk of the Commons for 1605, made on the side of a list of committee members, describing finding 36 barrels of gunpowder. And then the report of Elizabeth 1st's complaint, 20 years earlier, that her ministers had ordered an Act of Worship. It was her job to do that, not theirs. The report decided the ministers' mistake was an Excess of Zeal, nothing worse. All the same, they apologise.

Saturday, 22nd March

We get to the house. There is a dead wether lamb in the field. It stinks. Roger comes and drives it away in his all-purpose vehicle. Its friend, who is hanging around in some anxiety, he will pick up on Monday.

The beagles come up the valley. That is, six beagles and a collection of other dogs. The men (only) range themselves round the earths with double-barrelled shotguns. I explain that this is more humane than tearing foxes apart. No shot is fired. No fox is caught. Three hours later, two beaglers return: they have lost a four-month-old bitch. We set off to find her. We find some shoes we lost last summer, but no puppy. When we get home, the Chief Beagler's daughter has rung: walkers picked the puppy up and drove her home.

The mole is active. New hills appear each time I turn my back. The daffodils are coming into flower and the nettles are beginning their rampage. There is work to do. The wind blows but it is not cold and the ground is dry.

We try to see the Hale-Bopp comet, but there is mist and the sky is low at night.

Sunday, 23rd March

The dog finds another dead sheep. I find her chewing hooves. If I keep her out of the house, she finds more to chew. If I let her in, she brings smears of dead sheep with her. She will be out of control again soon.

John Major is filmed campaigning in a shop called SLEES. Norma Major's mother has cancer. They will be wondering what else can go wrong.

I meet our neighbour at the farm. That Blair does not know what he is doing. There will be war in Europe. We will all starve ... or (he turns to William) there will be nothing but spaghetti bolognaise. William says he likes spaghetti bolognaise. Our neighbour says there will be another Conservative Government by the time William is grown up. Then we will all be saved.

I advise Ivor not to talk politics in local circles. 'When have I ever?'

I get a letter from my mother, Jones The Pictures, reassuring me that she does not know anybody who is voting Labour.

At quarter to eight this evening, in the north-western sky, we see the double-barrelled comet, Hale-Bopp. We remember the Egyptians 4,000 years ago who saw it last. It is above the old rowan and we watch it from the back door. When I go out again later the moonlight is bright and I could find my way anywhere by its light.

Tuesday, 25th March

There are eight fresh molehills to be seen from one window. I haven't counted from any other window.

We take Ivor to the station. He has the meeting of the Shadow Cabinet and the National Executive to adopt the manifesto. They are allowed it at nine o'clock tomorrow morning. The meeting starts at nine thirty. He will have to check his words again.

Wednesday, 26th March

The dog is Out of Control. Too many hooves.

Thursday, 27th March

Ivor got back from his meeting last night. The manifesto arrived at ten past nine in numbered, sealed envelopes. This was to check that each copy was returned after the meeting. At half past nine Robin Cook started to lead (or push) them through it. Every time Dennis Skinner proposed an amendment Robin Cook asked:

'Seconder? ...' Nobody moved. 'OK.' And Robin Cook went on to the next page and Dennis Skinner shrugged and laughed. On the retention of Trident, Dennis Skinner asked rhetorically:

'That was accepted at conference?' Everybody agreed it was and that was that. The death of Old Labour was endorsed and Robin Cook had done to the meeting exactly what the Government had done to him with the Scott Report: allowed him limited access for a limited time. Robin Cook complained with vigour and volume when it happened to him.

Ivor reckons Dennis Skinner and Diane Abbott had a deal: neither would second the other's amendments so they can both say they Stood Alone. Diane Abbott had 'some balls-aching point' about moving an immigration matter into a family matter. She got nowhere. The smell of Victory and Power has silenced them all.

Ivor describes the manifesto as bland, with discrepancies between the Scottish and English versions, especially over NHS trusts. When he tried to pick them up, Robin Cook raised his arms and said:

'Too late.'

Ivor then went and saw Donald Dewar.

'Tony really must get his head round who is going to do what after the election.'

There have to be six Ministers of State in the Lords. Blair doesn't even know them all.

'Write to him.'

'But I don't know what I'll be doing.'

'Nobody knows what. they'll be doing ... Tony hasn't told any of us what we'll be doing.'

Donald Dewar made it clear that he didn't know he had a job after May 1st. So Blair is keeping them all on edge and ruling them by their fear of failing.

'Robin Cook must know he's going to be Foreign Secretary,' Ivor says to me.

'He may not, by the sound of it,' say I.

Donald Dewar, on the matter of Ivor's job, says:

'I haven't heard that you won't be Leader of the Lords.' That's Lord Privy Seal. The Locker of Lavatories.

'In that, case,' says Ivor, 'I need Lords to work.'

The reason for his and Donald Dewar's meeting is that John Major is appointing 20 new peers: ten Tories, seven Labour and three Liberals, and Donald Dewar needs to list their seven. They manage Peter Shore, Roy Hattersley, Joan Lester and Doug Hoyle and then their list grinds to a halt.

'... and you won't get any work out of many of them,' says Donald Dewar.

New Labour will have to get legislation through quickly to have referendums on devolution in time with their promises. Ivor makes the point that he can't expect the octogenarians in his team to sit up night after night.

'How many do you need?' asks Donald Dewar.

'Is that a real question or are we bargaining?'

'No ... no ... seriously.'

'25.'

Ivor comes away as satisfied as he could expect to be but worried that Ted Graham won't be Chief Whip though Donald Dewar has said he will represent Ivor's point of view.

Ivor meets Maurice Peston in a state of apoplexy. The night before, the

Pestons had a dinner in their daughter's restaurant to mark the anniversary of Maurice's year's intake to the Lords. Among them was Derry Irvine, Blair's Head of Chambers and prospective Lord Chancellor.

'Helen says,' says Maurice of his wife, 'she will Never Have Dinner with That Man again.'

Apparently he was tired.

'He's going to be A Problem,' say I.

'Not to me,' says Ivor. Blair's Achilles Heel? I wonder. As Maurice Peston should be one of the six Ministers of State in the New Labour Government, along with Tessa Blackstone, Pat Hollis, Bernard Donaghue and Margaret Jay, there are omens of unrest among the team. This would be carried into a New Labour Cabinet: Derry Irvine distinguished himself a while back with Donald Dewar's wife and Robin Cook and Gordon Brown have had a feud running since their days in Scottish student politics.

After his day in town, Ivor observed of the people at that table: 'a lot of them will be very disappointed ... they won't have jobs for long ... Frank Dobson will be a very disappointed man.' Maurice believes the House will reassemble on 7th May and the First Betrayal will be alleged on 8th May.

Things are getting worse for John Major. Last week there was Hogg and Beef, this week there is Sleaze. On Monday the safest Scottish Tory resigned because of a 'relationship' with 'a married mother of four'; on Wednesday Tim Smith resigned because he accepted cash in brown envelopes and did not declare it; today. *The Sun* tells of Piers Merchant's affair with a girl of 17.

It is known as corruption; sex out-of-line with heterosexual marriage and money out-of-line with declared income make politicians vulnerable. They are supposed to stay in line if they want votes. Personal Purity and Public Responsibility go together. These definitions of Personal Purity can be bigoted and merciless as far as sex is concerned. On the other hand we do not want the country run by crooks. Think of the fall of Rome ... of Albania.

16 more molehills out of the window. It's mild today. I've had the window open. The better to count the molehills. The only sounds are the dog breathing and the river running. All the flowers have gone from all the daffodils. I blame the sheep.

Friday, 28th March, Good Friday

Our water supply has packed up. Sometimes a little trickles in. Spend a great deal of time turning taps on and off and listening to gurgles and hisses and drips.

Monday, 31st March, Easter Monday

We have water.

The Chairman of the Scottish Conservatives resigns. Sex again.

The Opposition are proposing an independent, anti-corruption candidate stands against Neil Hamilton, who is refusing to resign.

Tuesday, 1st April

A summer's day. Bare feet … the dog dozing in the sun …laundry on the line … waiting for bees and butterflies.

Monday, 7th April

We left the house and came back to London. I finished the first draft of *The Everywhere Chair* before we left. I am very pleased.

Ivor has gone into the House today to keep in touch. He was not invited to launch the New Labour Manifesto. The plans for peers to campaign for 1st May are collapsing. The peers have nothing to do. Blair, it is said, is continuing to see Roy Jenkins and continuing not to see James Callaghan.

There is Bad Feeling…

Ivor says the House of Lords is his constituency and he will spend his time looking after it.

I picture New Labour in the New Millennium: the second chamber, without the hereditary peers, leaves the Labour peers with more power. The Labour peers find New Labour, next door, somewhat extreme. The Labour peers become the New Left in the turn of the millennium and fight New Labour.

I describe this picture to Ivor. He remarks that it is difficult not to be left of Blair. He thinks he will have to keep his head down. This was sparked off by Blair plunging into privatisation in a speech in the city; he has gone out alone, further than the manifesto.

'If you asked people in the Shadow Cabinet about it, they would not agree.'

'Were they asked?'

'No.'

'But if he is Prime Minister, he won't be able to run all the ministries.

'No.'

'So he'll have to delegate.'

'Yes.'

'And he won't like what they do.'

'No.'
'But if he sacks them, ...'
'He'll have a lot ...'
' ... of enemies.'
The Thatcher Story.

Tuesday, 8th April

We all had lunch in the House. Ivor, Ted and Andrew were hopping with excitement at the opinion polls. Then trying hard not to hop. After 18 years, it must be a bit exciting. (Ted is the opposition Chief Whip, Andrew Deputy Leader.) Ted came and played I-Spy while we ate in the dining-room. He gave us 'M' for monitor (most of us would call it a television) and 'BT' for the waiter's bow tie. He beat us. At the next table was David Hacking with his son, Alexander. They then did a tour of the building. I thought how things could change: in the olden days Alexander would take over his father's place, while William's father would not even be there by royal patronage.

The staff are worried that they will miss their holidays with the election and the New Labour rush on legislation. Ted says the week at the end of May will be holiday, but the House will sit into August and return in the third week of September. He also says that today is the last day of pay: the House is dissolved today. There is no pay until it sits again on 7th May. This is A Blow. Yet the state can't pay politicians to campaign for themselves.

Thursday, 10th April

Marianne Morris, who has run the Opposition Whips' Office in the Lords for years, is fulminating. She has been transferred to Blair's office in Millbank for the election. She says it is A Shambles. There are a great many people with mobile phones and nothing to do. At the same time, there is no system for dealing with the correspondence. The letters come in and a standard answer sent in reply. As a result, there is a follow-up letter: You Have Not Answered My Question (or whatever). Marianne says it would take half an hour to sort out the mess; to write a set of standard replies according to the standard questions and send them off accordingly. She says 12 standard letters would deal with 95% of the questions.

Ivor is surprised that Peter Mandelson has not done that.

Friday, 11th April

A letter from Westminster Council. They have not accepted my parking appeal so I shall have another appointment in the Haymarket with the Parking Committee for London.

Ivor has found a constituency that would like him to do some work. He has gone to Brentford.

Agitation at work. Very Senior Management have announced there will be up to 68 redundancies: 20 support staff and 48 teaching staff— Very Senior Management have just got the budget for next year. The final figure depends on numbers going for premature retirement. The last time I heard there were two of them.

I hope I am safe. That is everybody's first thought, unless they are better people than me.

Norman (the Voice of Doom) tells me we will have to go out on strike. I tell Norman most of us cannot afford to. Norman says he can't either. He'll live off his partner. I forbear from telling him that my partner is earning nothing.

The plumbers never came back before Easter. All quiet and cool in the pipes.

There is a new drip. The top lavatory was overflowing into my pot of fuchsias in the backyard. I have moved the fuchsias.

Summer Term 1997

Saturday, 12th April

Ivor thinks New Labour will win Brentford. The candidate has fought the seat several times, is a district nurse and not very New Labour.

Eight Irishman are in the dock, charged with plotting to blow up London's electricity supply. I remark that it is strange how many IRA plots are foiled.

'Ssssh ... there are some very brave people out there ...'

'Who are they?'

'M15, M16 ... living on their nerves all the time.'

'They must have to sleep for years to get accepted.'

'Yes.'

'How are they paid?'

'It all piles up for them while they live on the dole in Belfast.'

'Their private lives must be a complete mess.'

'Yes.'

'And every now and then one of them must get caught and killed.'

'Yes.'

'Won't the eight in the dock wonder where the ninth is?'

'It's too late now. I hope he's a long way away. When it all started 25 years ago some sleepers went in then. You can talk about it in general terms to Merlyn but he won't tell you anything.'

Merlyn learnt a lot when he was Home Secretary and Secretary of State for Northern Ireland.

We have a conversation we have had a hundred times before. I have never voted Labour. I have voted Liberal, SDP, Green, Gay Liberation, even, in 1979, Tory.

'What I vote doesn't matter. I have never voted in a marginal seat.'

'Frivolous.'

'Whatever I do doesn't make any difference.'

'Not serious.'

Tuesday, 15th April

Ivor had lunch with Richard Faulkner yesterday. He is part of John Prescott's campaign team. John Prescott is not speaking to Gordon Brown. It is not clear who is in charge. Blair is uncontactable.

'So silly to upset so many people ... all these youngsters who have never run anything in their lives.'

Millbank is chaos with Young People doing nothing but talking on their mobile phones.

'When Blair becomes Prime Minister he won't have a clue what to do,' say I.

'Thank God for the Civil Service,' says Ivor.

'Robin Butler will have to be exactly like a schoolmaster.'

'He's only there for six months ... Blair won't be able to run the country like this. A Prime Minister is not a dictator.'

'Will cabinet meetings just rubber stamp what he says?'

'They can't. It's too important.'

'Who will disagree?'

'It'll be very interesting. If you sack everybody who disagrees you have the Thatcher way ...'

'She lasted ten years.'

'But it was bad government. Nearly everybody ... Attlee ... Wilson ... has tried to take account of other people's thoughts.'

Richard Faulkner found a brown envelope on his desk in Millbank yesterday morning. In it was a copy of the memo from Robin Butler to John Major, describing Heseltine's questioning of Neil Hamilton. Michael Heseltine asked Hamilton several times if he had taken any money. Each time, Hamilton said he had not.

Rumours flying at Lambeth College about the method of reducing us by sixty eight.

Wednesday, 16th April

Wake up to new affliction: sore arm.

In the Study Centre, making coffee for myself one-handed, when a colleague comes in with her head on one side ...

'Ooo ... I've cricked my neck.'

Tell her about my arm. Compare notes. Two hours later, another colleague limps in ...

'Ooo sciatic pain in my leg ... my thigh...'

I laugh. Explain why. I think she sees the joke.

When mirth has died down, attentive student informs us that with the changes in the weather—hot/cold/hot/cold—we sleep tightly curled to keep an even temperature. So we wake up hurting.

Hope the weather steadies itself.

Thursday, 17th April

Ivor has gone campaigning in Cardiff.

Lambeth College's in-house periodical, Lambeth Talk, has a black-bordered announcement: we will be closed to students next Thursday, the 24th, from 3 p.m. We are to be 'on site' until 5 p.m. There will be meetings where we will be informed of the 'staffing reviews' . In other words we will learn who will and who will not have a job. Bob, in the Study Centre, has seen figures that suggest that staff of 500 will have to be 350 by 2002.

Friday, 18th April

Graham Burton, Ivor's colleague from his days in New York, telephones. He has been in San Francisco, Jakarta ... he has four days in London before he is sent to Lagos as Our Man.

'He'll have a hell of a time.' (Ivor)

The man from Millbank's press office rings. *Newsnight* would like to talk to Ivor. The man from Millbank's press office would like to talk to Ivor first.

Saturday, 19th April

They think they are going to win Cardiff North. The 500 wooden stakes for posters-in-gardens have run out.

Go to Garden City and buy nine plants. Expect there will be one survivor this time next year.

Tuesday, 22nd April

The New Labour broadcast last night fed itself by mocking the Old Conservative idols: Land of Hope and Glory, The Flag, True Blue ... until the

Conservative sandcastle was washed away by the tide.

Ivor is on the phone ' ... upset people who are trying to help him ...' I offer my advice:

'It'll take him well into the second year to start learning how to do the job. He is very insecure, that's why he surrounds himself with people who know less than he does, it makes him feel bigger and stronger. He needs to prove that he has balls.'

'He's proved it.'

'Not to himself.'

'Oh ...' (sigh) 'we'll have to go through all that macho stuff. Must make Quick Firm Decisions. And they'll be wrong.'

Meeting at the school. We have to deal with a cut of £55,000 from a budget of about half a million. Somebody suggests children bring their own pencils.

Wednesday, 23rd April

Drive to Brixton Centre (of Lambeth College) for union meeting. About 70 of us. A battered gathering. Cheap clothes. Tired faces. Hair awry. We are frightened. The new poor. Mortgages. Dependent children. No salary rise for four years. Many without cars. Without holidays abroad. We want our children to have the opportunity to go to university, as we did. Will we be able to afford it? As for the single parents among us ...

We are told the redundancies are now 40/45. There is to be an improved 'voluntary severence' offer. If enough of us don't take it 'there are bound to be compulsory redundancies'. More fear in the air.

An envelope goes round to collect for our colleagues at our neighbouring college, Southwark, where they are on indefinite strike, faced with over 100 redundancies. Not much money goes in.

We debate whether or not we should ballot ourselves on indefinite strike action. I argue we should take any action short of strike action: if we ballot for strike action and get a 50/50ish result (likely) we are split down the middle. If the strikers win (just) a body of staff will strike-break. If the non-strikers win (just) we might as well have put our hands up and said Please Sack Us ... we won't do anything. All but me vote to ballot. I wonder if they will do that in secret. Mortgages ... milk ... they have to be paid for.

Ivor, Andrew and Ted see the Leader of the House of Lords' senior civil servant Simon Burton. They are given the procedures if New Labour is elected and are appointed Leader, Deputy Leader and Chief Whip: who telephones who, what decisions have to be made, how many jobs there are to be filled.

Thursday, 24th April
Just over 20 teaching jobs are to go at Lambeth College. 45 posts altogether. A few 'instructors' jobs are offered. Instructors are cheap teachers. Office staff have been downgraded, which means they cost less. The postwoman, who carries the mail between sites, is cut.

We are called to a meeting with The Throne. I have not seen him for two years - maybe longer.

Those whose jobs are affected have already seen The Power. They have been in the pub. About ten of them are at The Throne's meeting.

The Throne tries to cut through the emotion with figures. He tells us Lambeth College has to find cuts of £1.63 million and that if we don't our funding council (the FEFC) will impose its own rescue plan which would bring more cuts. There is a chance our funding will be cut further in the future. We are, he says the second most expensive college in the UK (he thanks God for Hackney). He tells us that he and the Throne of another expensive college are having a meeting at Education to put their case for being expensive. This is because there is a lobby in the opposite direction: the Thrones at the cheaper colleges are stirred up at the inequity of it.

There is some shouting and finger-pointing from the floor. I ask the question I want to ask: if we are losing 45 posts for 97/98, and if we have the same amount of money next year, how many posts will we lose in 98/99?

The Throne says he does not have those figures. He will get hold of them.

Nearly-Doctor-Cousin comes to babysit. She has been working in North and Central America. She had a loaded gun held to her head in casualty in Washington DC.

Meet Our Man-to-be in Lagos and his wife for dinner. They will have armed guards and steel doors to their bedroom.

When we get home Nearly-Doctor-Cousin is looking at photographs of bent feet. She admits that she and William have, between them, broken his sword.

Friday, 25th April
Discuss sword at 6 a.m. Get letter from Parking Committee for London: they will decide my appeal in the week of 20th May.

Saturday, 26th April

Drive to Ealing with a box of salad—my contribution for lunch. There are 12 of us who left Oxford High School in 1970. 27 years ago. There are four of us who started at Oxford High School in 1955. 41 years ago. The three others from 1955 are an architect in Newark; the mother of three adopted children in Grenoble; a charity-worker for the unemployed in London with three children in Oxford. There is a sweetness in the long connection in our pasts. 14 years together, from when we were four, are a bond. There is the open question—nearing competition—to see who will have the last baby. Liz, whose house we are in, has a two-year-old who has been ousted as youngest by somebody who is not there. On the other hand, Melinda's eldest is 27. A number have never married. Watching us now, I realise how much was decided long ago: the homes we came from have made their mark harder and more conspicuously than all that education. (The Oxford High School and the House of Lords have something in common.)

The division that existed between us is still there: between those who were sent to the school to have the advantages their parents had and those who were sent there to have the advantages their parents did not have.

The charity worker remembers our bitter-tongued music teacher accusing us of being 'like those girls who hang around Woolworths and paint their nails'. I remember too, and when the charity worker met one of the 'free place' girls at the last gathering she talked of it: she described looking down at her painted nails and feeling seared for life by the snobbery. Perhaps it is the education that means 30 years later we can talk about it across the old division.

There is Talk about Boys among those who always Talked about Boys (who used to Go Out With which cabinet minister) and I am reminded why I was one of the Founder Members of The Spinsters' Union.

As we start to go our separate ways, there is a sweetness—not quite a sadness—in the extraordinariness of our meeting after 30 years. And the unspoken thought that in another thirty years we we will be in our 70s and who knows? ... It'll be first to die, not last to have a baby ... and then last to live.

We were educated to compete.

Monday, 28th April

Ivor spends more time in Brentford. New Labour is going to win Brentford.

Dishwasher breaks. Use plates twice.

Still dazed by Saturday in Ealing.

Tuesday, 29th April

Ivor goes to Northampton. I get back from Lambeth College to find a message for him to ring Jonathan Powell. I ring Jonathan Powell to tell him Ivor is in Northampton.

Derek the Plumber cannot come until next week.

Ivor gets back from Northampton and rings Jonathan Powell who says:

'If we win on Thursday, Tony will need to talk to you on Saturday about who does what in the Lords. Can you let him have a piece of paper with your thoughts on this tomorrow ... so that when he's in Sedgefield on Thursday he can think about it?'

This fits the picture of cobbling a government together on the back of an envelope at the last moment. The Prime Minister who begins to think about governing on polling day.

So. It looks as if Ivor is going to get 'The lowly cabinet position of Leader of the Lords' as he calls it. And when Blair told him he did want him to do the job before this diary started, he meant it.

Break news about plumber.

William makes the point that politics is taking over his life.

Ivor starts plotting his thoughts for Blair. They remain the same as months ago.

I begin to worry about security ... holidays ... the things that affect Life.

Papers talk of Landslides. The biggest change since 1945. The New Labour Government of 1997 will be remembered. The 1945 majority was 147.

Wednesday, 30th April

Sunny.

Fire drill at Lambeth College. The Power is Chief Fire Marshal.

Work with two hairdressers. Try to find out how much they do not know. Put four pencils on the table. Ask them to pick up half of them. There is a pause. One of the hairdressers picks up one of the pencils. The hairdressers are in their 20s, have small children and were educated in this country. They are not stupid.

The Times says that Blair has resisted pressure to make Tessa Blackstone Leader of the Lords. It also says Pat Hollis is one of the Blair Mob. She was telling Ivor the other day she has never met him.

Ivor and Ted have put together their Thoughts for Blair. Marianne has typed them. I have them here:

POSSIBLE MINISTERIAL APPOINTMENTS IN THE HOUSE OF LORDS

CHIEF WHIP

Ted Graham is the obvious and best candidate for this job. He knows the Lords intimately. He has negotiated with the Tories solidly now for seven years as the Opposition Chief Whip and is trusted by the backbenchers.

We are going to have some very difficult times, particularly in the initial stages until everything settles down. Frankly, I think he is the only person who can be guaranteed to produce the attendance necessary from our somewhat elderly troops to make sure that we can keep a House.

How long he remains Chief Whip is another matter but to start off with, he is the obvious candidate.

DEPUTY CHIEF WHIP

Brian Morris has been doing this job in Opposition and doing it well. The post of Deputy Chief Whip here tends to be under-used and there is no reason at all why he should not couple it with being responsible for Welsh Affairs and taking the Welsh Devolution Bill through. The only other Welsh speaker we have got is Gareth Williams and you may have something else in mind for him.

Ministerial Appointments

Health	Margaret Jay
Social Security	Patricia Hollis
Home Office	Andrew McIntosh
Trade & Industry / Treasury	Maurice Peston
Agriculture	Denis Carter
Heritage	Bernard Donoughue
Scotland	John Sewell

These posts to a certain extent pick themselves since they are already the Opposition spokespersons.

There is a difficulty about Education and Employment. Brian Morris has been doing this up to now but it will clearly need a powerful voice. One possibility might be Tessa Blackstone if she would do it and if you thought she would be more useful there than at the Foreign Office. If she went to the FCO, then there is no obvious person to do it but either Stanley

Clinton-Davis or, possibly, Frank Judd might do. Of the two, I would on balance prefer Stanley.

Environment may also cause a problem. At the moment, Charles Williams does it and might be prepared to do it in Government but perhaps only if his status would be, as he would see it, fully recognised. At the moment, he doubles it with Defence. If Frank Judd were available, he could do that.

At the moment, Gareth Williams does Northern Ireland and Wales. As you know, he is a highly competent man and would, I think, be quite prepared to go on with that portfolio. On the other hand, there is no reason why the Solicitor General should not be in the Lords and he clearly would be more than capable of doing that job. The present Northern Ireland Minister, Baroness Denton, has quite a high profile in Northern Ireland and in the absence of Gareth, one of the newer entrants such as Larry Whitty or Liz Symons (both of whom have settled in here well) could, I think, handle it up here. There remains the question of Whips. Whips in the Lords are vocal and frequently have to speak on Departmental matters. The Tories have six at the moment. Given the difficulties of running this place with the small numbers that we have, I think we should have seven. My candidates would be Josie Farrington, Joyce Gould, Alf Dubs, Derek Gladwin, Brenda Dean, Simon Haskel and Helen Hayman.

Transport does not, I think, merit a separate portfolio in the Lords and it could either go to Environment or, alternatively, be handled by one of the Whips. If, however, you thought it should have a separate Minister, then Tony Berkeley, who is one of the present spokespersons, would do it well.

The other difficult problem is that of status. At the moment, the Tories have six Ministers of State and six Parliamentary Secretaries. I am told that there would be no great problem in having an extra Parliamentary Secretary but, obviously, the number of Ministers of State is a matter for you. The names that come to mind at that level are Patricia Hollis, Andrew McIntosh, Tessa Blackstone, Maurice Peston, Charles Williams and Stanley Clinton-Davis (if he has a major portfolio).

RICHARD
30 April 1997

Thursday, 1st May

Sunny.

Quiet at Lambeth College.

Vote Labour for the first time in my life.

About 10 o'clock our party assembles. We are thirteen-and-a-bit people, two dogs and William asleep at the top of the house. The bit-of-a-person is my second step-grandchild who is due to be born at Christmas. This bit-of-a-person's mother is my stepdaughter. The second dog is hers too.

The exit poll suggests the Conservatives have lost. By midnight it is clear that they have. Younger stepson says the undecideds have decided a long time ago that they were not going to vote Conservative. They were undecided about what they were going to vote.

I cannot believe what I am watching. Ivor spends a lot of time sitting out in the backyard. The fewest Tories since 1832. Since George Eliot's days.

I don't think anybody else believes what they are watching ... Historic Night ... not 18 years ... 165 years.

The dishwasher is still not working.

I get to bed about 4 in the morning.

Friday, 2nd May

William is up by six. There is more news: the Independent, Martin Bell, has won Tatton, as Mrs Gaskell's Captain Brown won Cranford; Michael Portillo has lost; Norman Lamont has lost ... names that may mean nothing in a few months time.

Stagger through the routine and to Lambeth College.

My colleagues are buzzing. Hoarse from shouting through the night. One said '... and people are just sitting on the bus!' Meet the Head of Art and Design lost on the stairs ... 'it's the Labour Government.'

Hear the story of the Smoker at a party in North London: he was in the garden having a smoke when Michael Portillo's result came through. When he came in the others turned to tell him but 'I knew something had happened; I could hear cheering and shouting coming out of all the houses all around.'

9.05 p.m. the telephone rings. Ivor answers it. His voice is measured and sedate but he keeps thrusting his thumb into the air.

'Is that Lord Richard?'

'Yes.'

'10 Downing Street here. Can you hold a moment?'

'The Prime Minister's Private Secretary comes on: 'The Prime Minister ... 12.15 ... tomorrow.'

There is concern for Ivor's transport. Ivor says he will walk: 'It's not a very long walk.'

Saturday, 3rd May

Ivor considers his ties. He goes out and buys new ones. He finds rows of golden apples on dark blue. He sets off bedecked for 10 Downing Street.

My friend Taffy, whom I have known since university, and Tom, whom I have known since he was born, arrive for the day with a Marble Run. We run marbles. Ivor comes home with two files and runs marbles too. Between runs he mutters:

'Blair looked terrible ... terrible ... staring eyes ... white face ... puffy ... manic ... but, typical Blair, he wouldn't discuss anything. He had my piece of paper in front of him ... I don't know if he'd read it. He asked: 'who do you want for Chief Whip?' I said 'Ted.' He said, 'I'm not sure I can meet you on that.'

'Poor Ted.'

'Yes, he's very hurt ... Blair also said he didn't think Tessa wanted to leave Birkbeck ... and he made it clear he didn't think abolishing the hereditary peers a first priority ... he is keener on devolution.'

'If he'd sorted all this out beforehand he wouldn't have to waste time on it now ... he hasn't got the time now and by being so slow, he's starting all sorts of rumours and difficulties ... this Minister for Europe ...'

'Margaret's putting her foot down ... however good David Simon is he has never stood at a despatch box ... she doesn't want him.'

'What else did Blair say?'

'That I was to keep close to Derry.'

'What does that mean?'

'Say the same as Derry. I expect I will have to look after him.'

Taffy, Tom, William and I walk along the river.

Denise, Ivor's driver, picks him up to take him to Buckingham Palace. She is a Government driver. She was driving Cranborne until the election. A glance at the set of her jaw would tell you she is Very Sorry Indeed not to be driving Cranborne today.

Janet, Taffy and Tom's driver, picks them up and takes them to King's Cross to catch their train to Cambridge.

Rain at last.

William runs marbles. I read Ivor's two files:

1. Black plastic with gold letters: *EIIR LORD PRIVY SEAL*
2. Brown manilla, *LORD PRIVY SEAL* typed on a white label.

The Civil Service is in charge.
Black Plastic contains:

1. Private Office and daily routine in the Privy Council Office (ie who works there and what they do)
2. A copy of the 'History of the office of Lord Privy Seal' which starts with a sheet headed *PRECEDENCE* which I shall copy here. Notice particularly the Civil Service's understated final 13 words:

Strictly speaking, the Lord Privy Seal is fifteenth on the List of Precedence in England:
The Sovereign
The Prince Philip, Duke of Edinburgh
The Prince of Wales
The Prince Andrew, Duke of York
The Prince Edward
The Princess Royal
The Duke of Gloucester
The Duke of Kent
Archbishop of Canterbury
Lord High Chancellor
Archbishop of York
The Prime Minister
The Lord President of the Council
Speaker of the House of Commons
Lord Privy Seal
The Lord Privy Seal therefore comes above the High Commissioners, Ambassadors, other Archbishops and the Secretaries of State. However, although the Lord Privy Seal has been for a long time an office enjoying considerable prestige, he has not for centuries been quite of the first rank in practice.

It goes on to explain that it started with King John (1199–1216) when the

Lord Privy Seal looked after the King's private seal. After the middle of the 16th century he stopped using it in his own name and power moved to the newly-created secretaries of state. Then in 1884 the Great Seal Act got rid of it.

The first Privy Seals have been lost. The oldest survivor is Henry III's. Some medieval ones survive but unbroken ones are rare. The last one, made on Queen Victoria's accession in 1837, is four inches in diameter and a bit thicker than that. It is silver and lives in a velvet box in a leather case.

3. The role of the Lord Privy Seal on the boards of trustees for Chequers, Chevening and Dorneywood.

So Ivor chairs committees that keep houses.

4. A brief for the Leader of the House of Lords.

Again, Ivor is told what the offices are, what he has to do, and who else works there and what they have to do. There are lists of all the Members and statistics on how long they 'sat' from 1993 until now: how long the House sat; how long individuals sat. Ted managed 78 of the 79 sits last session. So did Longford. Derry got to 35.

Peerage type is listed:

Archbishop
Countess
Bishop
Viscount
Duke
Baron/Lord
Marquess
Baroness
Earl
Lady

Sittings are timed to the minute and shown in graphics and pie charts.

Jane Hope is the civil servant in charge of the Lord Privy Seal. Simon Burton is the civil servant in charge of the Leader of the House of Lords. Ivor wonders if they are keeping smiles off their faces. They are good civil servants and he can't be sure.

Brown Manilla contains:

1.   handwritten numbers: office+home+mobile for Jane Hope. Home+mobile+carphone for Denise Mordue (the driver who can easily keep the smile off her face – Ivor does not think she is a member of the Labour Party). Office+home+pager for Simon Burton.
2.   the order for Ivor to go to Her Majesty's Most Honourable Privy Council (that is where he is now) in 'ordinary clothes' (what did they think New Labour might wear?).
3.   Matters for Decision
The first of these is whether or not the Lord Privy seal will carry the Cap of Maintenance at the State opening of Parliament on the 14th May.

What kind of circus is Ivor joining?

Next is the order and content of debates followed by which bills come first then whether or not to have a Whitsun holiday. Last, Ivor has to put peers on committees.

There is a note at the end explaining the duties of the Chief Whip as Captain of the Gentlemen. He has to have a uniform fitted and made for 14th May. Blair had better hurry up. Ted is languishing. He needs to be told whether or not he is Captain of the Gentlemen.

Next there is an order from Blair:

> *'... the Prime Minister draws the attention of his colleagues to chapter 8 of QPM which deals with the rules on private interests and would be grateful if ministers would ensure that they order their affairs, so that no conflict arises or could be thought to arise between their private interests and their public duties.'*

Ivor has no affairs to order.

Then come five Guiding Principles and 25 Rules on Travel of Ministers.

Then five points on who can or cannot be appointed to jobs and paid for or not paid for by public funds.

Next, a parliamentary private secretary cannot be appointed without the permission of:

a.   the Chief Whip and

b.   the Prime Minister.

Next I find a copy of Questions of Procedure for Ministers. It is dated May 1992 and blue. You can go out and buy it if you want to.

Last of all is a hand-drawn and hand-coloured map. 10 Downing Street is coloured-in in orange. The Privy Council offices are in blue. The Lord Privy Seal's Offices (five of them) are in yellow and the Judicial Committee is pink. Sir Robin Butler's office has not been coloured-in. There are two Xs:

1.   to mark the entrance from Downing Street
2.   to mark the connecting door to 10 Downing Street

Ivor will not get lost.

It is clear that, as the civil service puts it, Ivor has two hats: Lord Privy Seal and Leader of the House of Lords. He has a set of offices with each job. The civil service expect that over time, he will decide how to divide his time and his presence. It is hard to see how he can spend much time chairing houses' committees. They seem to meet twice a year. With three houses that is six meetings. None of them are in any of these offices.

Ivor comes home again. He has Knelt and Kissed Hands (instructed to 'brush with lips'). Also kneeling and kissing hands were Margaret Becket, Mo Mowlam and other hard-line anti-establishmenters of the past. My mind boggles at what the smell of power causes people to do. And they swore their oaths:

OATH TO BE TAKEN IN THE PRESENCE OF THE QUEEN IN COUNCIL

You do swear by Almighty God that you will well
and truly serve Her Majesty Queen Elizabeth the Second
in the office of (office filled in by hand)
SO HELP YOU GOD.

There is a memorandum to go with this:

The Lord Privy Seal, on his name being called by the Lord President, will leave his place in the line of Privy Counsellors and kneeling (right knee) on the footstool facing Her Majesty, with a Testament uplifted in his right hand take the Oath of Office which will be administered by the Clerk of the Council.

> *He will then rise, move forward, kneel (right knee) on the second footstool
> in front of Her Majesty and kiss hands on appointment.*
> *Her Majesty will then hand to him the Seal of Office. Thereafter the Lord
> Privy Seal will return to his original position in the line of Privy Counsellors.*

Some of them chose to affirm. The Lord President is, for the first time in
history, a woman.

I go and get Chinese Takeaway.

Ivor is still muttering that Blair has got to learn to delegate. That he is
remote ... unfriendly ... won't discuss. I try my usual explanation that Blair
needs to assert himself ... he is frightened of Ivor's age and experience, ... as
the others in the new cabinet are.

'Then it's time they all bloody well grew up. He's the Prime Minister for
God's sake.'

There is a trickle of calls through the evening: congratulations which are
an undisguised 'Have I got a job?' It is Very Nasty Not Knowing. Remember
Lambeth College ...

Sunday, 4th May

The Lord Privy Seal has gone swimming with his son while I write this.
People might assume that was what he did all the time. Seals are known to be
an aquatic species.

New Labour have a majority of 254 over the Conservatives. If New
Labour lose 100 seats in the election of 2002 they will have a majority of 154
to take them to 2007.

The New Labour Cabinet is announced. Ivor is the eldest and earns the
least.

Cherie Booth/Blair is photographed on her doorstep with her hair on
end, her eyes shut and in sleepwear. Hope she doesn't mind.

Listen to the one o'clock news. A few more jobs are announced. Harriet
Harman can't have chosen Frank Field as her Minister. Nobody is being consulted. No news of Ted. He has waited to hear through Friday, Saturday and
now Sunday.

'It's cruel,' say I.

'Yes, compassion is not a sign of weakness.'

'Common humanity,' I add a cliché.

Ivor rings Merlyn who comments:

'What a way to run a ship.'

'Why's he doing it?' Ivor is rhetorical.

'He wants power,' I try, 'wants to keep control.'

'In that case he doesn't understand the nature of power. He'll lose it. The way to do it is to hand over the job. Let them get on with it. Let them know you're watching.'

William and I and the Lord Privy Seal go to the Natural History Museum. Another of the seal's habitats, one might suppose, albeit posthumous.

Look at layers in volcanic ash; rings in trees; layers in a staligmite; layers in a scallop shell, marks of time.

Find a plaster skeleton of a giant American sloth, extinct for 10,000 years.

'That's young' says Ivor.

Observe geology's R.I.P: Restless in Perpetuity. Could apply that to all of us.

Go home and look at the defunct dishwasher.

Ivor rings Ted:

'Ted, I've heard nothing.' Neither has Ted.

'Glad to know you're as concerned as me' he says.

Ivor tries the defunct dishwasher. It works.

Monday, 5th May, Bank Holiday

Telephone rings every five minutes all day. I get congratulated. Refrain from asking what for.

Callers include Margaret Becket ... 'I would very much like to speak to Ivor ...' She is fighting off the imposition of David Simon. She foresees trouble.

Put in and take out the laundry when not answering the telephone. A schoolfriend comes to spend the day with William. They play more than they quarrel. The Schoolfriend's mother comes for the day too.

Ivor rings. Denis Carter has been given Ted's job.

'Unnecessary and unkind.'

'Will he be good at the job?'

'All right. No better than Ted.'

'Is he a lot younger than Ted?'

' No. He's my age. I had another go at Blair but he's not having it ... he asked me if I wanted to tell Ted ... I told him "You tell him."'

'Can't he have it for a year?'

'Not even for a year.'

Ted rings. I say how sorry I am. Then I realise Ted may not know. Ted says:

'At least I won't have the responsibility. The thing that's beginning to irk is the humiliation in front of colleagues ... who know I've been dropped.'

I think he did know ... but I'm not certain.

He has had to wait for four days by the telephone for this humiliation. The son of the meat porter, paid in beer, is not to be New Labour's Captain of the Gentlemen.

I ring Ivor to tell him Ted rang. To tell him I assumed Ted knew.

'Bloody hell ... did he know?'

'I think so.'

'I was waiting for Blair to ring him. Then I was going to ring him. What did he say?' I repeat Ted's words. 'He's not the only one who's going to be humiliated. There are lots of them.'

It will be a relief to get back to Lambeth College tomorrow.

Ivor gets home with a scribbled list. Ted (who was Chief Whip) and Andrew (who was Deputy Leader) are dumped. So are Maurice Peston, Charles Williams and Brian Morris. They were all on the front bench too. Blair has dumped the older men from Ivor's list and juggled around with the others. Liz Symons, with little experience of any bench, will find herself at the despatch box arguing Foreign Affairs with ex-foreign secretaries.

However good she is (and she's not touched Foreign Affairs before) she cannot yet be that good. Ivor had suggested she start with Northern Ireland. Derry wants to be friendly '... but they have all got to learn that you cannot govern a country from a mobile phone ... they've never had drivers ... never had red boxes ...' In fact Ivor does not have a red box. He has a brown box.

Derry has been given two jobs. Robin Butler has said he will not be able to do both.

Read Ivor's papers from the Committee for Constitutional Reform. Nothing new.

Spare several thoughts for the older men who worked for this day for 18 years, to be dumped.

Tuesday, 6th May

Cold. Snow in Wales.

Liz and Richard take us to Covent Garden. Half way through L'Elisir d'Amore I realise it means the Elixir of Love. This turns out to be bordeaux.

On the way out Ivor meets Damien Welfare whom he would like as his political adviser. So New Labour does go to the opera.

On getting home, learn that Ivor has been at five meetings where the same people have talked about the same things. Peter Mandelson has drifted in and out of all of them.

'He enjoys looking sinister.'

Robin Butler is Having Difficulty with Derry Irvine.

'He is trying to be the Prime Minister's Right Hand Man ... he can't go on as he is. He talked for an hour and a half. It'll settle down ... they'll all settle down. They're intelligent men. They'll work it out. Otherwise he'll get up everybody's noses with "the PM wants ... the PM says ... the PM has told me ..." ... he won't like being stuck on the woolsack.'

Also learn that Ivor saw Cranborne. Denise-The- Driver was Very Upset by the election results. Cranborne has told Denise not to be rude.

Finally learn that 'Andrew has been forgotten.'

'Forgotten?'

'Yes. Forgotten.'

'?!'

'Denis remembered. Rang Jonathan Powell. Jonathan Powell said 'Oh God!' and now Andrew is Deputy Chief Whip. Deputy Chief Whip had been forgotten too.'

Wednesday, 7th May

All quiet at Lambeth College. So quiet that I am the only person in the Study Centre.

Rush home to Derek the plumber. Walk dog. Liz turns up. Derek mends overflowing lavatory, mends other, leaking lavatory, mends side of bath. Leave him mending and Liz and I walk over the river to St Margaret's Church.

Nick Hinton's memorial service is terrible and beautiful. Terrible because he was 54 and his daughter who is at the front is 12. Beautiful because Nick was a good man and the words and music remind us of this life's limitations. It would take a monster not to be distressed.

> *Blest are the pure in heart;*
> *For they shall see our God*
>
> *Lord, we thy presence seek;*
> *May ours this blessing be.'*

Tom Burke talks of Nick the warrior, but his voice breaks when he talks of 'my friend'.

'Lass dich nur nichts nicht dauren mit Trauren, sei stille'. We finish with Fauré: May the angels lead thee into paradise.'

I sit there and cry. I cannot think I am alone. Don't look.

As the congregation waits to leave there is a downpour and the smell of it wafts over us.

Go and get William. Sara has bought him a bow and arrows. She has bought Florence a bow and arrows too.

Ivor is not late. He is on more Cabinet Committees: Europe, Public Expenditure, the Constitution. I am beginning to see that this is the purpose of his Cabinet Office rooms. His job has scope which may or may not be used by the Prime Minister—who may or may not put him on Cabinet Committees.

David Simon's appointment has been announced. Margaret Beckett has partially got him out from under her feet. There have been several appointments to the Lords announced which must have got through the Scrutiny Committee in double-quick time!

The Daily Telegraph has asked to interview Lady Richard. Alastair Campbell does not think it is a good idea. Janet Jones does not mind one way or the other what Alastair Campbell thinks. Lady Richard can be the property of the Government for the moment. Janet Jones is writing her own version of Lady Richard. She will decide when to offer Lady Richard to the public. The only person to be consulted will be Ivor Richard.

Next Wednesday, when the Queen opens the new Parliament, Lady Richard has been booked a seat in the Chamber. I do not want to dress up as Lady Richard (evening dress ... decorations ... tiaras ... a wife once told me not to worry that I was not wearing a tiara) and I am trying to find a compromise. This is partly in the interests of Marital Harmony, partly out of curiosity.

Can I go, as me, and watch from a gallery? I'll be respectable. Ivor is suspicious:

'They'll think that a very *odd* request.'

'Who are 'they?'

'Black Rod ...'

If 'Black Rod' doesn't sound odd, I don't know what does. Not something you would want in a children's home. (In fact, Black Rod is the Facilities Manager of the House of Lords.)

Ivor will make enquiries. I repeat that I will Be Respectable but continue to resist the picture of myself dressed as Lady Richard. Remember colleague who was watching satellite news in Poland and spotted me, dressed as Lady Richard, meeting Nelson Mandela:

'That's Janet Jones.' And she laughed. Exactly.

Ivor has appointed Margaret Jay as his Deputy. He tells Jim Callaghan who says:

'Our Margaret?'

'Yes ... do you want to know why?'

'Yes.'

'I had a choice: Stanley Clinton-Davies, Tessa Blackstone or Margaret.'

'I quite see.'

Southwark College, Lambeth College's neighbour, is on indefinite strike and is in the headlines. The £69million deficit in Further Education is a problem. Yet I work in a part-empty building and that is a problem too. The students don't come. Many of those who do come can't do. The schools have hardly touched some of them in the 11 years they were there.

Ask Ivor for his new telephone numbers so I can ring him at work.

'I don't know,' he says, 'I can't ring myself up yet.'

Break backdoor handle.

Thursday, 8th May

Ivor puts on the Golden Apple Tie for his first Cabinet Meeting, the first for 18 years.

I take William to school on my way to Lambeth College.

On the way home from school, William asks me if I was around in the days of the dodo. I tell him I was not.

The Cabinet Meeting was 'jolly'. They started with photographs.

Ivor asked Robin Butler, 'How many of these have you done before?'

'18 ... 20 ... but this is a bit special.'

Ivor is next to Harriet Harman.

'You don't like her.'

'It's mutual ... She was complaining about the civil servants.'

The Cabinet Committee on Europe is going to be the most interesting: 'a lot of decisions have to be made quickly.'

Any committee that Derry is on, he continues to talk: 'I don't want to sound like a lawyer, but ...'

'Don't then,' said Mo, to Ivor.

'He does sound like a lawyer,' says Ivor to me, 'he keeps talking as if he's in court.'

'He's never been anywhere else.'

Later, Derry 'complained bitterly' that people are complaining to him about what has been done to the Lords.

'Nobody consulted me,' said Ivor.

Some of the dumped and therefore malcontent will have tackled Derry. Charles Williams and Maurice Peston are both angry: 'If they think we will sit here night after night and vote for the government ...' Derry said he did not talk to Blair about it:

'Sally Morgan has a lot of contact with the Lords.' Sally Morgan works in 10 Downing Street.

'He can't have it both ways,' says Ivor, 'if he is the Prime Minister's Right Hand Man one moment ... and knows nothing about any appointment the next ...'

Ivor asked Jim Callaghan to propose the formal address next Wednesday. Jim tells him he would rather not. He has lost confidence. Merlyn will do it instead.

Ivor has got a ticket for me to sit in a gallery next Wednesday, so I can go dressed as myself.

'Was that OK?'

'I don't know. As Leader of the House I can sort it.'

I will not have to spend a morning behaving like, and dressed as, a nineteenth-century Cheer Leader.

'What do you think I will look like?' asks Ivor.

Get my hair cut. The haircutter tells me the subjects she is told not to touch: religion, politics, sex and money.

Come out into a wall of rain. No umbrella. No coat. No bus. No taxi. See a taxi. Get it. Lady with talons (scarlet) elbows in:

'It's mine.'

Tell her she is charming, Madam. Get a bus in Regent Street. Haircut has survived: rained on, steamed and showered. It is a good haircut.

The dishwasher has stopped. Again.

Must remember to return pot of fuchsias to where they belong now we have no drip.

Friday, 9th May

Derry, Ivor and the Duke of Norfolk (the Earl Marshal, the senior peer in England) go through the ceremony for the opening of Parliament. The Duke says: 'Of course we're a Liberal family. Glad to see you boys. Couldn't have had you with those unions. But now ...'

Derry has to walk downstairs backwards wearing a long skirt.

'He doesn't want to fall down in front of ten million people,' says Ivor.

Saturday, 10th May

William and I take a train to Warrington and my old friend The Cheshire Barrister. (She was renowned for keeping gerbils and brewing beer in her student rooms. The two did not go well together.) He asks me how to spell 'pony.' I cannot remember. 'Pony'? 'Poney'? All fellow passengers seem to be reading newspapers that have long words in them. They assume that look: I Am Not Listening.

Sunday, 11th May

It turns out that the Cheshire Barrister's youngest daughter has a pony and a horse. Take a train back to London. William makes the point, several times, that he has neither a horse nor a pony.

The *Sunday Times* has drawn up Blair's first reshuffle. Ivor's job goes to Liz Symons. He has had it for a week.

'What is interesting is seeing who will be any good as a minister. You never know. Some you think will be splendid are a disaster and some you think will be a disaster are splendid. Look at Merlyn and Shirley Williams. She could not take decisions. He took a decision and moved on.'

The backdoor handle has come off.

The dishwasher is functioning.

Monday, 12th May

Getting back to normal. Beginning to believe that the Labour Party won the election, that Ivor was given a job and that he is in local, pensionable employment. Good news is as much of a shock as bad news.

I try to ring Ivor at work. The switchboard is in disarray: they are handling the biggest upheaval for years. I ask to be put through to the Leader of the House of Lords. Get an answering machine that says it will not take any messages. That any messages left there will not be answered.

Ivor got a message from the Romanian Ambassador in Washington. He would like a word with him. He rang him. The Romanian Ambassador in Washington had had a message that Ivor would like a word with him. They had a word.

Tuesday, 13th May

Ask Ivor if he believes what has happened. He says Robin Butler wants a word with him today: 'I have a ghastly feeling he's going to take it all away.'

Sara has found mouse droppings in the Study Centre. Survey them and wonder what the mice are finding to eat. Remark that the droppings resemble little black beetles that are falling through our top ceiling. We are finding them in the bath, over the floor, the window sills. They look like mouse droppings, but they move. Sara says I should speak to Len. They could be furniture beetles (woodworm). Len walks through the door. Tell him. Furniture beetles come out to mate May–September. They lay eggs in wood. Those then hatch and start to consume the house and its contents ... oh the havoc.

Try to think what would be left. Slates on the roof . Quarry tiles on the basement floor. In between a very great deal of wood.

Experts are needed to assess and spray.

Robin Butler had his word. Are the civil service doing their bit? Very much so. It is good to have Ivor on the Public Expenditure Committee: not coming from a spending ministry he can add Weight without Baggage. Cabinet Meetings have lost their purpose. The Cabinet has got too big. Decisions are made by the Prime Minister or groups of ministers. Rows are in private. The real decisions and business now take place in Cabinet Committees. Then they talked about Europe.

Ivor had to write to Jack Straw about his plan for 'fast-track' legislation. There is no 'fast-track' in the Lords.

He also had to write a 'stiff letter' to Mo: she had said there would be two short uncontroversial Northern Ireland Bills. One is long and controversial throughout. The other is not short and controversial in part.

Delaying reforming the Lords may yet be seen to be an error. The Government is in a tiny minority there. Although the Lords cannot stop legislation, they can delay it by as much as eighteen months.

We have a copy of the Queen's Speech for tomorrow. Education comes first:

'The education of young people will be my Government's first priority. They will work to raise standards in schools, colleges and universities ...'

Thus my world meets Ivor's world. Southwark College's strike is on the news. I do not want to join them.

Wednesday, 14th May

The Queen is opening Parliament. I drive William to school before the roads start closing.

I get dressed as myself. There is a touch of Chairman Mao about my jacket and trousers. My amber earrings are intended to relieve the sobriety. When I am put in the West Gallery the ranks of peers' wives below me reinforce my instinct to recoil at the thought of joining them. Their seats are so sought after, they have to be balloted for.

I sit for three-quarters of an hour before the procession reaches us. I am next to the Lord Mayor of Westminster and Jane Ashdown. The Mayor and I talk about his ward—Ladbroke Grove—and Jane Ashdown and I talk about Paddy's election successes (she says 'It hasn't really sunk in'); whether or not Jane should be wearing a hat; how the Blairs are going to protect their children from the ravages of their father's public life. I don't see how they can. Jane tells of how one of their sons was tormented and hounded at school in Yeovil. And I remember 'young' Parkinsons, Jenkinses and Healeys—my generation—perpetually subject to scrutiny and gossip. We also talk about our lives in Lambeth and the Ashdowns' new grandchild who took three days to be born.

Cherie Blair appears next to us in the Gallery. She spies Jane Ashdown and they embrace and start animated conversation. I smile politely but Cherie and I have never met (I can see her processing that fact—getting it right but wondering who I am) and I decide now is not the moment to introduce myself. When Jane sits down again, I explain that I have never met Cherie—Jane must have thought we were not on speaking terms: 'Oh my dear!' she exclaims. She is surprised. And feels she should have introduced us ... but I go on and explain that I hardly ever go to things so it is not surprising.

'We only know each other from meeting in our spousely roles,' she says.

The Queen arrives, walking frontwards—unlike some unfortunates who are walking backwards. In front of her is the Cap of Maintenance. The Cap of Maintenance is red velvet with white trim, stuck on a pole. Carrying this, and underneath a gargantuan red blanket, also with white trim, is Ivor. I give the apparition glances to signal solidarity, but do not risk more for fear of overstretching my composure. It is an extraordinary way to spend a morning.

We have all been given a programme and the Dramatis Personae read like any one of Shakespeare's (or Marlowe's for that matter) history plays. There are 57 characters, ranging from the Monarch and Howard Pursuivant Extraordinary and Garter King of Arms through Woman of the Bedchamber and the Mistress of the Robes and the Master of the Horse to Gold Stick in Waiting and Silver Stick in Waiting. There are even four Pages of Honour. The cast are a motley crew of royalty, politicians, aristocrats, civil servants and servicemen. Some of them are playing the parts of their ancestors—The Queen for one. There are also a Percy, a Howard—Shakespeare had Percys and Howards— and a clutch of other 'old' names: Vestey, Cholmondeley, Fellowes, Fitzpatrick, Havergal, Somerleyton, Chesshyre, Burgess, Belcher ... until we have moved into Restoration Comedy, for 'old' England is still here and breeding.

Duty may volunteer them for this performance. But I look at the Queen, small and tired on her throne, doing this tens of times over the past 40 years and feel sorry for her. I know you can make jokes about this—how can you be sorry for somebody with palaces and castles and diamonds—but we have a constitution which imposes ceremonial (and lots of other things) upon her and her children and their children. She has been cornered by us and her duty and accidents of birth and family history and is hemmed in here, in front of me, by flunkies and politicians and the electorate and the tourist industry and the Church of England, most of whom think she is where she should be, doing what she should be doing. It seems to me a specialised cruelty. This sunny morning in May, countrywomen of her age will be in their gardens or walking their dogs or doing their housework or their shopping; maybe stopping to watch this on television—but then they can switch it off and go away.

After a while the Commons come along and the Queen reads the speech. It is two and a half minutes longer than the one she read last time. Then everybody goes away.

We go away to the Lord Chancellor's (Derry's) reception. Liz Symons is full of push and anxiety: she has to make her first speech of her new job. She keeps turning her back to me to talk to Ivor. When she realises why he has kept trying to introduce me she is embarrassed. I chat with a high court judge who is still wrapped in her red blanket and says she is hot.

Derry addresses us with the information that the Queen is a Very Nice Woman - so sympathetic about his chances of falling over that he felt more nervous than ever. He speaks as if he has known the Queen well for years and the rest of us have never met her. Can see why Ivor feels old and wise.

We go and queue for lunch.

Denise-The-Driver is a careful two minutes late to pick me up. 'I wasn't late, was I?' Barely a question.

'I don't think so. I was early.'

I am not Viscountess Cranborne.

The man from the pest control company comes to diagnose our beetles. He puts dead ones and live ones from our bedroom in his test-tube. He will have the results from the lab in two days and will let me know.

Ivor is late home. Tells me Ann Taylor has been late for two meetings—one of them her own.

Jane is surprised at the number of committees that he is on. He's now on Home Office. It's his Independent Weight.

'I am above it.'

'Not partisan.'

'That's right.'

'Wasn't Cranborne on a lot of committees?'

'Yes – but he was a friend of the Prime Minister's.'

The Lords are threatening not to let Government legislation through. Ivor will not be sorry if they prove his point that the Lords has great nuisance power. They would hasten their own demise.

'They must have thought of that. That if they are good they will last longer.'

'I'm not sure.'

Ivor has to be seen to try to smooth the way but he has a fine line to travel: too smooth and reform will be left; too rough and he will be failing in his job. Bill Rodgers tells him the Liberals will put down a private member's bill and start the process if the Government don't get on with it.

The Lords cannot prevent legislation but they can delay it.

In his speech, Ivor has said how pleased he is that Jim Callaghan is here to see Labour's return after 18 years and Jim wrote a note to say thank you. Ivor was Nice to the Tories. They were not Nice to him:

'They are pretty sick.'

'Nobody likes losing.

'

Thursday, 15th May

'I hope there aren't too many of these 8:30 meetings,' says Ivor as he gets going.

'Whose is it?'

'Derry's. He's taken on so much. He won't be able to do it.'

'What'll happen?'

'He'll live on his nerves, afraid of making mistakes, and half do it.'

I walk the dog, take William to school and get myself to Lambeth College.

Kenneth Clarke announces good politicians are not dangerous, good politicians are decisive.

Cabinet Meeting discussed Zaire, where there are British Troops. George Robertson is exercised by the fact that the Belgians are getting all the credit.

Ivor went in to the Chamber to make his speech, to discover he had been sent with an empty folder.

William comes home with a piece of paper saying they have a half-day tomorrow as a reward for working so hard on their SATS. William says it is really a reward for Miss B. so she can go home early. Struggle to plan to give William his half-day. Ivor got his paperwork done by staying in the Lords until 11.15 p.m. He can be at the school gate tomorrow lunchtime.

Friday, 16th May

The pest control people have not got the lab's diagnosis of our beetles.

Go and get Florence for swimming. Leave Len with another sample of our beetles. He will put them under his microscope.

Ivor thinks he can see what Gordon Brown is doing: he is setting the Big Spenders against each other: Education / Health / Social Security / Defence / Foreign Office will have to vie for money. There are six of them on the Public Expenditure Committee and none of them are Big Spenders.

Difficulties at Chequers, where Ivor is Chairman of the Trustees. The woman who runs it has her own way of doing things. John Major was watching television at 10 o'clock one evening and she walked in and turned the television off. It was time to put the house to bed for the night. John Major said he thought he could turn the television off for himself.

Denise-The-Driver continues Very Unhappy. Ivor continues to drive himself to work.

Saturday, 17th May

Go to Geffrye Museum. Shell of 17th century almshouses filled with a history of English domestic interiors, fronted by lawn and backed by herb garden. The interiors run from Elizabeth I to the 1950s and we place each according to houses we know: my childhood home in Oxford and the Cheshire Barrister's first, then our London house, then Alexander's, then Florence's, then Harriet's, then Jones The Business's and Helen of the Treasury's and Homer's, then Ivor's childhood home and then the days that I was born into. Enjoy the drawings of cross-sections and spot the privies.

Walk into the herb garden and savour it. Fountain for splashing on to the brick paths. Clematis bowers to sit underneath. Meet the gardener. They have trouble getting money: 'It's no good going to the Government, they want to take over. We got some lottery money but we have to match it. Come back later in the summer and it will look different.'

Chelsea play Middlesborough in the Cup Final. The roads and the park are empty.

'A billion people are watching this.' Ivor is one of them.

Sunday, 18th May

Ivor and William met Monica when they were swimming. She will babysit tomorrow. Jones The Business and Helen of the Treasury and Homer come up to London and we eat roast chicken and apple crumble and go to the park.

Monday, 19th May

Phone call from pest control. They are biscuit beetles. He wants me to, pay £200+ for him to get rid of them. There is no guarantee that he will succeed. I ask him to send me a written estimate.

Go and see Tom and Clem at the Aldwych with Liz. The 1945/1997 comparison is laboured. Laugh on and off. A diversion but not Theatre.

Ivor gets home at 11.30 p.m. He has had permission from Number 10 to have Marianne (who spent the election in Millbank) and Damien (of Covent Garden) as his researchers. He has had permission from the Cabinet Office to have one researcher. The Cabinet Office has a tiny budget.

Chelsea ribbons are all over London. I think Chelsea beat Middlesborough.

Tuesday, 22nd May

Len can't find his microscope. l tell him they are biscuit beetles.

Frank Dobson said to Ivor: 'I went to talk to the nurses, said there was no, money and everybody cheered.'

Ivor is reading and reading and; learning what he has to read, learning what he does not have to read:

'There's a lot of paperwork ... Cabinet Committee papers. They are beginning to realise how important the Lords is, how it slows legislation. Derry will be telling Blair.'

He is on ten Cabinet Committees. Jane has told him not to take on too much. I now understand the purpose of the five offices in the Cabinet Office. His job is very flexible in its potential.

Gordon Brown has had to ring him, trying to get legislation through the Lords.

Wednesday, 23rd May

Black Rod came to see Ivor. Derry has been to see him. Derry's flat, which is within the Palace of Westminster and goes with being Lord Chancellor, needs doing-up, says Derry. He says he needs new curtains, new carpets, new decoration. He says he needs half a million pounds. I say he is a bloody fool. Ivor says that is his reaction too. I say that half a million pounds would rescue the jobs going at Lambeth College or that it would provide Ivor with 20 political researchers.

Ivor adds that the Mackays did nothing to the flat, that nothing has been done to it for some years.

'So! ...' say I. 'When he's been there for a fortnight!' I stomp about.

'Calm down,' says Ivor.

Derry is riding for a fall. Hope he has the sense to dismount first.

Thursday, 24th May

Art and Design student shows me his work, including spelling mistakes and wild punctuation, saying he wants to do better. We start with when to use capital letters. Across the top of his page, headed 'Interelation of Coulers', he has scribbled 'my dick so hard it float away when the wind blow.' He does not know it is there.

Go into school and get three secondhand sweatshirts. William comes out with a letter. The teacher who came in to replace the teacher who was the Weak Link and disappeared one day in November, is leaving tomorrow. Miss Godfry is taking over. Wonder if she will last for the remainder of term. Wonder if William will have time to wear out the sweatshirts. We cannot leave him there to drown.

Friday, 25th May

Planning for Blair's first European meeting, the Cabinet Committee (Europe) is settling to Stephen Walls' advice to accept decisions by partial majority instead of unanimity, when Peter Mandelson walks in. Oh, he's not sure ... and he stirs everybody up. It looks as if the decision may be reversed. Robin Cook is starting to worry. Ivor decided to speak:

'We can't send the Prime Minister to Europe to act against the policy we had in Opposition and against the advice of the Ambassador.' That was the end of it. Robin Cook thanked him afterwards.

John Prescott stopped Tony Blair leaving a meeting (the Ministerial Teams have been called in to see him one by one)—'Wait! ... No! ...You must meet

Superwoman!' Superwoman (alias Helene Hayman) describes herself as wondering what she was doing there at all.

Ivor is pleased with his Power Women: Margaret Jay, Pat Hollis, Tessa Blackstone, Liz Symons and Helene Hayman: 'They are formidable. Formidable. They're good.'

The Opposition is struggling:

'All over the place. Can't handle it.'

There will be 30 more New Labour peers but Ivor would like to know who they are.

Tuesday, 27th May

We are at the house.

The only disruption is the cuckoo. After singing thirds for twelve hours on Sunday it went flat with weariness and sang fourths.

Cattle have been in the field while we were in London. Cowpats and chewed trees tell the tale. Sad about William's oak, planted to mark his birth, and two apple trees. The larches and the lime were big and strong enough to withstand the munching. Cattle may be rough but they cannot open gates. Jones The Business suggests chains and padlocks. Nobody can pretend cattle can manage keys.

I have had the time to read the last 27 days of this. You can see the fractured way I am making sense of what Ivor tells me about taking over Government and you can see the fractured way in which he is learning how Government works. Each of these processes has its variables: I have to sieve everything to make sense of it and relay what I think is interesting or important and he has to sieve everything to make sense of it and work out what matters, what could change, what should change, what should not change. Nobody wants to dispense with a whole system but they need to get a grip on the system at the same time as making it their own system. What is the system? What was a Conservative system? What should be New Labour's system?

And there is his own job to work out too.

There was a film last night of Martin Bell's Independent campaign and victory in Tatton. Nobody has mentioned—anywhere that I have come across—that Tatton is Knutsford and that Knutsford is Cranford and Cranford is Mrs Gaskell's vignette of 19th century middle England. And into that Amazon world came Captain Brown who somehow 'made himself accepted in Cranford'.

20th century Knutsford would not be quite sure about Cranford.

Ivor said of the film: 'That's yesterday's story ... sleaze.' I do not agree. We will always enjoy the story of the off-white knight standing against Corruption in Public Life, and winning.

High wind and sun. Too cold to bathe. Dig out overflowing stream instead. Dig out thistles and nettles.

28th May

The stream has stopped overflowing. The wind is even higher. The cuckoo is defeated when it tries to fly. Ivor walks over the hill to pick up the taxi to take him to the station to his train to London. Bill Clinton will address the Cabinet tomorrow morning.

Tuesday, 3rd June

And we are in London. In that Cabinet Meeting ('the Tories will be spitting') there was an empty seat in front of where Bill Clinton would be, because Robin Cook was abroad. There was a suggestion that everybody should shuffle along to fill the central space. Before there was time to do that, Harriet Harman had moved herself from the edge to the middle.

Tragedy. A group of design students are on a course in Holland. One of them, on a bicycle, turns into the path of a lorry. She is a single mother with small children. She is thirty-two. She is in a coma.

Go to a meeting at the Brixton Centre. Room 52B is so hot when I arrive I try and open windows. One opens. When others arrive, we realise the radiator is fixed on. Have our meeting under a tree in the garden. Look at students' work. Learn how to mark it—that is how to fill in the form—and go and pick up William. He and Florence are catching bees in boxes on the grass in Florence's square.

Ivor is reading and deciding. How to incorporate the European Bill of Human Rights into English law? What should be a devolved Scotland's relations with the EU?

From 8.30 to 10.30 Derry chaired a meeting. From 4 to 6.30 he did the same thing.

'The problem is he's not a very good chairman. He walks in like a judge to a courtroom. He has decided what he wants, and does not want interruptions. I have to stick up my pencil and when I'm ignored I interrupt.'

At one interruption, Derry muttered under his breath.

'If you want to insult me Derry, at least do it audibly.'

Everybody laughed except Derry.

'Why do you interrupt?'

'There are things they haven't thought of that need to be thought of ... what powers should a devolved Scotland have the in the EU?'

Wednesday, 4th June

The design student got worse during the night. Her sister has got there.

Ivor opened a bottle of champagne for his office. Denise-The-Driver drank some. He thinks she is thawing. She gave him photographs of horses to bring home to William.

Thursday, 5th June

Ivor's favourite Cabinet Committee: Europe. 'Robin Cook is good. He has a feel for it ... a nose. He's good.'

Ted chaired his first Peers' Meeting. The Labour Peers elected him their Chairman.

Memorial concert for John Smith tomorrow. Ivor discovers I have been booked a seat.

Ring very-nearly-doctor (exams next week) cousin. She is not on the pub rota. She can babysit.

William has a burgeoning cough.

Friday, 6th June

The cough has burgeoned. William cannot go to school. The last time I sent him to school with such a cough the school rang me up, and told me to come and take him home. Go to Lambeth College very early with William. He coughs in the Study Centre for three quarters of an hour while I write a review of my first year's Assisted Learning Support. The Study Centre begins to fill and William and I leave. Hope half-written review can be substitute for day's work.

Check my pigeonhole on the way out. Communication from the Union. Southwark are still on strike. The result of the secret ballot we have just had – on whether or not to follow their example—will be out on Friday night. When the ballot was not secret it was 70 in favour of balloting for a strike and 1 (me) against. A full union meeting is called for next Tuesday where, depending on the ballot result, we will decide what to do. We need to 'get answers from the Government on FE's funding problems'. Don't think I will be approaching Tessa. Ivor's contribution is to say that if the Government has any sense it will stay well away from the problems.

The problems, in my view, are not to do with funding. The problem is Management. Some staff are overworked while others are idle. Some space is used, much is empty. Some equipment is used, some is not. Some buildings are too full others are empty.

Sit behind Derry at John Smith's concert who tells us that Nick Brown, Government Chief Whip in the Commons, is a thug who is keeping his head down. Meet Nick Brown who is alarmed at a Private Member's Bill to ban hunting – which could damage the Government timetable – and fears he may have to put his head up and thereby lose political capital. Ivor reveals that the Lords would defeat a hunting ban. Do not think anybody is surprised. None of this spoils the concert, some of which (especially the Mendelssohn 'Hebrides') I enjoy and some of which (especially the Keats) makes me think:

> 'To one who has long in city pent
> 'Tis very sweet to look into the full and open face of Heaven,'

And the Hopkins:

> 'O let them be left, wildness and wet,
> Long live the weeds and the wilderness yet.'

Some of Keith Burstein's music, with these words, I also enjoy. We come out into a downpour and we paddle to Planet Hollywood and white wine and pizza.

Sunday, 8th June

My friend Jo and I have supper together in Pimlico. Strange that she should teach English at one of the 'best' places in the country and I should teach it at one of the 'worst'.

Monday, 9th June

The student in Holland has been declared brain-dead.

68 have voted against balloting for a strike; 48 have voted in favour.

Tomorrow's Cabinet Committee meeting has to decide whether or not to cancel the Millennium Event at Greenwich; the Treasury is worried about money. I agree with the Treasury. I think most of us will be pleased to see New Labour not venturing into Glitz and Expense.

Tuesday, 10th June

Meet Norman, the Voice of Doom, and a few more of the 48 strike support-ers on their way to the union meeting at Brixton. Wish I had chosen a dif-ferent moment to go and get my sandwich. 'What I want to know,' said Roger, 'is where are the 68?'

'I'm one of them,' I say. They know this perfectly well ... I was the only one who owned up at the first vote. 'What are we going to do to work together?' I try. I do try. A divided union might as well be no union.

'We have to fight,' says Norman. The fact that two thirds of the votes were against 'fighting' has not touched him.

'We have to negotiate,' I say.

'Management won't talk to us. We saw them four times last week. They won't discuss anything.'

'We have to try.'

'Janet, you're winding me up.' Norman is wound up.

I go and get my sandwich.

A piece of Private Eye is enlarged and on the wall by the sandwiches: a lec-turer at Lewisham (I think) has been forbidden by her Throne to have any contact with politicians or the media. This could be a recipe for divorce.

The Cabinet Committee has decided to continue with the Millennium Extravaganza. Ivor votes for it (such is my influence). Jack Straw and Peter Mandelson vote for it. Gavin Strang and the Treasury are against. Harriet Harman is silent.

Ivor is now on his eleventh Cabinet Committee. He wonders why he has been put on the environment one.

'The Voice of Common Sense' says Jane.

The Independent tells us today that Peter Mandelson 'is on more commit-tees than any other minister, apart from John Prescott, the Deputy Prime Minister, who sits on 12.'

'They have got the arithmetic wrong,' says Ivor.

The chairmen of most cabinet committees understand that the Lord Privy Seal does not have a department or have people to read cabinet committee papers for him, so they send him their chairmen's papers. John Prescott does this. Ann Taylor does this ... Derry says He Won't.

Denise-The-Driver has handed in her resignation. Ivor says to Jane, 'She seemed unhappy.' Jane says to Ivor, 'Nothing personal.' Jane will organise sev-eral drivers from the Government car service to give Ivor a go.

Nick Brown is alarmed again. He has had sight of Jonathan Powell's list of 50 peers for Blair who has to pick 30 of these 50 to be the New Labour Peers.

The list includes a Footballer and a Media Man.

'No use to you,' says Nick Brown, 'we need people who will work.'

And vote. Ivor has not had sight of Jonathan Powell's list. What kind of place is the Lords to be? They have got to make their minds up.

Ivor is also alarmed at news of names being included of people who have funded the Party or been persuaded to leave their parliamentary seats.

Wednesday, 11th June

Norman, the Voice of Doom, tells me I am dishonest. I think this is because I do not agree with him. If I was not fond of him I might punch him on the nose.

The house–next–door is for sale.

Thursday, 12th June

My elder stepson and my step-granddaughter Kirsty Elizabeth arrive from the U.S.

Ivor says the Press Do Get Things Wrong. There was a verbatim report of what Penny said in one cabinet committee that Ivor attended. There was no Penny at that meeting. He has never seen an outsider at a cabinet committee. 'The press make it up.'

Today's Cabinet Meeting was one and a half hours long after two hours' cabinet committee on Devolution.

The Granddaughter Kirsty Elizabeth is on American time. She is tired, hyped up but cannot sleep. Therefore none of the rest of us can either.

Friday, 13th June

Shortage of sleep hurts Some more than Others. I am one of the Some.

Charles Williams has been elected as the Peer on the Parliamentary Committee. People voted for him because they think he should have been put in the Government. Ivor suggested Junior Minister of Defence because he is Good On His Feet and that would Keep Him Out of Trouble. Instead, the Parliamentary Committee find themselves with Charles Williams. The Parliamentary Committee is also Blair, Prescott, Nick Brown and Margaret Jay. After their first meeting Margaret Jay apologised to John Prescott for C. Williams who had complained, prevaricated, wanted things in writing and interrupted.

Prescott found Ivor later: 'This Charles Williams? ...Why? ...'

'If you'd given him a job as I suggested ...'

Another Running Difficulty is Simon Haskell, put in the Lords by Gordon Brown who had noticed his ability and talent. Nobody doubts his ability and talent, but it turns out he is No Good On His Feet. Ask him a question out loud, when he is standing up and people are watching, and his ability and talent dissolve. Ivor has written to Gordon Brown to say This Cannot Go On. The Government has to have a Treasury Spokesperson who can Speak. Echoes of Margaret Beckett on David Simon: she did not care how brilliant David Simon was—she needed someone with Despatch Box Experience.

Liz Symons collapsed at the despatch box; freshly injected for a trip to the Caribbean, she was overtaken by fever. 'A man could not have got away with it,' said Ivor.

Jonathan Powell asked to see Ivor today. Ivor went along with Denis Carter and Simon Burton.

Jonathan says he has got to get Tony to focus on the Lords. (My guess is that Jonathan Powell is just starting to focus on the Lords himself, propelled by Nick Brown.)

The Government is most vulnerable in the Lords. It has a majority of hundreds in the Commons. And a minority by hundreds in the Lords. (Ivor must feel oceans of irony swirling round him as he hears his own theme coming back at him after these years of saying the Lords Has Great Nuisance Value.)

Does Ivor want another 50 peers?

No. He could not control them. He wants to see how the first 30 behave themselves. He wants the first 30 to work first.

'... the architect is no good to you.'

'Great man and all that but he doesn't do any work.'

Ivor would like to talk to each new peer before their appointment is announced so they understand that they are required to work. And if they are not able or prepared to work they do not take the peerage. Ivor will take 30 peers now and another 30 next spring.

'I need some Welsh too ...'

'How are the Tories going to play it?' Jonathan Powell wanted to know.

'I don't think they have decided.'

'Have you started negotiating with Cranborne yet?' About the reform of the House of Lords.

'No. It's much too early.' It was not in the Queen's Speech—so it cannot come for 18 months at least.

Nick Brown's alarm at the Government's Weak Point—the Lords' power to Mess Up Government Business and Throw the Whole Programme askew is getting through.

According to the papers, Derry's refurbishment of his quarters is up to £2million.

Saturday, 14th June

Gwen's friend rings up. Gwen was Granny's friend. She is in Addenbrookes Hospital and very low. She was 90 in November—and she last came to stay with us in the early spring. She is the last of that generation for me.

Sunday, 15th June

Catch the train to Cambridge to see Gwen. She is frail but herself. All the etiquette has gone; the consultant sits on her bed. When she was a hospital almoner, nobody sat on a patient's bed, unless they were a visitor. She wants to go home.

On Cambridge platform, see Charles Williams and his wife. They are walking towards me. Decide I must say hello in case they recognise me and I have not said hello. I am dressed as Janet Jones and I am Out of Context, but all the same ...

'Hello,' I say. I grin. Can see them thinking Who is This Woman? 'Hello,' I say again. 'My name's Janet Jones. I'm Ivor's wife.' Jane Williams is friendly. They have been in Cambridge taking her mother out for her 92nd birthday lunch. The train is crowded. The Williamses are in First Class. I am not. However, at King's Cross, they get a tube to South Kensington while I get a taxi to Lambeth.

Wonder aloud why Mandelson's eleven cabinet committees are noticed and Ivor's are not.

'Nobody's interested once you are in the Lords. The Lords is a side-show. Who has heard of Cranborne?'

'How many cabinet committees was he on?'

' I don't know but he chaired half of them.'

Drink too much wine. Hope Gwen can go home soon.

Monday, 16th June

Heavy rain, lightning, thunder. The grass in the park is glad.

Alistair Darling has written to George Robertson. People rescued by the British from Zaire should be sent a bill. Before we enter any peace-keeping operation, any manoeuvre, any rescue—it should be costed and considered. 'The world ain't like that.' Ivor is not impressed.

Blair has got what he wants from Amsterdam—the maintenance of borders—if only to prove that when the Tories can't get something, he can.

There is a row between Blair and Brown over the Millennium Junket. Blair wants it, Brown does not. The final decision will be taken in Cabinet. Ivor is intrigued to see who wins the clash of Public (Blair) versus Purse (Brown).

Tuesday, 17th June

Ivor does not get home until a quarter to midnight.

Wednesday, 18th June

Pat Hollis is not happy: there is a chasm and a schism between Harriet Harman and Frank Field, no way the twain will meet and Pat Hollis is caught in the middle. HH makes decisions and then denies them and changes them. 'Pat has no respect for Harriet whatsoever,' says Ivor.

Tessa Blackstone is Totally Silent'—I never see her'—buried in Higher Education.

Ivor has to catch Gordon Brown tomorrow: he has not replied to The Letter about Simon Haskell: Simon Haskell made a Balls Up of Treasury Questions, fellow peers are getting restive and 'Simon is waiting for The Chop.'

Two Foreign Office officials, who had been working with Blair in Amsterdam until three o'clock this morning, came and briefed Ivor before he made the Amsterdam Statement in the Lords. One of them remembered his first posting in New York, when Ivor was UK Representative there. Ivor had been wondering where he had met him before. They all thought the Lords' Statement should have been left until tomorrow. Blair wanted to get it out of the way. It turned out that Cranborne had a more detailed brief than Ivor did; Ivor could not answer some of Cranborne's questions.

'He must have been pleased.'

'Not really.'

The Tories are in turmoil. Clarke and Redwood have been named 'The Odd Couple'; Redwood's acolytes are 'The Barmy Army'.

William Hague is the other contender left in the scrum.

Thursday, 19th June

The dog is Not Very Well again. Throw out front door mat.

William Hague has won the Tory Leadership and I do not see how he can win the next election. This country will not vote for a right wing government, nor for one split amongst itself. The Tories will have to wait for their next crop of MPs and see how they change their constitution, and re-group for 2007. New Labour will be running until it becomes Old. Ivor comes home: 'What a shambles! A shambles! A disgrace! Disgraceful! I hope it doesn't leak.' The Shambles is today's Cabinet Meeting. Blair said he was in favour of the Millennium Dome and then disappeared, leaving John Prescott in charge. The meeting fell apart. People talked and talked and did not agree. 'The worst kind of Parish Council Meeting. Like the National Executive. More were against the Dome than for it. They thought if they talked long enough they would agree but they would not. It's not like that. We left it that we were not in agreement - most did not want it—but if you want the Dome, have the Dome.' When the meeting ended, Robin Butler's Number Two caught Ivor's eye: 'Oh Dear.' he said.

'Yes,' said Ivor. 'Oh Dear.'

Ivor goes out to a dinner for the Australian Prime Minister. I eat Greek salad and talk to my friend Mandy on the telephone. She teaches in a university.

'This Dome,' she says.

'I know,' I say, 'would you visit a dome?'

'No,' says Mandy. I don't think the Dome will miss Mandy and me.

Ivor comes back from his dinner. Peter Mandelson was there because, Ivor guesses, Mrs Prescott was not there and John Prescott was hosting it, and found Ivor: 'I gather Cabinet did not go very well?'

'No,' said Ivor, 'it did not.' And told him his version of the tale.

'Tony said he didn't think he handled his introduction right,' said Peter.

'Hm.' said Ivor. Then John Prescott found him.

'Thank you for what you tried to do today.'

'I tried.'

'Well, thank you for your Try.'

From what, I can gather, Ivor's Try was to spread harmony and accord. I ask Ivor if he thinks John Prescott could do Blair's job.

'I used to think so. Until today. I'm not so sure now. What's Peter Mandelson doing asking me what I think of Cabinet ... and Harriet has start-ed being Very Friendly ...'

'People think you have Power.'

'I haven't ... I'm on The Fringe.'

'Everybody thinks they are on the fringe ... they're all sitting on their fringes ... when Jonathan Powell and Peter Mandelson ask you things it's because they think you know things they don't know or have things they don't have ...'

'Softly, softly,' says Ivor, 'anyway, I don't see what else I can do.'

John Prescott was sitting at his desk, minding his own ministry, when Blair rang. Come on John, we're off to Greenwich. And off to Greenwich they went, with Mandelson and Chris Smith and all, in green wellington boots and blue plastic helmets, photocalling on the site for the Dome. Looking forward to three years from now when the Eyes of the World will be on Britain (and New Labour) at the moment the millennium turns. What could go wrong?

Friday, 20th June

Tessa has emerged and Ivor has talked to her about her job. She says she likes David Blunkett, finds him a good minister and approachable. There is so much to her job. Higher Education, Further Education. Ivor says Further Education in London is in a Mess.

'Yes,' sighs Tessa, 'Southwark ... the union is weak ... should sort them out ... SWP run the union ...'

'So, she's not sympathetic to the strike?'

'Not at all ... when the students should be doing their exams.'

'Management can run them ... and some of the strikers are very high-minded; they will be teaching the students in their homes.'

'I told her Lambeth was in a mess too.'

'Yes, but I don't think it's as bad as Southwark. The day should come when the schools are doing their jobs so well that FE is redundant and can be part of Adult Education...'

'I'm sure David Blunkett would agree with you.'

I remember the laboratories ripped out of the Vauxhall Centre about three years ago in favour of hairdressing salons; now laboratories are being built in the Clapham Centre for 1998. I remember the Marketing (or Enterprise) Suite built at the Vauxhall Centre about eight years ago, which was rumoured to have made no money at all; three days ago it was announced that the staff common room is being converted into a Marketing Suite. The staff are organising a petition. They want their coffee and sandwiches. How will building a new Marketing Suite bring in any money?

Ivor met Tommy Strathclyde who has Ted's old job as Opposition Chief Whip in the Lords.

'Our problem is making sure we let you win,' he says.

'So they understand that if they are good they will be allowed to stay?' I say.

'Oh yes. They understand very well.'

'So they are all right for this session?'

'They think they may be all right for the next session too – and they might be if Blair doesn't think it's very important.' Ivor doesn't want that. He treads his fine line – not getting Government legislation through too painlessly and not being seen to fail at his job.

Sunday, 21st June

Lightning, thunder and RAIN. A wet English June, the grass glowing green.

Meet people deciding whether or not to buy the house-next-door. 'What's it like living round here?' They watch us setting off to the park with dog and bicycle and all.

Monday, 22 June

Sara has decided to leave Lambeth College. Personnel have doubled the money they offered her last week if she would go.

Black Rod comes to see Ivor. Trouble continues to bubble over Derry's Doing-up his Dwelling. Black Rod offers to Square the Tories … if that would help.

Ivor and Denis Carter go to see Derry. The estimates are running at £730,000. Derry believes Black Rod has caused the trouble by Plotting and Telling. 'I am not going to fall on this one.' Ivor and Denis, 'with great difficulty', persuade Derry to Do-up the public rooms only, which would halve the cost. Apart from blaming Black Rod, Derry also blames Michael Havers who did up the flat eleven years ago in Sloane rather than Pugin. Derry will be blaming Ivor soon.

Ivor says he is surprised Derry has so little political nous: 'We have explained to him there will be criticism of him for doing any refurbishment at all … he doesn't believe us.'

Dick Marsh has had a letter from Jonathan Aitken's solicitor. (Jonathan Aitken has abandoned his libel action and fled the country in disgrace while there is talk of him being stripped of his privy-councillorship.) Dick Marsh was going to give evidence for Jonathan Aitken. The solicitor thanks him and goes on to say that Aitken's dropping of the case was the Act of an Honourable Man. The solicitor has the evidence that proves it but is not at liberty to reveal it. But he can assure Lord Marsh that Jonathan Aitken never lied. 'An odd letter to write,' says Ivor.

Tuesday, 23rd June

I am Appraised at Lambeth College. This means Sara has to interview me about my teaching, watch and take notes. I have one student at the time.

Meet Norman, the Voice of Doom, by the pigeonholes. He looks tired. Supporting Southwark will be a strain. Southwark are talking of staying out over the summer. They will be out forever if they are not careful.

At Denise-The-Driver's leaving party, Jane made the speech and told the story of Denise, waiting to pick up Cranborne, seeing an unmarked van waiting too. She called the police and Cranborne on her mobile phone and kept Cranborne lying on the floor of his house, away from the windows, until the police had checked the van. It was empty.

It reminds Ivor of the time when one of his bodyguards in Brussels noticed a car parking by his flat at the same time every morning. He took it's number and gave it to the police who failed to trace it and decided it must be bogus. They planned to swoop one morning when Ivor was in Strasbourg. Ivor's car came to collect him as if he were there and at the same time a pack of police cars surrounded the parked car. The police leapt out, their weaponry at the ready, and gave a substantial shock to an amorous couple. The couple were in the habit of taking time together on their way to work and, unfortunately for them, had chosen to do so outside Ivor's flat and, even more unfortunately for them, Ivor's bodyguard had misread their number which was not bogus at all.

These stories are less funny when I remember that Christopher Tugendhat, doing the same job as Ivor in Brussels, was shot at on his doorstep. The bullets missed. Less funny still when I remember the Wakehams. John Wakeham and his wife were staying in the hotel at Brighton when the IRA blew it up. John Wakeham was hurt. His wife was killed. He was Ivor's pre-predecessor as Lord Privy Seal.

Ivor found himself defending one of the Brighton bombers when the case came to court. The trial was in May and the defendants signed a birthday card for him. He had done his professional best; that was the acknowledgement.

The police had found plans to pack children's plastic lunch-boxes with explosives and leave them on English beaches that summer. I think I remember photographs of the lunch-boxes ... red ... yellow ... blue ... enticing.

Nick Brown has faced Gordon Brown with the Simon Haskell problem. Gordon Brown let it be known Ivor & Co could do what they liked ... there was a shrug and a backward step.

Wednesday, 24th June

Term is coming to an end. Less and less to do at Lambeth College.

Meet some of Sunday's people. They have made an offer on the house next-door and had it accepted.

Dishwasher failing once more.

The Man of Honour (J. Aitken) has resigned from the Privy Council.

William Hague is reinstating some People with Pasts in his shadow cabinet. His problem is most of his people have pasts. Ivor is delighted.

Speak to Oldest Friend, in Scotland, about their visit to the house this summer. Explain that Ivor, because of his New Job, may not be there.

'Has Ivor got a New Job?'

'Yes.'

'What is it?'

'He is called Lord Privy Seal.'

Blasts of laughter. Oldest Friend has No Respect. Explain that Ivor is 'quite busy'. More semi-coherent spluttering ... same sort of bad jokes about seals that only I am supposed to make.

Feed dog rice and chicken. Feed gerbils half a mange-tout apiece. Cook macaroni (fresh) cheese (mature cheddar) and mange-tout for William. Cook pork and apple and beans for Ivor and me.

Derry is writing to Black Rod. He wants Ivor to look at the letter tomorrow.

Cranborne has written to Ivor. He upbraids him for having rude ministers. 'This is not the House of Commons.'

Thursday, 26th June

The rain is relentless.

The union have told Southwark they are running out of money for their strike pay.

The Labour front bench have their weekly meeting. Ivor reads out Cranborne's letter. There is hilarity. They enjoy it. Simon Burton is instructed to draft a 'brief and bitter' reply. Ivor wonders if Simon will enjoy himself.

Derry's cabinet colleagues are less and less enchanted with him. 'The way he speaks to them. As if he were a high court judge. You should have heard him at Donald Dewar today ... as if he were some junior barrister who had not read his brief.'

Ivor meets Black Rod. He has had a long letter from Derry. (Not seen by

Ivor after all.)

'Does he make it clear you should talk to the Tories?' asks Ivor.

'Yes,' says Black Rod.

'Does Black Rod realise it's an embarrassment for you?' I ask.

'Black Rod and I have no problems ... we see eye to eye.'

'So Derry still doesn't realise.'

'No,' Ivor shakes his head, 'and his timing is terrible.' (Ivor has noticed holes in the chairs in his office. He might have them re-covered.)

Ivor also sees eye to eye with Nick Brown who is arranging to be present when Jonathan Powell gets 'Tony to focus on the Lords' and presents him with his List from which to pick the 30 peers. 'You want workers.' says Nick. 'When you see my list and your list you won't see much difference.' Ivor has still not seen Jonathan Powell's List. 'Why,' says Ivor, ' is the Chief Whip in the Commons consulted on the Lords? ... I shall keep my head down.'

The Cabinet have a Presentation of the Millennium Project. They are all Very Enthusiastic. A public holiday for 31st December 1999 is announced. I crank up my disapproval and cynicism over lamb brochettes and French burgundy:

'And here we are in London, England .. the millennium is turning ... the eyes of the world are on the British Dome ... the Greatest Environmental Experience in History ... The Biggest Show on Earth ... (Vote New Labour Next Time Too).'

'That sounds rather good,' says Ivor.

If you want an Environmental Experience you should walk out into the rain we have today.

Ivor has to view Chevening tomorrow. It is the Government's Country House for the Foreign Secretary. Robin Cook is given £250.00 a month for the expense of using it—flowers, papers, laundry. John Prescott has decided he wishes to use it too. The novelty of Ministers sharing has thrown the trustees into a flutter and a quandary.

'This is the kind of thing,' says Ivor, 'that is going to waste a great deal of my time.'

Friday, 27th June

More rain.

The house-next-door has SOLD over its For Sale sign.

When we are sloshing home, William asks me if I am as old as the River Nile.

Gordon Brown has gone quiet. His first budget is due on Wednesday. He has found a bigger Black Hole than he expected in the Treasury's figures.

Ivor is pleased with Simon's reply to Cranborne ...

Roy Jenkins has also found something to complain about. He has written to say that his Liberal Democrat peers are not getting their fair share of the money for opposition parties. (There are no more Liberal Democrat peers after the election than there were before it.)

These cries of You're Rude ... Mean ... It's Not Fair ... are identical to a seven-year-old's fury at parental power: the subject matter is not the point, the situation is the point. If you give way to one complaint, another will take its place. If Ivor agrees he is Rude, Mean and Not Fair, Cranborne and Jenkins will continue to feel cheated as Ivor is in the Government and they are not.

Saturday 28th June

Spend the day in Oxfordshire with Jones The Business, Helen of the Treasury and Homer and nearly A.N. Other. The new cat was called Clem, 'in expectation of a Labour victory'.

Sunday, 29th June

The Hippo Willow is opened at the zoo. Swaraj Paul paid for it, Frank Dobson made a speech ('I speak for the children ...') and Ivor pulled back the curtains over the plaque while William and I found a pygmy hippo.

At the end of the day, we talk over what New Labour will do: 'hard decisions ... have to do some nasty things ... have to be done by a Labour Government ... nasty things in the first two years ... sweeter before the election ... Frank Field and Harriet Harman are silent ... There's a lot going on in that ministry.' FF can't run things; HH has no ideas; Pat Hollis is in the middle. 'We'll have to stop benefit for those who won't work.'

Suggest that tickets for the Dome are £11.00 not £10.00 so that every ticket sold plants a Millennium Tree. Glastonbury had a Tree Levy, so why not Greenwich?

Monday, 30th June

Southwark votes 2:1 to return to work and 'marched' back in at 10 o'clock this morning. Find a note on my desk in Norman's writing saying so. I don't think he put it there. Find Norman.

'New Labour are Bastards. Bastards. Nothing between the ears. When Southwark went out on strike two years ago, Harriet Harman was there supporting. Now she doesn't want to know. They are all Bastards.'

I say I am glad it's all over.

'You don't like strikes, Janet.'

'No, I don't. I can see that sometimes they are necessary, but not always.'

Have dinner with old friends of Ivor's. Her daughter was David Blunkett's political researcher before the election and lost her job at the election. 'David Blunkett behaved with great honour. He put up her salary before the election so she would earn more in her next job. And he gave her excellent references'.

'Does she enjoy her new job?'

'No. She is bored out of her mind.'

Tuesday, 1st July

It was the wettest June since 1860.

Learn from Bob in the Study Centre that the Southwark Strikers each had a letter telling them that if they did not return to work last Friday they would be sacked. And they had got the message that the union was running out of strike pay. The strikers have lost £3,000 a head.

Quote Norman, 'New Labour are Bastards', to Ivor. Ivor does not see why Lecturers should not have the same problems as everybody else. And he tells me what he knows about Gordon Brown's budget tomorrow: the £6.00 a week for Lone Parents is to go, saving £50 million. And benefit claims can be back-dated for one month. It was a year, then three months ... That is all Ivor knows, today.

Margaret Thatcher was heard to say in Hong Kong: 'William? ... Oh, William .... He'll only be around for 18 months. Until we get Michael back.'

Ivor and I agree Blair is tough enough to be Prime Minister. He flew to Hong Kong (12 hours), spent 12 hours in Hong Kong, flew to London (12 hours) and then did a day's work.

'He hasn't put a foot wrong,' says Ivor.

'Yet.' say I.

Ivor was embroiled in more meetings with Derry. Ivor kept raising points.

'I know what I am doing,' said Derry.

'Share it with us said Ivor. There were guffaws. Except from Derry.

'I thought it was clear.' said Derry.

Wednesday, 2nd July

Plan my work timetable for next year. It seems that if I don't stop for lunch, I will be able to pick William up from school most days.

Sit in my car and listen to Gordon Brown's budget while William has his piano lesson. The commentators are not picking up the draconian moves on the long-term unemployed. You will no longer be able to sit and do nothing and get unemployment benefit for more than six months.

Gordon Brown was cheered at the pre-budget Cabinet Meeting. 'It was a good speech.' said Ivor.

Jane has told Ivor she is leaving him to go back to the Department of the Environment. A job has come up on a project of John Prescott's, and she is afraid that if she does not get her foot back through the door of the Department, she may fall under the knife of the next round of cuts. Running Ivor's office could be a dead-end job. Ivor is very sorry. He will miss her.

'You've got your feet under the table,' she said, 'it's not as if I'd gone six weeks ago.'

Ivor will have three candidates to choose from to replace her.

Ivor's day was also discommoded by Chevening. It is the problem house with the problem trustees (except for Robin Leigh-Pemberton who 'lives in the world and was appalled'). The Prime Minister has nominated Robin Cook to have the use of Chevening. He is happy to share it with John Prescott but this gang of trustees, headed by their Secretary, Captain Husband (RN retired) will not countenance John Prescott using it too. They have dug up The Act which, with tight interpretation, suits their stand. They say John Prescott can use Chevening on the same terms as everybody else (except Robin Cook).

'Do you mean to say,' Ivor addressed The Gang, 'if the Deputy Prime Minister would like to use Chevening for the weekend, you will charge him £1,500 for opening the house up and more for each room that he uses?'

The Gang shuffled about a bit. If worst comes to worst, Ivor will try to get The Act amended. What irritates him is that the root of all this is the fact that neither Robin Cook nor John Prescott are Tories: if Douglas Hurd was the nominated person and Michael Heseltine had come down for the weekend, The Gang would have been delighted.

Captain Husband (Gang Leader) has put in a bid to buy the house on the estate which only goes with being Secretary. I take in my breath at this information. 'Maybe he would only have a life interest,' says Ivor kindly.

Dorneywood, the no-problem house, has interpreted its rules allowing exactly such sharing to take place.

Derry's housing problems are not over either. He is not living in his flat. He is living at home. He will not move unless the flat is done up, and it looks as if the Tories will not blink at the £730,000 doing-up—they will be happy to let the media do the blinking for them. Meanwhile, Derry has invited David Blunkett to use the flat. David Blunkett is blind. This is a humane and practical offer. It is not so simple though. Oh no. Terry Boston, who chairs committees which decide these things, has said That Will Not Do. We cannot have a member of the Commons loose in the Lords.

'Such,' said Ivor, 'are the great affairs of state I had to deal with today.'

Thursday, 3rd July

Lambeth College has a new union banner. Bob has hung it, large and red and shining, along my teaching space in the Study Centre. My teaching space is known as the Goldfish Bowl because it is a glass-walled cage within the Study Centre itself.

Get notice of Lambeth College's next union meeting: 'Although New Labour may be acting like Old Tories the pressure is on them to find some money for FE.'

Go to the Assisted Learning Support meeting at the Clapham Centre. The Centre has a swimming pool and tennis courts (48 staff are now 'leaving' at the end of term). We meet upstairs overlooking the tennis courts. Nobody is playing. Danny (Study Centre Supremo) tells us there are so many of us, 'and you are all lecturers,' that he has a meeting with The Throne at 4.30 at which he hopes (and then he laughs)—as we do too—because we all know The Throne has been known to wield an axe) the status of ALS and Study Centres (and our Supremo) may be raised. We go through the plans for next year and our Supremo leaves us with his present of wine and crisps while he encounters The Throne. I do not wait to see what happens next.

Ivor has had a good day. At the Cabinet Meeting this morning he gave, as he always does, the Lords' business for the week ahead and added: 'There will be defeats.'

There were intakes of breaths.

He was asked questions—'They know nothing about the Lords.'

'How many hereditary peers do we have?'

'15.'

'How many hereditary peers do they have?'

'400 odd.'

'How many peers do we have in all?'

'126.'

'How many peers do they have in all?'

'About 500 taking the Whip.'

There was interest and 'people are friendly'.

'They realise you are not a threat; you are not in competition with them.'

Denis Carter and Tommy Strathclyde are in cahoots. This suits everybody. The Tories are trying hard not to win. New Labour don't want to win too much either. If the Tories win they draw attention to the fact that they should not be there. If New Labour win they lose the argument for reforming the Lords. Denis and Tommy are meeting and sharing out the unwanted victories in advance.

'I don't know how' says Ivor, 'Tommy is stopping his people voting.'

Ivor had a word with John Prescott about The Gang of Chevening trustees and their leader, Captain Husband (RN retired). The plot thickens.

'It was his idea that I should use it.' John Prescott's eyebrows rose.

'Oh!' Up went Ivor's eyebrows.

The Prescotts were at Chevening for something else and Captain Husband proposed the Prescotts stay in the place. 'You don't want to waste your time on this,' said John Prescott, 'we won't go there.'

'No,' said Ivor. He does not want Captain Husband to get away with these machinations.

'The Liar!' was Jane's reaction. 'The two-faced ...'

But Ivor thinks he may have found a way round Captain Husband: Blair can nominate Robin Cook and, if he is not using it, John Prescott.

Terry Boston was asked to see Ivor about his aversion to a commoner loose in the Lords. (David Blunkett using Derry's flat.) 'There is a precedent,' said Ivor, 'Sarah Hogg stayed there when Quentin was Chancellor.' Precedent is all. Terry Boston did not know that.

David Blunkett addressed the nation today on the options for the young unemployed. They can take a subsidized job, join the environmental task force, do voluntary work or go into full-time education/training. 'Staying in bed is not an option.' There is a piquancy in this coming from a blind man. New Labour are aiming high. Icarus did too.

We hear on the news 'the Government has reaffirmed its commitment to abolishing the hereditary peerage in the House of Lords.'

'If they want to read my press release like that, that's fine by me.'

The builders starting the Dome are threatening to strike.

Ivor says if this diary is published he will have to move to the Isle of Skye.

Friday, 4th July

8 a.m. the phone rings. I expect it to be Jones The Business to tell me his and

Helen's A.N. Other, due three days ago, has been born. It is Merlyn Rees. Can he give our phone number to BBC Wales? Of course he can. The phone rings again.

'This is 'Good Morning Wales'. Could we speak to Lord Richard?' I was still hoping for the baby.

While Ivor is locked in, live, to 'Good Morning Wales', William and I indulge ourselves in the idea of picking up the extension and shouting 'Wotcha you Wallies' or similar. We don't do it.

The Study Centre is closed. I do not go to work. Enjoy myself instead.

Put ant-killer round the front door as we are being invaded.

Fail to get on with *The Everywhere Chair*. Could grumble a lot about this. Sustained and concentrated work is impossible against the rest of life. I think *The Everywhere Chair* may remain in three-quarters of a first draft until I retire or am pushed from Lambeth College.

Meet Martin Bell at the American Independence Day party at the residence in Regent's Park. Ask him if he has read Cranford. He has a copy but hasn't read it. His opponent in Tatton, Neil Hamilton, has not been exonerated by the Downey Report into sleaze. 'He made my life a misery,' says Martin Bell, 'the first week of the campaign was hell. Absolute hell. I was not prepared for the brutality of it. Of politics.'

There is film of Martin Bell being shot in Bosnia.

Walk in the gardens: expanses of moulded lawns, given to the American people by the richest woman in the world at the time.

'Isn't it lovely,' I say to an hereditary peer's wife.

'What would you do with it?' she asks. A People's Playground? Loaves and fishes for the homeless?—are the thoughts behind her question.

'Dogs?' I say. 'Children?'

The men from two newspapers appear: should the Man of Honour (J. Aitken) be prosecuted? (*The Guardian.*) Which Government minister described Gordon Brown's budget—in advance—as 'bonkers?' (The *Financial Times.*) Ivor makes well ... yes noises to both. I say the 'bonkers' remark could not have come from one of the Scots because 'bonkers' is not Scottish vernacular. 'Nor a woman,' says Ivor. I say 'bonkers' is not 'gender-based'.

'Who would have known in advance?' asks the FT (rhetorically).

'Who?' I ask (not rhetorically).

The FT starts a list: the PM ... the Deputy PM ... of course, it could have been John Prescott ... he would say 'bonkers'.

Nick Brown appears. I begin to remember the days when Ivor last had a job that meant that when he went to a function, all he had to do was stand there and people kept appearing. This is starting up again. There have been many years when the only people who have come near him have been the Old-Time's-Sakers or the Chums. Nick Brown, however, is doing his job: 'You need working peers,' he says.

'Yes,' says Ivor.

'Not Jonathan's list' Nick Brown shakes his head, 'I'm trying to get my list to Blair ... my list, your list and Denis's list are the same. We've wrapped it in lots of special ribbons ... made it look terribly important.'

'What would you think,' Ivor asks him, 'if we got an agreement with the hereditaries that we leave them alone for three years and then they go without a fuss?'

'Yes,' says Nick Brown, 'yes...' There are intonations of ambiguity in the 'yes'. It could mean anything. He mutters about the 'one-chamber proposal.'

'Do you want a second chamber?' Ivor asks.

'Yes. I want a second chamber.'

Over our supper afterwards Ivor tries his 'three year agreement' on me. I say there is no guarantee it would not be reneged on.

'Ah ... but if it was agreed with William Hague publicly.'

'Ah ... but if he was no longer the leader ... different leader equals different circumstances.'

'Then we'd have to vote them out.'

'You might not have time.'

'We'd need two years.'

'You might not have two years.' I stick to my view that Cranborne and co. would see it as their duty to do anything to keep their seats. Any means would justify that end. Ivor imagines something more like the Hong Kong handover: New Labour would march in and behave themselves as the Chinese are doing while the hereditaries retreated as the Britannia did, worrying about democracy the while.

Saturday, 5th July

Jones The Pictures' 70th birthday. At her dinner, one of her guests regales us with how he found a pile of remaindered copies of Princess Anne and Mark Phillips's list of wedding presents. He bought them up as Christmas presents for his friends. Everything they had been sent was listed with honesty and precision, including a heart-shaped potato, a pair of novelty handcuffs and a book on cystitis (donated by the author). A few years later he bought a copy of Prince Charles and Diana Spencer's wedding list, hoping for further gems.

Not to be. The Palace has not recorded the bizarre, the eccentric or the idiosyncratic. He was left smiling at the Abel-Smiths' 'two wastepaper baskets' in among the jewellery given by the other VIP donors.

We walk home through the floodlights in St James's. People are feeding the ducks at 11 p.m.

Sunday, 6th July

After his perusal of the papers, Ivor is pleased to observe that the Opposition's policy platforms are:

1. against Europe
2. in favour of fox-hunting and
3. in favour of the hereditary peers.

He feels these provide the nation with no alternative but to continue voting Labour. There is a by-election at the end of this month and the Tories had the seat with a small majority. It will be interesting to see whether or not they keep it.

I am sorry for William Hague. He is in the wrong place at the wrong time.

Monday, 7th July

HOT.

Ivor gets home for supper but has to go back again. Derry is not on speaking terms with his private secretary. He does not trust her. Derry has also decided to ignore Ivor's advice and to refurbish all the rooms in his flat - not just the public ones.

Northern Ireland is stirring up. Neither side will make compromises and Mo is jammed in the middle taking the flak. HH told Ivor she would not have the job 'for all the tea in China'.

British Airways have a strike in the offing. One day New Labour will be blamed for such things. Not yet.

Tuesday, 8th July

Hotter and sticky.

Go to the meeting of lecturers in journalism, where and when scheduled, to find the room full of people lying on the floor. Are they journalists? No. They are First Aid. Go and find Norman instead. He is being moved to the Brixton Centre for next term. I shall miss him. Vauxhall will be quiet. He says he is going to be quiet in Brixton. I will believe that when I hear it. He is cutting pieces from the papers to keep for his teaching next year. He is scornful of the journalists' hubris over the change of government—but for them, you might think, we would still have the Tories. _The Observer's_ headline, 'End of Xenophobia', was, he thought, the worst front page you could imagine.

He asks me if we have any security. I say not. He says we should have. I say we are 'pretty anonymous'. He says 'the state should protect you'. I am left wondering if Norman knows something I don't know. Or if Norman is being Norman. Discuss it with Ivor at the end of the day. 'I don't want the police crawling round,' he says, 'and Norman wouldn't want the police talking to him.'

Denise-The-Driver has not left the Government Car Service. She has been 'made an offer she couldn't refuse,' and is driving John Prescott.

'Hope she enjoys driving up and down to Hull,' says Ivor.

The Devolution Committee today was 'angry and ill-tempered'.

'Derry thinks it is his job to come in having worked out what he wants or thinks is right, and to bully and push it through.'

'Bully?'

'Yes. Bully. That is not the way to do it. At least, I don't think it is. He gave Donald Dewar a very hard time. A very hard time.' Ivor has a great deal of respect for DD. He knows a lot and has been around for a long time. He is an experienced politician. 'Last time that happened, I was on Derry's side, but not today. He'll say to Donald 'Got that?'—of some wording—Donald says 'Yes.' 'Agreed?' 'No—I reserve my rights. I'll look at it.' And he knows Fuck All. Fuck All. Donald and I had some time together afterwards, waiting for the next meeting, and I said 'That was a rough meeting.'

As far as I can interpret, Donald's answer was a mixture of a shrug and an expletive.

Jack Straw and Jack Cunningham have got together as a group of nit-pickers. The Welsh Devolution Bill may be ready first.

'What happens to people like Derry who make so many enemies?'

'Nothing if they've got the Prime Minister's Ear.'

'Is he New Labour's David Owen?'

'No. He does his homework.'

'Who then?'

'Cardinal Wolsey.'

'What happened to him?'

'He got his head chopped off—no he didn't but he got too big for his boots.'

There was a written question in the Commons. How much are the Lord Chancellor's refurbishments going to cost? £650,000.

Simon Burton has been asked to go and see Jonathan Powell, who is looking for a deputy.

'Shit,' says Ivor to Simon, 'you must take it.'

The money for two political researchers has been found, so Marianne and Damien are ensconced.

Wednesday, 9th July

A colleague who is leaving, under I do not know how much duress, comes into the Study Centre with the news that the Lambeth College Plan is foundering: the decision to close and sell the Tower Bridge Centre (the most valuable piece of real estate) and use the proceeds to shore up the rest of the sites (and build new labs) is blocked. The Guy's School of Dentistry, who are Tower Bridge's chief customers, will not move to Clapham. Very Senior Management have a Very Serious Problem this is correct. Lambeth College will have more empty buildings crumbling round it.

Departing colleague goes on to expand on the details of the redoing of the Clapham Centre swimming pool. He does not know how many thousands of pounds went into that. He does know that the pool is nearly always closed.

He rounds off with the Lambeth College clocks. Our Throne was at a two-week Anglo-American college jamboree in California. It is the custom for thrones to exchange presents when visiting other colleges. Our Throne arrived without the clocks, decorated with the words 'Lambeth College', which were to be his tokens. There was much exchanging of faxes until the clocks were despatched as air freight to join him. By this time, he had visited three colleges and left them clockless. He handed three clocks to a fellow (but female) throne and asked her to see to their delivery. She looked at them. She said nothing. When it was time to pack up and go home, observers wondered how she had handled the clocks. They investigated. In her room and in her wastepaper basket were three Lambeth College clocks.

Spot a memo in which ALSters are referred to as belonging to a 'school'. Our status has been raised. Our Supremo's meeting with the Throne bore fruit.

'Derry and I have crossed swords,' says Ivor as he comes through our door. Blair wanted the Cabinet Committee to discuss PR in the European elections. Ann Taylor (Leader of the House of Commons) had a point which Ivor disagreed with. Derry said the Commons business was not Ivor's business (? by that argument it's not Derry's either) to which Ivor said 'What's the point of this bloody meeting then?' He is getting crosser and crosser cooped up listening to Derry's hectoring.

'Are the others all totally silent?'

'More or less. But Derry needs me. He needs me tomorrow. David Clark's White Paper on FOI has to be left until the autumn. We haven't even met yet. We are meeting tomorrow for the first time. We must put it off.'

Ivor's tomorrow is David Clark's White Paper, the Cabinet Meeting and then HH's problem. HH's problem out-ranks Lambeth College's. The courts are in the process of deciding the scope of housing benefit. Does it cover other services or does it cover housing alone? If it covers other services, these have to be provided. If it covers housing alone, the other services still have to be provided. Either way, HH is worrying about £500million. 'Another left-over from the last government.'

The good news is Simon Burton went to see Jonathan Powell and they agreed Simon might move to 10 Downing Street, but not yet. Not until he has seen the reform of the House of Lords go through. Simon knows more than anybody else about the Lords, its workings and its members.

Ivor now has the idea of setting up a select committee to advise on the removal of the hereditary peers simultaneously with the rest of the reform. I describe my Hong Kong analogy (4th July), and Ivor says that is not a good analogy at all: from the papers, it looks as if the Chinese were expecting Britain to continue in Hong Kong and were very surprised when Margaret Thatcher offered to give it back. They would not have minded another 60 year lease.

The Chequers' trustees are meeting at the weekend. Central to this is the Chequers' swimming pool. Its roof needs looking at. 'The least we can do for those Blair children is keep the roof on the swimming pool. Why didn't the last government do anything about it?' They knew they were going to lose the election.

Thursday, 10th July

Sara leaves her 0.6 of a job while Bob's 0.4 of the same job is uncertain. He will apply for the whole job and we will see if he gets it. That would be the sensible appointment. Our Supremo's mother is too ill for our Supremo to contribute to making sensible appointments.

David Clark was sat on by Derry, by Ivor, by Jack, by all and his white paper will be delayed until the summer is over.

It is announced that Blair is creating a clutch of New Labour peers. Ivor did not know that it was being announced. Individuals start ringing him up to tell him that they are one of the clutch and to ask what they should do next. The names had not been announced either to the public or to Ivor. Belatedly, he manages to get the list from 10 Downing Street and finds there are about six who had been on his list. There must be tens of people out there sitting by their telephones waiting to be told if they are on the list. Ivor has been getting letters at the rate of two or three a week asking 'Can I be a peer too?' Some say they were promised a peerage by Neil Kinnock. Ivor is having to say, truthfully, that he does not know what is happening. Since he is Leader of the Lords, this is making him look a fool.

We have a quarrel.

Friday, 11th July

Quarrel continues. I would not like readers to think we live a life devoid of quarrels.

SUMMER 1997

Saturday, 12th July

6 a.m. the phone rings. At one minute past nine last night Jones The Business's and Helen of the Treasury's baby was born. Homer's little brother. Pack. Walk dog. Get teddy bear for baby, soft red bus for Homer and William and I leave for Oxford at 7.30. See baby just after 9. Twelve hours old. Human. Alive. Nameless. I said we would stay for ten minutes and we stayed for twenty-five. Then we drove on to the house.

There was plenty of traffic but, coming the other way, there had been an accident (a car on its roof, skewed across the road) and there was very heavy traffic. From Taunton to Bristol, nothing was moving. People were resting on the verges, talking in groups, eating and drinking—unwisely: there are no bushes to squat behind. Most people in this country would submit themselves to many things (traffic, for example) but not squatting in front of a motorway-full of stationary traffic. I wonder how they are managing.

We get ourselves into the house by three. Ivor rings: 'I'm just leaving Chequers.' He has been chairing the Chequers' trustees. His car has a mobile phone. I think it is the first time he has used it.

Tell him about the traffic.

Ivor arrives and I hear about Chequers' problem. There is no Captain Husband (RN retired) on the trustees but there is a Miss Uff (also RN retired) in the house. It was Miss Uff who told the last Prime Minister that it was time for bed. Ivor has also been forewarned by a letter to Jane from JH Holroyd CB (the Secretary for Appointments, 10 Downing Street) that the main issue was what should be done about the future employment of the Curator. The key point being that, because of her own illness, the Curator had not been in the house at all when the Prime Minister and Mrs Blair and family were there. 'They have settled into a good routine with the house staff and a number of us are nervous about the potential re-introduction of the Curator into this happy scene.'

The Chequers' trustees are as follows:

Lord Privy Seal (Chairman)	Ivor
Appointee of the P.M.	Sir R Verney
Appointee of the Environment Secretary	Lord Camoys
Chairman of the National Trust	C Nunnerly
The Public Trustee	Ms J Lomas

They also have to consider some minor house improvements and the swimming pool.

JH Holroyd has also written to say 'how much the Prime Minister and his family enjoyed themselves at Chequers last weekend. They appear to have plans to make a good deal of use of Chequers as a family—so it looks as if it will be back to the Callaghan days. The fact that they warmed to Chequers so quickly surely justifies all the steps that the Trustees have taken to preserve its particular charm and calmness.'

And so the Trustees met. Sir Ralph Verney (leaving after twenty-seven years) has wanted (for some years) to solve the swimming pool heating problem with solar panels. They agree. They agree to everything else. But they cannot solve Miss Uff. She is ill. The house has run well without her. There is no other job for her. All turned to the Chairman of the National Trust. 'I thought you might look at me.' He will see if he can find anything for her.

And then the Trustees were given lunch by Cherie Blair. Smoked salmon. They chatted rather than talked. Cherie Blair assumed Ivor had been to Chequers many times before.

'Oh no,' he told her, 'I've never been here in my life. I was in New York during the last Labour Government.' She was surprised. (Oddly, I have been there—William's other Godmother's uncle was head gardener with Callaghan and Heath and Thatcher.)

The Blairs are enjoying Chequers. Their eldest child swims a mile in the pool. Their youngest is being taught to cook in the kitchens. Last weekend she made rolls and gingerbread. Granny is there most of the time.

Monday, 21st July

William broke his arm on Saturday. The pony he was riding was attacked by a wild stallion. He was filled with morphine and admitted to Wildgoose Ward. They could not decide whether to nail or plate his arm. The Consultant descended. Don't nail or plate seven-years-olds. Gravity is the Great Healer. William was discharged in a Collar and Cuff.

The stoicism William showed on Saturday—riding on for half an hour, his wrecked arm dangling—is needed now: no running, jumping, swimming, climbing, riding or swinging for the whole summer.

I trace the owner of the wild stallion and speak to him. He does not know that we are not going to sue him.

Tuesday, 22nd July

The stallion has been put down. Reflect how lucky we were that it was 'only' William's arm that was broken.

Politics is fading from our rural stockade. All I gleaned last week was that journalists' accounts of Cabinet meetings are 'so wide of the mark as to be unrecognisable'.

Dearing has not been discussed in Cabinet, yet if you Believed What You Read in the Papers it was the subject of prolonged debate the other day. 'It is not like that at all' —Ivor is reading that when Blair's view is announced all the others wriggle round to join it in silence —'Not at all.'

Buy a great many two-inch cowboys and indians on two-inch horses.

Wednesday, 23rd July

Ivor - 'it was a seminar'—spoke to the Parliamentary Labour Party on the House of Lords. 'If they were there they learnt.'

'How many were there?'

'About 150. I spoke to them immediately after Blair—so a lot had left with him.'

Ted Short (Lord Glenamara) spent the day deciding whether or not to leave the Labour Party over the Dearing Report. The Report wants students to pay £1,000 a year of their tuition fees, and grants towards living expenses are being phased out. This is the end of Labour as Ted Short believes it should be. Ivor spent the day trying to persuade Ted Short not to leave the Party. Blair was also concerned that Ted Short should not leave. He approached Ivor. Had Ivor considered bringing in Jim Callaghan? 'I've already done that,' Ivor told him. Blair may not appreciate the historical nuances: a long time ago, Jim Callaghan sacked Ted Short, and Ivor (and Jim) had been calculating which were the least inflammatory tactics. 'It was a very long time ago,' says Ivor, but if Ivor remembers it and Jim Callaghan remembers it, it is likely that Ted Short remembers it too. Callaghan's exertions might be counterproductive. 'Blair was bothered about it,' said Ivor. Blair sees Ivor as a bridge between himself and the Labour peers. And he must also see that, although few in numbers and many in years, the Labour peers have the power to hurt the Labour Party. What surprises me, is that Blair let himself appear so clueless as to suggest that Ivor would not have brought Jim Callaghan into the problem. What does Blair think Ivor spends his time doing?

Saturday, 26th July

Ivor is home at the house for the weekend. Blair is still exasperated by Ted Short. But Ted Short was once Education Secretary and Deputy Leader of the Party so it is not good if he does go. Ivor believes Blair went so far as to describe his Noble Lords as 'Buggers'. 'Yes,' said Ivor, 'but what am I supposed to do about them?'

The list of 30 new Labour Lords—presumably assumed not to be prospective 'Buggers'— is shorter than it was.

Jim Callaghan told Ivor that Blair sought him out for half an hour. Callaghan took the opportunity to tell Blair that he should show more consideration and sensitivity towards the 'Buggers': the 'Buggers' held the Party together through the 18 years: without the 'Buggers' (among others) Blair would have had no vehicle on which to ride into power. 'Blair just doesn't think it's very important,' says Ivor.

I can see why Blair does not enjoy half hours with Jim Callaghan and his ilk. They do not tell him he is perfect and he is already loaded with enough insecurities as it is and not many people enjoy home truths.

The Scottish Devolution White Paper is out and is being promoted as Donald Dewar's Triumph. Ivor agrees ... 'and he is so funny. Those newspaper reports of the cabinet committees are crap. Absolute crap. All that rubbish about Jack Straw fighting Donald all the time. It was not like that at all. We hardly discussed the reduction of the Scottish MPs in Westminster. And that is what the Tories have latched on to.'

One happy fallout of this is that there are no more early morning meetings chaired by Derry.

'The press are just waiting for him (Derry). He has upset everybody except the Prime Minister ... he is so bumptuous.' Ivor shakes his head. 'And next week's problem is that Derry's refurbishments are coming up in the House.

Derry doesn't know whether or not to be there. To begin with I thought he shouldn't be there and we were looking for reasons why he couldn't be, but now I think it will draw less attention if he is there.'

Ivor's mind-changing cannot be quelling Derry's quest for a clash: 'When I'm attacked, I fight back.' Ivor did not tell him, in so many words, that starting these refurbishments within a fortnight of coming into office was as good as asking to be attacked.

Monday, 28th July

Ivor has left the house for the House for another week, having acquired a gash on his leg from a rock.

A Senior Tory ex-Minister has been to see Denis Carter and Denis has been to see Ivor. It is a matter of some delicacy. The Senior Tory ex-Minister has great affection for the House. He does not wish to see the House brought into disrepute but Denis should know that people are talking about the Lord Chancellor and alcohol. And he is falling asleep on the woolsack. Ivor says that sort of gossip has been around for centuries and it doesn't amount to much.

Denis and Ivor do not see what they can do. Anything they do could be seen as making trouble or even Doing Derry Down in order to Do Themselves Up.

'The only risk,' says Ivor, 'is that one day Blair will say to, me why didn't you tell, me?'

'But you can't tell him.'

'I can't.'

'Derry must have a lot of enemies.'

'Yes.'

'Will Blair know that?'

'He's not going to hear it from me.'

Derry came to see Ivor for ten minutes. He was confirming that he will be present for The Question on his Housing Arrangements. He spent the remaining nine minutes telling Ivor of the strength of his (Derry's) relationship with Blair.

'His feet are not on the ground,' says Ivor.

'Oh dear,' say I.

Cranborne is throwing punches in his crusade to Keep the Hereditaries.

'I am told,' says Ivor, 'his side are fed up with him ... don't like his arrogance.'

'Sounds a bit like Derry.'

'He would hate to hear you say that.'

'So would Derry ... that may be a reflection of the accuracy of my remark.'

Tuesday, 29th July

The Times tells me Ivor is a member of Grillion's Club.

Wednesday, 30th July

Ivor tells me he is a member of Grillion's Club. He says it costs him £15 a year.

The Times gives Ivor 7/10 for his Cabinet performance so far. Blair gets 9/10, Derry 8/10 and six of them less than 7/10. I tell Ivor he is in the middle which is the safest place to be. He is described as 'A solid, calming influence in the Lords.' Derry's power, we are told, 'is underlined by his membership of seven cabinet committees and sub-committees' and 'he has even given up his beloved whisky.' The five who are tipped to be sacked are Chris Smith, David Clark, Frank Dobson, Ron Davies and Gavin Strang. (Harriet Harman is next-most-wobbly.) And the five who are tipped to succeed are Stephen Byers, Tessa Jowell (who has not answered her letters from Lambeth College in her constituency), Alan Millburn, Alun Michael and Peter Mandelson ... 'his influence is underlined by membership of eleven cabinet committees'. Just like Ivor.

Long ago, when Ivor was MP for Barons Court, a schoolboy arrived at the House of Commons and asked to be shown round. Ivor took him round. Recently, the schoolboy, now grown up, reminded Ivor of this. He is Peter Mandelson.

Thursday, 31st July

The Times gives Cranborne 6/10 for his shadow cabinet performance so far. 'You got more than him,' said Jane.

William fell on his arm. He felt the bones move.

The Tories win the by-election.

Saturday, 2nd August

Ivor's gash is infected. The Cottage Hospital Casualty says he must not walk.

Sunday, 3rd August
The dog wins first prize in 'Best Veteran,' at the village dog show, deaf and blind as she is.

Thursday, 7th August
William's appointment at the fracture clinic. X-rays show how much the bones moved when he fell. They are not aligned 'as we would wish'. Consultant repeats his refusal to operate. Collar and Cuff for two months.

Ivor tells me Derry got his money.

Saturday, 9th August
Ivor's leg is beginning to mend.

Gwen has come home from Addenbrookes.

Peter Mandelson is hated by all the papers. 'Because he did so well,' says Ivor.

Ivor has found himself reassuring Derry: 'He was sitting in my office in a twitch ... 'it is all right,' I said, 'calm down, you are doing fine.' "I work very hard," he said.' And then Ivor heard, again, how close Derry is to Blair. How he will discuss XYZ with Blair when he goes to Chequers. So Ivor sent information through to 10 Downing Street to go to Chequers for him. Number 10 did not know anything about the Lord Chancellor going to Chequers. Oh the insecurity ... burning insecurity.

'I wonder what Derry will do once his Devolution is through.'

'Start being Lord Chancellor, I suppose,' says Ivor.

Ivor's new driver, John, has to find his way to the house with a Brown Box. Is Denise happy with John Prescott?' I ask.

'She's showing signs of wanting to come back.'

Jane's successor will be Simon Burton's Number Two, Leslie Bainsfair.

Muse on the fact that most of us die in winter but most members of the House of Lords die in the summer - when there is the long recess and they have nothing to do.

Sunday, 10th August
The dog no longer recognises William and is distressed by most things that move..

Monday, 11th August

The dog is put down. It is a sunny day.

Tuesday, 12th August

Ivor reads this diary up to Chequers' roof for the first time. 'Inevitably you make me look more important and powerful than I am but since I am the only Cabinet Minister you talk to ...' and 'I was wrong that Frank Dobson would be disappointed ... he is not disappointed at all. And I was wrong that Blair would not be able to run things on the basis that what he says goes ... he is centralising.'

'Surely the Cabinet are keeping quiet because they are worried about their next jobs. If they cross Blair they risk their futures.'

'Um...'

In the deep of the night there is rain. I am up. I think I have locked the dog out. Then I recognise the sad little pastiche of Wuthering Heights: the paw at the window in the storm.

Thursday, 14th August

All visitors are gone. William is at the farms, Ivor is shopping, the sun is out and this is up to date.

On the re-read at the beginning of this week, I read that I had finished the first draft of *The Everywhere Chair* on 7th April. I had forgotten. I must be ready to write the second draft. I settled at this desk and started to unpack *The Everywhere Chair*. I found the first handwritten volume. I cannot find the second or the third. I have left them in London. I do not have them in my head and I cannot manage the second draft without having the first in front of me. I cannot work. There will be another 12 month delay. There is never space except in the summer ... I am not reconciled to leaving it until I retire. This diary does not replace it.

Thursday, 21st August

A pigeon has taken to this place. She is building her nest in the senior beech with twigs from the larches. She flies to and fro all morning. The woodpeckers are braver. They hid when we arrived in July. Now they are out. And we have a pair of magpies.

We buried the dog's ashes with a boulder for her headstone. We had to dig two holes to get deep enough among the rocks. We sweated. We picked her yarrow and wrapped it in bracken. The summer flowers are tired. And we read some Lucy poetry, since that was her name:

Thy mornings show'd, thy night conceal'd,
The bowers where Lucy play'd;
And thine too is the last green field
That Lucy's eyes survey'd ...
She seemed a thing that could not feel

The touch of earthly years.
No motion has she now, no force;

She neither hears nor sees;
Roll'd round in earth's diurnal course,
With rocks, and stones, and trees.

Later:

The Government is quarrelling while Blair's away, as when Prescott was left to chair that Cabinet meeting. 'The key to government,' says Ivor, 'is the relationship between the Prime Minister and the Chancellor. As long as that's all right ... Blair and Brown know each other well. Blair owes Brown a great deal. He may think it doesn't matter.'

Sunday, 31st August

Ivor comes in with a cup of tea: 'Princess Diana's been killed in a car crash.'
    We go back to London.

Monday, 1st September

And back to Lambeth College.

Lambeth Talk tells us the Study Centre Supremo has been moved on to another job. Our new Supremo is also the Library Supremo. Bob of the Study Centre is now Bob-my-Boss.

The thousands of Assessments (not tests), that we ALSters have to give to every student, have been misprinted to include the answers.

Robin Cook is coming to see Ivor—'He must be having very great problems with Chevening'—and with Captain Husband.

Ivor wonders who will be asked to Princess Diana's funeral. A great many other people will be wondering too.

George Tambone, Ivor's driver from his New York days, calls: it would not have happened if he had been driving. He once drove the Queen Mother for three weeks: 'They kept trying to make me go faster—shit man, I told them, it doesn't matter if we're late: we are going to get there.'

Tuesday, 2nd September

The Library Supremo does not know anything about also being the Study Centre Supremo ... the Study Centre Supremo does not know anything about doing another job. All assume they remain with the status quo.

Many hours are spent tearing answers out of the assessments and putting in questions.

Captain Husband told Robin Cook he could not use Chevening in August because that is when the staff have their holidays, and he cannot have it in September because that is when maintenance work is done. Chevening seems run for the convenience of Captain Husband: he paid £100,000 for a life-time tenancy, for him and his wife, of a house in the middle of the Chevening Estate. A house, not a cottage. We believe he was there in August and is there in September.

Wednesday, 3rd September

8.15 a.m. the phone rings:

'This is the Lord Chamberlain's office. Could I speak to Viscount Cranborne?'

I do not hear the name because it is unexpected: 'I'm sorry, who would you like to speak to?'

'Viscount Cranborne?'

'Oh...' I begin to make sense of what is happening, 'This is Lord Richard's home, Viscount Cranborne is Lord Richard's opposite number.'

'This computer! I'm only a serviceman called in to do this ... I don't know who all these people are .'

'Are you trying to ask Viscount Cranborne to the funeral on Saturday?'

'Yes.'

'I don't think I can help you—I don't have Viscount Cranborne's home number.'

Poor serviceman. A difficult day. I can't believe the Lord Chamberlain believes he will find Viscount Cranborne and Lord Richard snuggling up together at breakfast time.

Friday 5th September

The postman put two funeral invitations through the letterbox, addressed to the Lord Privy Seal. They were sent by special delivery and should have been signed for. When I see the postman in the street later, I run after him and thank him. 'I cleared it with the office,' he says, 'I thought you would need them.'

Saturday, 6th September

The funeral of a girl of 36 is even more of a funeral. I have never been to one before. I hope I never go to one again. We were sitting at the top of the choir stalls, by the people who knew and loved her. I suffered for the people who were suffering and felt I should not have been there as I didn't know her.

The only other observation I will make is on the curtseying. Curtseying is a courtesy still practised in this country: if you are a woman, when a member of the Royal Family passes or meets you, you curtsey. You put one foot in front of the other and bend your knees. The congregation was told, in the order of service, to stand for the entries of the members of the Royal Family. We did so. As they walked by us, the women bent their knees. Some dipped until they creaked. I decided to ignore what was going on. This was easy with the less senior members of the Royal Family. But as we came to the Queen, I began to worry. The women bent very low indeed. There seemed to be rows and rows of sinking women. Cherie Blair, straight opposite me (we have still never met), had been doing the same as me: not noticing, not bobbing up and down. But as the Queen came towards us my tension mounted, a decision had to be made on whether or not to curtsey. Elderly wives were curtseying (of Field Marshal Bramall, of the Duke of Norfolk), women in their own right were curtseying (Margaret Thatcher). The Queen was reaching where I stood opposite Cherie Blair. We caught each other's eye for the first time. Neither of us bent our knees.

Trivial. Yet we are moving into a different world.

AUTUMN TERM 1997

Sunday, 7th September

We go to Jones The Business's and Helen of the Treasury's party for new baby, Nelson. Play rounders. Four fathers get hurt. Ivor is one of them.

Monday, 8th September

Distressing blah in the papers; despite all the requests for privacy, journalists have pried and told; who cried, when they cried, how they cried. A funeral is a funeral and there is not much more to be said.

> *'Whether we fall by ambition, blood or lust,*
> *Like diamonds, we are cut with our own dust.'*

The unfolding of tragedy is always the same: love, ambition, betrayal, revenge, death. Once it was duals and poisoning. Now we have car accidents. The heart of the story does not change from the ancient Greeks through Shakespeare to the tunnels of Paris, when people continue to live their lives of passion and danger and risk.

The public are as interested in its aristocracy as it ever was.

None of us would have heard of Diana Spencer if she had not married the heir to the throne. None of us would have heard of Ophelia if she had not been Hamlet's girl.

Ivor was concerned to see that Jim Callaghan had been excluded from the row of ex-Prime Ministers in the Abbey.

'Can I ask you something?' he asked Jim later.

'Anything you like.'

'Were you happy with where you were in the Abbey?'

'No, I wasn't.'

Ivor started an enquiry. He was told it was a mistake by the Abbey. The Abbey is writing to apologise.

I don't get as far as having lunch at work. I am busy, busy meeting and assessing all the new students in my School. This is a grouping I have not explained. I belong to the Study Centre and I service the School of Creative Studies. Lambeth College is divided into several schools (the number varies from time to time, along with the names). Each student joins a course (of study) and each course is attached to one of the schools. The School of Creative Studies is journalists, artists, designers and hairdressers. (There are a few more I do not work with.)

I tell each new group my name, where I belong (the Study Centre), where the Study Centre is, what the Study Centre is (it is not the library), what I do there, where they can find me and how it is my job to support them on their course (help them with their work). Finally, I tell them I am an English teacher - that is the part that makes sense. The assessments tell me, their tutors and teachers, Lambeth College and the Basic Skills Agency, their levels of literacy and numeracy (how well they can read, write and do sums).

I weave in and out of the jargon.

This year, like last year—like the last 23 years—I find students who cannot read or write or do sums. Sometimes this is because English is not their language, sometimes because they are dyslexic—letters and numbers tangle themselves between the eye, the brain and the page ('tangle' might appear as 'hagel'). Sometimes this is because they have never learnt or because they have never been taught.

At the end of the day I remember hearing two hairdressing students: 'the Queen is an old bag' while 'the only one who was any good is dead.'

Wednesday, 10th September

Our chief babysitter, since Dr Cousin is removed to Devonshire for doctoring, has broken her elbow. The chief calamity is that our chief babysitter is also chief ironer and chief house controller.

Thursday, 11 September

Ivor irons. I attempt to control the house.

Blair has seen Denis Carter about the House of Lords' reform ... not Ivor:

'Why?'

'He wants to find out more without asking you ... He finds you as remote as you find him.'

Lambeth College is hotting up. I know of three quarrels among staff about teaching.

And as for the quarrels over contracts! I am losing over £2000 a year by being on the old contract—known as the silver book. The perk of the silver book is that I have to be given a year's notice of redundancy.

Monday, 15th September

We went to Paris for the weekend. Ivor was limping from his rounders' injury.

Tuesday, 16th September

The papers say that Blair will take his pay rise next year. Blair says he will not take his pay rise next year.

I go out to supper with Priscilla, my friend from publishing. When I come back Ivor, who has been watching all the news programmes with close attention, is steaming: 'They said on the news John Prescott has consulted the Cabinet and we have all agreed not to take our pay rises next year.' He throws his hands about. 'Nobody has consulted me.' The phone has not rung all evening. And Ivor earns less than anybody else in the Cabinet so these untaken pay rises are proportionately bigger for him.

Priscilla and I had a Greek supper. Tell her *The Magic Blob* has got nowhere. That reminds her: she has just seen her old boss's old children's editor - who is also her old friend. She is reading for Scholastic Children's Books. Priscilla could ask her to look at *The Magic Blob*. I remember that Scholastic Children's Books' rejection slip had three handwritten paragraphs of advice:

1. Give a title
2. Explain where the Blob comes from
3. Give a synopsis and
4. Word count.

It was the only kind rejection I had. I cannot remember the writer's name so we do not know whether or not it was Priscilla's friend. I will check. It will be a further blow to my pride if the only way *The Magic Blob* gets anywhere is through Priscilla's old boss's old children's editor.

Wednesday, 16th September

Jonathan Powell rings, replying to Ivor's call out. I hear ... 'John didn't speak to me ... I'm not included? ... it's a grey area? ... Is it going to be mentioned in Cabinet tomorrow? It's not? Then I won't say anything.'

Thursday, 17th September

It was mentioned in Cabinet. Blair mentioned it. Mea culpa. They were unprepared. They had not thought it through. They will think it through. John Prescott and Ann Taylor have been given the job of thinking it through, a job for losers. There was a head of steam: 'HH is furious. Ann and I agreed it should have been sorted out in May. We won't take the pay rise this year but we will take it next year ... there's never a good time.' David Blunkett was first to follow Blair as the discussion widened.

Assessments are done. Find myself the English Teacher for over 200. I don't think there is one to whom I could not be some use.

Friday, 18th September

We are talking about the expense of sending a child to university. Ivor is not able to see what this Labour Government stands for, 'even through a glass darkly'.

Sunday, 20th September

Find my rejection slip from Scholastic Children's Books. Ring Priscilla. It is not her friend. I will incorporate all Scholastic's advice into *The Magic Blob*. Priscilla offers to hand the result to her friend when she next sees her. I have a fortnight.

Calculate that I have to stay at Lambeth College for at least another 11 years, if it will have me. Ivor points out there will always be a job for me there 'unless there's an outbreak of literacy in Lambeth'.

Monday, 21st September

Struggle to find time to write synopsis. (I can't leave it for 11 years.) All (Ivor and me) agree *The Magic Blob* is a terrible title. Start a list of alternatives..

Tuesday, 22nd September

Wonder why Peter Mandelson is quite so rude to the Liberal Democrats in

The Times. Ivor has been reading the minutes of the New Labour/Lib Dem cabinet sub-committee and thinks there was an understanding that Paddy Ashdown would find it helpful if there was some public dispute. He has to deal with his Neanderthals and public division would help private accord.

Wednesday, 23rd September

Rewrite first page of *The Magic Blob.* Go to work. Work. Teach. Come home to milk, biscuits and this.

Ivor is too late to book a hotel in Brighton for the Labour Party Conference. He has a hotel in Worthing instead. Andrew will be in Lewes. It will be a good week for cab drivers.

Go to school to meet Mr Thomas. Enquire about homework. This should be happening but the photocopier has broken down. What maths will William learn in the course of the year? He is doing numbers up to 20 at the moment (he could get up to 100 two years ago). Then adding and subtracting. Tables? Oh, he'll be doing his two times table ... and his fives and tens. He has been able to do them for two years too. Surge of panic. Hope it is good for children to be left dozing for much of the day.

Ivor returns: after today's meeting, John Prescott asked Cabinet Ministers to remain behind. He is FURIOUS with Blair and Brown over the Cabinet pay freeze. He said he told Blair:

'If you want to be fucking Jesus Christ and not take your pay rise ...'

'Everybody is hopping,' says Ivor, '... someone said "What about those of us with overdrafts?" ... Frank Dobson is more philosophical. When he heard Blair's announcement he reckoned that was the end of all pay rises for the five years of this Government ... I think I've got my point across.' Ivor's point is that he earns least.

9.50 p.m. John Prescott rings. He's spoken to Blair about Ivor's situation. Blair is 'very sympathetic.'

Thursday, 24th September

Derry and Ivor meet to discuss the reform of the Lords. They agree on the way forward.

'I assume I'll be seeing the Bill through,' says Ivor, not at all sure that he will be.

'Oh yes,' says Derry.

Derry is 'vitriolic' about the 'Hairshirt Chancellor' as he calls Brown: 'Bloody puritanical hairshirt son-of-the-manse'. Derry is taking his pay rise.

After Ivor has given me these epithets, he tells me they can't be recorded for posterity.

I spend every spare moment putting Scholastic's advice into *The Magic Blob*. And then typing it in.

Find myself:

1. The English Teacher for over 200
2. Rewriting *The Magic Blob*
3. Writing this
4. Mother
5. Wife
6. Part-controller of two houses
7. Catching my breath

Don't see how I can be doing anything properly.

Friday, 25th September

Re-title *The Magic Blob: Mud, Magic and More*. List another 20 alternatives.

Take William to St Thomas's Fracture Clinic. In another month the broken arm can be treated as a normal arm. That will be three months and one week since he broke it.

Complain to Ivor that I have too much to do.

'I know the problem,' he says. 'It happens to a lot of us.' But he is not a Hairshirt Husband.

Saturday, 26th September

Pollocks 'Toy Museum. Disconcerting to see what could be one's own old toys in a museum.

Jo, who continues teaching in a Top London Day School, and I have supper and go and see *Mrs Brown*, an enjoyable film. Don't see how it could be much on paper. Jo and I compare our educational institutions. Her sixth formers drive themselves to school, park in the car park for the day and drive home. Her 13 year-olds are reading the first pages of the finalists for the Booker Prize and deciding who should win and why.

Monday, 28th September

Ivor has gone to Brighton (well, Worthing).

William comes home with his first English homework: 'Answer the following questions with a sentance' The teacher meant to say: 'Answer each question in one sentence.'

Despair.

Tuesday, 29th September

The first cheers for Blair's speech are for the reform of the Lords.

William sees a kestrel land on the roundabout on the way home. I nearly drive into the roundabout in the excitement.

Thursday, 2nd October

Keep looking out for the kestrel.

Ivor returns from Brighton and Worthing. On the surface, it was the least quarrelsome conference he has ever been to. He thinks there is trouble afoot in the Department of Social Security. Andrew, who has an old friend high up within its civil service, tells him John Denham does one quarter of the work, Pat Hollis does three-quarters of the work, FF contributes nothing and HH flaps. HH is skilled at taking credit for other people's ideas ('good for morale', says Ivor) and is desperate for publicity; she was in 'physical distress' when the cameras swung on to Peter Mandelson who was near her - and she was left out of the picture.

Meanwhile, Pat Hollis tells Ivor that FF is A Disaster. He is not a Team Player. He produces nothing workable and creates trouble. He is meant to be having Radical Thoughts. He went to Exeter for two days and told the staff they would be responsible for their own budget. He proposed that all pensions should be in the hands of the Friendly Societies ('it worked in the 19th century') who are in the process of being fined by the Treasury for their bungling of pensions. All FF's evidence is anecdotal (that is what damns him in Pat Hollis's eyes) and he knows little about how the whole thing works. On top of this, FF has told Pat Hollis (which he should not have done) that he had been to see Blair (which he should not have done) to give him his assessment of ministers' performances (which he should not have done).

'Blair should not have asked him,' says Ivor.

'Perhaps he didn't.'

'Well ... Frank certainly shouldn't have said anything to Pat, telling her that if she is good he will be nice about her to Blair!'

'Harriet has problems.'

'She does ... and it's Frank who has been complaining about her to the press saying she's blocking him.'

Ivor has been having his own Radical Thoughts about House of Lords' Reform. Perhaps it should all be done at once instead of in two stages. (Stage One: removing the hereditary peers; Stage Two: setting up an elected and/or nominated second chamber.) That would stymie the Tories: they have been arguing that the hereditaries should not be removed until the alternatives are in place. To oppose an all-in-one reform, they would have to own up to their argument that the hereditaries should be preserved. Or they would have to keep silent.

'I wonder,' says Ivor, 'how they would organise a No Campaign.' Cranborne would have to make those placards. Hague, who said last week he would abandon the hereditaries, changed his mind this week. He was summoned to Cranborne's castle where, Ivor guesses, he was sat upon – 'Poor sod'.

Friday, 3rd October

School's Harvest Festival. The organist speeds hymns along. The Singing Teacher sustains every last note deep into the organist's next phrase. The children keep up with the organist.

Get all sorts of demands from the Inland Revenue. This could be the most tedious tale of all. Readers' tolerance has its limits. So does my sense of humour. Given the sums of money involved, it would be cheaper not to employ somebody to ask me for them.

Reading this I notice how politicians make enemies of each other. 'Today's enemy is tomorrow's friend,' says Ivor.

Tuesday, 7th October

I have lost two copies of two printed pages of this. I look through everything I can think of at home several times. I tell Ivor. We both look everywhere we can think of, several times.

'The worst case scenario,' I say, several times, 'is that a newspaper gets hold of it.' Ivor does not say anything. I cannot have lost those two pieces of paper. I do not lose paper. Who could have snooped, pried, taken? Begin to suspect everybody I can think of. Wish I could suspect the dog. But she is dead.

Priscilla would like to see the synopsis of *Mud, Magic and More*. She will read that and decide whether or not she can send it on to her friend at Scholastic.

Wednesday, 8th October

Hunt through my filing cabinet and the Study Centre rubbish for my two pieces of paper. Several times. Do not find them. Harbour suspicions about everybody I see. And people I do not see.

Hear colleague describing Gordon Brown as 'the Socialist Woman's Crumpet'. Hear journalist-teaching colleague discussing Peter Mandelson: how he is hated; how he deserves to be hated. Regale Ivor with the details— how Peter Mandelson prevented Jo Richardson from getting heard—to which Ivor says, 'I am delighted to hear it.'

Thursday, 9th October

No sign of my two missing pieces of paper. 'We'll cross our fingers,' says Ivor.

Garcia is my biggest student problem at the moment. He is the noisiest member of my biggest and noisiest group. He throws a chair around and says fuck.

Have dinner at the Belgian Ambassador's in Belgrave Square. Nobody throws a chair or says fuck.

Friday, 10th October

Liz and Richard, our friends who take us to the opera, take us to Rameau's Plateé, which is at the Royal Opera House at the Barbican. We are a po-faced opera audience. We take three quarters of the performance to realise that an 18th century masque has been turned into a pantomime masque-pastiche and it is funny. Even when the audience does grasp the funniness, it is not sure it should do anything as risque or overt as laugh. Some of the audience manage to get through the whole performance without laughing. Tortoises mate with the thrust of the violins' bows. Satyrs hobble mock ballet. We have a formal 18th century dance, its sexual yum-yum-yum acted out within it. Plateé herself absorbs the pantomime dame into Caliban so we can relish the funniness without being swamped by the pathos. Still there are sections (especially of the expensive seats) which cannot laugh. The fact that Plateé can sing (I mean SING) should not make us earnest. Caliban's poetry and Rameau's music colour and enlarge the creation; they do not dry up the humour.

Saturday, 11th October

Walt Disney's Hercules. This audience is brimming with little children who can neither follow the story nor get the jokes. The ironic swipes at Greek Tragedy and being famous, at Popular Culture and mock-heroism are missed. We are told you do not have to be famous to be a hero. Hercules is reproduced millions of times in plastic as an Action Figure but that does not earn him his seat with the Immortals. He has to go on labouring until he is dead to join them. Hercules is not a nice story.

Tuesday, 14th October

Ivor has been mustering opinion to move on from 1621 which is when the ceremony for introducing new peers to the House began. It involves dressing up, processing, saying things in Latin and taking one's hat off and bowing three times. It takes up to 13 minutes per peer. Roy Jenkins agrees with Ivor so opinion is part-mustered. But Roy Jenkins is in the US so opinion will not be present at the Lords' Procedure Committee Meeting.

Wednesday, 15th October

Ivor is interviewed at 7.10 a.m. in a van in our street about his procedural reforms. The press are interested. 'This is just the kind of trivia that gives the Lords a bad name,' says Ivor, not in the interview. By the end of the day the committee has met and agreed to investigate. Moving on after 376 years on a small matter may be a symbol of what is happening to the Lords on bigger matters.

Thursday, 16th October

The Public Expenditure Committee has its first meeting. There sat Gordon Brown, Alistair Darling, Ann Taylor, Derry, Margaret Beckett, David Clarke, Ivor and (this is a mystery to Ivor) Frank Field. The plan is that each of the big-spending ministers will appear before the Committee in turn, to put their case. The Committee will listen to and question ('grill' says Ivor) each suppli- cant. It will then decide how the public purse will be shared among those ministeries. It is more of a court than a committee. Ivor is worried. He can- not see how this will work. He does not think the Public Expenditure Committee will know enough to make these judgements. Who is qualified to play Solomon?

Experts have to be brought in. The Treasury Experts provide briefings, have their heads round the nation's finances, but how far should the nation be run by the Treasury?

'Gordon's only interested in saving money and he's quite right. As he keeps saying, this is the only opportunity we will have to do this ... after this it will all get bogged down...'

'How long will it take?'

'Oh months and months ... we're meeting three or four times a week for months.'

'Will it have to be done by next March?'

'About then.'

'No expert can come in without a point of view.'

'The Treasury are very good but they are the Treasury. George Robertson did very well today ... HH won't do so well. Frank Dobson will have a hard time ... I might write Frank a personal note.'

'David Blunkett will be all right.'

'Yes.'

George Robertson was the first to face the Committee: there was a manifesto commitment to carry out an internal defence review, and while this is going on George Robertson can argue that he does not need to plead. Derry tried to cross-examine him but George Robertson swatted him off.

The problem with Defence, as Ivor sees it, is that the last Government 'cut it to the bone' and, unless you are going to make a Huge Decision (e.g. No tanks), there is little left to cut. A Huge Decision could bring the UK out of the international community, off its seat on the UN Security Council and, in unforeseeable circumstances, lead to death and destruction. The British put 40,000 troops into the Gulf War; they have 15,000 in Northern Ireland; they have 10,000 in Bosnia. Who could have foreseen Bosnia? The expenses are people and equipment.

Should New Labour extract itself from international defence responsibilities? Or—Ivor turns his mind to Frank Dobson—should there be a £2 charge for seeing a GP? Or a Health Tax? Or means-tested health care?

Where and who is New Labour's Solomon?

Mo was wearing a headscarf instead of a wig in Cabinet. Her radiotherapy-ravaged hair must be returning. She did not look well.

Ivor announced that they would lose the votes on guns in the Lords.

Garcia, the biggest noise and nuisance to me last Thursday, is quiet and industrious today.

I see a copy of Lambeth College's Study Centres' budget—money for Learning Aids for this year (CDs, tapes, videos, books)—set at £50,000. Westminster has cut William's school of £50,000. I disapprove. Ivor says it is a human tendency to think that the money should go wherever one's own child is within the system. 'And that wouldn't save money anyway.'

'Perhaps the whole problem could be resolved with the Redistribution of Resources,' I try irony.

Ivor tuts.

The hereditary peers did defeat the Government on guns.

Friday, 17th October

Meeting at Lambeth College. A directive from the FEFC (Solomon for all the colleges) says all us teachers must be assessed—and graded—by each other. We protest. We have to work together. We cannot make public judgements on each other. Propose we assess ourselves in groups.

Tackle my tax. Make one phone call. Write two cheques. Fill in three forms. Am poorer and no wiser.

Saturday, 18th October

The television is on the blink. It had taken to turning itself off every now and then. The every now and then is increasing to every five minutes.

Monday, 20th October

Bob-my-Boss tells me there is a proposal to turn the Study Centre into the Student Canteen. According to the document, this is part of Giving The Vauxhall Centre A Heart.

Tuesday, 21st October

Find a crack in the wall at the back of the London house. Can see daylight through the crack. Blinking television doesn't seem to matter now. Priscilla rings. She has spoken to her old friend at Scholastic. Can I send her *Mud, Magic and More*?

Ivor is late and with a brown box. Paper work is mounting. His tomorrow is one meeting after another and each meeting has its papers. There is one file and a series of bundles. I spread them out.

'You'd never make a minister.'

'I can only read one thing at a time.'

'Then you'd certainly never make a minister.'

I start reading one thing at a time. Freedom of Information (FOI) is the biggest bundle. The detail of every possibility thought up is listed, considered in turn, cross-referenced; questions are listed, problems are listed, decisions-to-be-taken are listed. The Prime Minister has written an introduction which I think is intended to be a mixture of rousing and policy-affirming.

The other bundles include HH's minutiae on providing for Slav refugees in Kent and then there are all the letters. Ministers write each other letters when they think they have something to say. These letters are then circulated. Jack Straw writes a lot of letters. So does Derry. He adds a hand-written 'ever' to his civil servant's 'yours'.

Margaret Beckett has written a letter because she won't be at a meeting and there are two points she wants to make.

Get the impression that some ministers make work for themselves—and for others—unnecessarily; other ministers are getting their heads round minuscule details on paper which may have major effects in practice.

A minister without an imagination can get bogged down in theories which are not worth a row of beans in the allotment of life. A minister with an imagination may not be able to translate into systems and paper—or the red laptops, which are now mooted.

'Blair can't read all this,' I say.

'A couple of boxes a night—he should have more of a filter than some of us. The thing is there are only me, Derry, Peter Mandelson and perhaps Ann who don't have their own ministerial brief—who once they have looked after that don't have to worry about all the rest.'

'Is Peter Mandelson reading all this?' Pause.

'Not the detail ... Derry certainly does his homework ... he really does his homework.'

There is the agenda for tomorrow's Cabinet Meeting:

1. Parliamentary Affairs
2. Economic Affairs
3. Foreign Affairs
4. European Affairs

I ask about EMU.

'Don't ask.'

I ask about defence.

'Don't ask.'

The bad news today is that it is colder and I turned the central heating on (remember last winter) and nothing happened.

Thursday, 23rd October
One radiator is hot. We have eight other radiators.

'Blair's set up a new cabinet committee to reform the House of Lords. Derry's chairing it, I'm the Leading Minister, and there are Jack Straw, Nick Brown and Ann. It'll be a bill for the next session and I'll be seeing it through the Lords.'

'Is that what you wanted?'

'Yes.'

'Good.'

'It's all right with them. None of the big-spending ministers. We'll be all right ... it's all settling down ... gelling ... the Public Expenditure Committee with Gordon Brown today was fine.'

'Is it all right to have Derry chairing?'

'Derry and I work OK together, there's rude respect.'

'Did you talk to Blair about it?'

'No - it was arranged with Downing Street. It also means my job's all right for two years. Until 1999.'

'Perhaps you'll be left where you are for the whole five years. It's your twelfth cabinet committee.'

'Don't tell Peter Mandelson. Some of them don't meet for weeks at a time unless there's something specific like I showed you yesterday.' That was the refugees in Kent.

'What's your brief?'

'?'

'I mean is it just to get rid of the hereditaries or is it to reform the second chamber?'

'All of it.'

Wonder if this will be the first major reform for centuries. I guess that, apart from the introduction of life peers and women, it is. Spare a thought for all those daughters. Who would like to be passed over in favour of their brother? All too close to the Divine Right of Kings. Even that allowed the occasional queen.

Friday, 24th October

The Chair Man comes to take away half our furniture which, after 20 years, needs mending or re-covering or both.

Beginning to realise the reaches of my ignorance. Start by looking up 'Lord' in our biggest dictionary. 'Lord' covers nearly three pages. It starts with a pre-historic form. And when we get to 950 'The development of sense has been largely influenced by the adoption of the word as the customary rendering of Dominus.' (Latin) The meaning is Master or Ruler.

'Baron' does not cover two columns. It comes to refer to those who 'personally attended the Great Council, or, from the time of Henry III, were summoned by writ to Parliament.'

A baroness is the wife of a baron until 1884, when she may be a baroness in her own right.

'Peer' has three columns. The first 'political' reference I can find is in French and is 1321.

Move to Winston Churchill: 'The structure into which the Norman enters (1066) ... was a kingdom ... governed, we may say, by the King in Council, and the Council consisted of his wise men, laymen and clerics; in other words, bishops and abbots, great landowners, Officers of the Household. In all this it departed in no way from the common pattern of all kingdoms which had been built out of fragments of the Roman Empire'. It gets better. 'On the whole the English doctrine was that a free man might choose his lord, following him in war, working for him in peace, and in return the lord must protect him against encroaching neighbours and back him in the courts of law. What is more, the man might go from one lord to another, and hold his land from his new lord. And these lords, taken together, were the ruling class. The greatest of them, as we have seen, sat in the King's Council....

We cannot yet speak of a nobility and gentry, because the Saxons distinguished sharply between nobles and peasants and there was no room for any middle rank.'

With the arrival of the Normans (pinned to 1066), the King's council is mainly French-born and French-speaking ... the governing class is a landowning class 'far more definitely' than in Saxon days. '... in the middle of the 13th century, we begin to have a new word, Parliament. It bears a very vague meaning, and some of those who first used it would have been startled if they could have foreseen what it would some day come to signify'.

In the 15th century the 'baronial structure perished' and we have Parliament: the Lords sitting in their own right, and the Commoners as representatives of the shires and boroughs.

As I understand all this, the 1999 Reform of the House of Lords will be the biggest change since Parliament was established 700 years ago. It is yet to be decided whether the 1999 peers will be elected or nominated. If they are elected we will be free for the first time since our Saxon forebears to go from one lord to another. This full circle over 933 years is incomplete in that we would make the lords by voting for them, whereas—theoretically—a Saxon lord could be a lord without any followers. He would not have lasted long without his army!

Churchill gives more detail of the Saxons: 'the idea still persisted that the tie of the lord and man was primarily personal, so that a free man could go from one lord to another and transfer his land with him. The essence of Norman feudalism, on the other hand, was that the land remained under the lord, whatever the man might do.' I had not realised we were so much under the Normans in 1997.

Saturday, 25th October

Discover that Ivor knows even less than me about the Saxon system. Recommend it to him, but 'I don't want a mob of independents ... I want something I can control'.

Make note of Churchill's comment on Henry II: 'The power of any Government depends ultimately on its finances.' This fits with Ivor's pragmatic version: the key to it all is the relationship between the Prime Minister and the Chancellor.

Sunday, 26th October

Get to the house for half-term. William has his first ride since he broke his arm. The pony rolls on him. He is trapped by one leg underneath the pony's back. Nothing is broken.

Monday, 27th October

Sun and high wind. The water supply is scant. Flash-boarding has come off the garage. One leaking pipe. And mice.

Read Alan Bullock's *The Forming of the Nation*, written for children and helpful for me. He first uses 'Lord' to describe the chiefs of the Celts who arrived here about 450 BC. They 'made themselves lords'—they were renowned for their flair for fighting from chariots—and they were the first people in the country to use a kind of money. So from them another kind of power evolved. They also preserved Christianity and the Church and started schools. Their fight turned into some sophisticated channels. Read on until Scotland and England are united in the 18th century. So Devolution, New Labour's first excitement, touches something a mere 200 years old.

Two mice come and take a look at me in the course of the evening. Try to follow them, to see where they come from. They are quicker than me.

Tuesday, 28th October

Get out *The Everywhere Chair*, where upon Environmental Health arrives. He is in a plain white van - in case we do not want the neighbours to know? He leave pots of poison in the house, the garage and the shed.

Ivor is busy. He and Damien are working out the new cabinet committee (on House of Lords Reform). They are worried that it will be taken over by the Cabinet Office. The normal procedure is for the minister's department to put up a paper to the committee, which the Cabinet Office then savages. However, Ivor has no department so he is left with the Cabinet Office putting up a paper. How can it savage its own paper? 'We've just got to work out a way of doing it.' Ivor then discusses the Way Forward with Derry. Derry is in favour of comprehensive reform, not reform in stages: removing the hereditaries and rethinking the whole place all at once.

'Good,' say I.

'Um,' says Ivor.

'Well, isn't it?'

'Um,' says Ivor.

'Does he want elections?'

'No.'

Oh.

Wednesday, 29th October

All the poison from the pot in the bathroom has been eaten. We have rare mice. Not fieldmice. Glossy dark creatures, with great round ears. Beatrix Potter mice.

Thursday, 30th October

The bathroom poison pot is empty once more. Will soon run out of poison despite Environmental Health's confidence that they had left me with too much.

Get out *The Everywhere Chair* again. Read the first draft. I had finished it. It had left my head completely.

Monday, 3rd November

Lambeth College once more. Isaac, a student, stabbed Michael, another student. Michael took himself down the corridor to the Head of Art and Design to complain. The Head of Art and Design saw the red staining Michael's shirt and told him it was time he stopped playing about and painting himself.

Ivor said he had a much quieter day. The Public Expenditure Committee has noticed that prison is expensive. Jack Straw does not agree that he is putting too many people in prison. He believes that prison is where the voters think such people should be.

Tuesday, 4th November

Derry has had an idea. The American Bar Association is having its annual gathering in London. 16,000 American lawyers are on their way. How about having a debate in the chamber of the House of Lords between Top American Lawyers and Top British Lawyers? Derry would sell tickets.

'Who would choose the Top British Lawyers?'

'Derry, I suppose.'

'It'd make a lot of money.'

'Yes. Derry's talking about selling television rights.'

'A lot of people would be horrified.'

'Yes.'

'What did you say?'

'I said I would make discreet enquiries ... and I had a word with Terry Boston.'

'What did he say?'

'He was polite. And will make discreet enquiries. And will come back with a big thumbs down.'

The central heating is proving as uncertain this year as it was last. Heat in one room. Call in our friend Mark who says there are two solutions:

1. to acid clean it through which might burn it to bits;
2. to put in a whole new system.

The crack in the wall of the house has not gone away.

Wednesday, 5th November

Half of the furniture comes back. The Chair Man has succeeded in re-upholstering the stool and the upright chair with the material upside down. The sofa leg breaks off as William (aged seven) sits on it. The Chair Man takes everything away again.

The police are not pressing charges against Isaac.

Thursday, 6th November

Blair tells the Cabinet that they should appreciate the importance of the Lords. There is 'quite a discussion'. HH tells Cabinet of Pat Hollis's skill in handling difficult matters. Ivor tells me how, if he was Leader of the Opposition in the Lords with 500 behind him, he would wreck Government business. 'The Lords has great nuisance value.'

Mark rings up and tells us he and his brother and his father will take out our central heating system on Saturday, start putting a new one in on Sunday and finish on Tuesday. Discuss arrangements for siege.

Friday, 7th November

Get a letter from Priscilla's friend at Scholastic Children's Books: *Mud, Magic and More* is no good. She is constructive. She tells me things I know: the lack of structure and pace; the difficulty of reconciling tragedy and a 'safe' world; the need to be 'sterner' for fiction, as opposed to storytelling, which I'm good at. I have to put it away and go on to *The Everywhere Chair*.

Tuesday, 11th November

We had a weekend first without water, then without hot water and entirely without heat. The schedule for the siege has been adjusted: we should have hot water by this afternoon and heat by Thursday. I am not too concerned about heat as it is mild but am increasingly concerned about hot water as I have not had a bath since Friday and I have got to dress up as Lady Richard tonight for a white tie dinner. Ivor has been having showers in the House. I can't find such things in Lambeth College.

> 3.45. Get home from work and school. We should have hot water in half an hour.
> 4.45. We should have hot water in 20 minutes.
> 5.45. We should have hot water in quarter of an hour.
> 6.45. We should have hot water very soon.
> 7.00. We should have hot water any time.
> 7.15. I run an inch of water that is not quite cold and do my best with it.
> 7.20 Leave for St James's Palace.

Sit among sworded, helmeted and breast-plated walls, between Our Man About-to-go-to-China and Our Man in Islamabad. Hope I smell OK. Think

I am still damp. They ask me about Lords' Reform. Find myself explaining the arguments in favour of retaining the hereditaries. 'Nobody outside can be in favour of them,' says China, 'but are they going to keep their right to use the building?'

'I don't think so,' I say, adding that 'as I understand it nothing has been decided; everything is open and up for discussion.'

When I report this to Ivor he says 'that's the line'. It also happens to be true.

Leave St James's Palace for Buckingham Palace and the annual reception for the diplomatic community in London. The diplomatic community and the rest of us (a mixed bag of representatives of local colour—religious, political, civil service and spouses) mingle for hours. Then the Queen comes through and we are divided: local colour one side; diplomatic community the other. She keeps her back to local colour. When the Queen has gone we mingle once more. Meet the Ashdowns and discuss Hague.

'... mustn't underestimate him,' says Paddy, 'the best orator there is ... far better than me, than Blair.'

'His party will crucify him,' says Ivor.

'Why does he go in for it—knowing he'll be dead in the end?' I wonder.

'You don't think of it like that, you don't think it through,' says Paddy.

He also tells us that Mohammed Al Fayed offered the Liberals £1million to fight the election. They refused it. And he offered New Labour £2million. Paddy does not know whether or not New Labour accepted. Neither does Ivor. He hopes not.

Meet Josie Farrington (the Lady Farrington, now a Government Whip). Hear how she was in the Ladies in the Lords (except they don't call them that there) and there was a group of hereditary peers' wives. They told her to go and get them clean towels. She told them she was on her way back to the Chamber but if she saw 'A Lady' who could help, she would mention it.

On the way out, meet Lord Carrington.

'Hello Ivor, how's it going?'

'It's fun. Isn't it?'

'Yes.' Pause. 'For a while.'

Ask Ivor who is the best politician alive. After some skirting of definitions, he comes up with Willie Whitelaw, Carrington, Jenkins and Callaghan.

Thursday, 13th November

The new central heating system is installed. It has Gone Off all on its own.

Jack Straw is fighting off the Department of Justice.

'Can the prisons be run by the Lord Chancellor?'

'I don't see why not.'

'And the police?'

'Yes.'

'It'd save a lot of money.'

Ivor is impatient with the Freedom of Information Committee '... to solemnly sit there considering whether or not civil servants' advice to ministers should be openly available ...'

'They couldn't do their jobs.'

Ivor nods: 'I'm in favour of efficient government, not open government.'

'Does anybody else see it like you?'

'Jack Straw. He's got the police and M15.'

Ivor also thinks Derry is stopping 'playing silly buggers.'

'He's learning?'

'Slowly.'

Cabinet discussed the Lords again. Blair has 'got the wind up'. He wants Denis Carter to come to cabinet meetings.

'Does Blair think he got his priorities wrong?'

'Eh?'

'In delaying the reform of the Lords?'

'I don't think so ... and I think he was right now ... the second session.'

The Chair Man brings back all the furniture. He breaks the leg off the sofa in the back of his van. He takes the sofa away again.

Friday, 14th November

Hear from the Inland Revenue. I have paid them too much. I have to write to them if I would like them to send me my money back.

Ivor had a Chequers meeting. They have to renew the whole roof. There was alarm last weekend: the Blair children were found climbing on it.

'It's a long way down,' says Ivor.

'It's been a bad week for the Government and a good week for me.' I'm told. The Government is failing to get rid of the story of the £1million it took from Formula One Racing, who are the only sport allowed to keep their tobacco advertising. Ivor, on the other hand, is succeeding in his bid to get the Nuisance Value of his constituency (the Lords) recognised.

Sunday, 16th November

Colleen and Merlyn Rees come to supper. All shake their heads over New Labour, tobacco and Formula One. It would not have happened in Nye's day. Nor in Jim's.

Ivor has had a phone call from Sigismund Sternberg. A Warning. Sigismund has heard that the pharmaceutical industry is in and out of Downing Street. And the industry is giving money to New Labour. Ivor has a word with Margaret Jay.

'Yes,' she says.

Cabinet Committee on Welsh Devolution. A lot of time was spent deciding on the English name for the new assembly's leader.

'I'm getting on better with Jack and Derry now ... they're getting used to me. Derry has realised that when I put my pencil up I have something to say.'

Jack continues to want to put people in prison.

Ivor resists: 'I've met more villains than you've had hot dinners.'

'That's your problem: you're an Old Labour Liberal.'

Wednesday, 19th November

The Privy Council are giving the Queen and the Duke of Edinburgh dinner in the House of Lords in honour of their golden wedding. Ivor was given a copy of the placement for his approval. He did not approve. He was next to Mrs Thatcher: 'Bloody Woman. She's done this country a lot of damage. A lot of damage. She sorted the unions out at the beginning. That needed doing. But after that she divided the country right down the middle. I'm not sitting next to her.'

The last time they met in the Lords' bar, she complained loudly that there were 'too many ex-commissioners in the Lords.' He countered: 'Some people might say there are too many ex-prime ministers.'

Thursday, 20th November

Transfer my students to other times of the week and go to the Abbey for the Queen and the Duke of Edinburgh's golden wedding anniversary service. I am next to Betty Boothroyd; fingering the service sheet she worries:

'There is rather a lot to get through ... difficult time of day ... parliamentary business ... haven't time to change...' (she is wearing her Speaker's uniform) 'I don't curtsey. Mrs Thatcher does a sweeping bend, almost to the ground. I couldn't get up if I did that.'

Thatcher is indeed to be seen sweeping away. And she's pretty busy because there is a ragtag and bobtail of European Royalty passing by. She sweeps at them all. Happy music. And another dozen couples who have also survived fifty years of marriage.

Tell Mrs Derry I'm glad to see she is not wearing a hat.

'There are two things I never wear: hats and tiaras,' she says. There is a long and hostile piece about Derry's refurbishments in today's *Times*. Tell Ivor in the lowest whisper I can muster. 'I know. I've seen it. And it's going to get worse.'

Friday, 21st November

Surveyor from insurance company comes to look at our crack. 'You have a crack.' If it is subsidence, the insurance company pays; if it is 'wear and tear' we pay. It will take a year to monitor before they can decide.

'Derry and I have locked horns.' Says Ivor.

'What about?' Say I.

'The reform of the Lords. He's produced a paper. He wants to clear out the hereditaries. No elections. An appointed chamber.'

'That's it?'

'That's it.' Pause. 'It'll have to go to Blair. We have to have a policy line. It would mean a U-turn on the manifesto. That would leave it all in the hands of the Prime Minister ... it still wouldn't be taken seriously ... I shall argue the case for elections within the Government ... if they go for a nominated chamber I don't know how I'll get it through ... there'd have to be an Act, I suppose ...'

Saturday, 22nd November

Take William to Oxford, where Jones The Business and Helen of the Treasury, Homer and Nelson have moved from Oxfordshire. Leave him for the night.

Sunday 23rd November

William rings. He has hurt his foot. Thinks he may have broken it. We are due to meet at the Zoo later. It looks as if we will spend the afternoon at St Thomas's rather than at the Zoo.

Papers full of Derry and his refurbishments.

'How long before he falls?' I wonder.

'You can never tell.'

'Five years? Ten years?'

'You never know ... I didn't think he was that daft.' Said Ivor.

'It says Jack Straw is the only one who stands up to him.'

'I'm delighted.' Ivor does not believe in drawing attention to himself.

Tuesday, 25th November

William *has* broken his foot. We spent Sunday afternoon in St Thomas's instead of at the Zoo. Logistical problems tower above us. Two full-time jobs, no child care and a one-footed child who cannot go anywhere, let alone to school. I did not go to work yesterday. Sara has offered to help. He will spend tomorrow and Thursday with her. Where would we be without her? And she is moving to Oxfordshire as soon as she can.

Wednesday, 26th November

St Thomas's Fracture Clinic. William will be mended in three weeks' time.

'But he can't go to school like this!' I point at the foot that has no protection and cannot be put to the ground.

'No, he can't.'

'Well?' I am going to have to make a point. 'Can you put him in plaster?'

'It would be sore when the plaster came off.'

'Yes.' But not as sore as three weeks stuck at home.

'We could put a plaster on. And give him crutches.'

'Yes.' I can only assume that this doctor has never tried to carry a fully-grown nearly-eight-year-old into a fracture clinic. Or, for that matter, into casualty, out of casualty or to any of the other places you need to go when you have broken your foot. And this doctor, like the casualty staff, has never spent even 24 hours with a one-footed child.

William's morale rises as we effect our three-legged walk into the plaster room and climaxes as crutches are revealed in the cupboard.

'Didn't they give you anything in casualty?' The Plaster Man obviously has spent time with a one-footed child.

'No.'

'Nothing?'

'Nothing.'

'I don't know what they are doing in casualty.' More muttering. We leave the plaster room on cloud nine and crutches. Crutches are not so easy when you smashed your right arm in July and won't have it back to full strength for two years. Therefore, although we leave the fracture clinic on crutches, we have reverted to piggy-back before we get to Ivor's car. I think piggy-backing eight-year-olds should be part of medical training.

Friday, 28th November.

Take William to school.

Get a cheque from the Inland Revenue, for much the same amount as one of my cheques to them.

Jack Straw told Ivor, '*The Guardian* will always have its finger on the pulse of betrayal.'

'What's happened to Derry's plan to sell tickets to the Lords?'

'Terry Boston has been to see him and sat on him. Told him no one is in favour. People are very much against.'

Monday, 1st December

Lambeth College has produced its Accommodation Strategy. We are to become a three-site college by 1999, if all goes according to plan. We were 13 sites and are now five sites. The two sites to go are Tower Bridge (handsome and valuable) and Norwood (hideous and in Norwood). Staff will go too. We all think ... not me ... no ... not me.

Mr Thomas at the school tells me that he has given up giving homework because only two or three children do it. Protest.

Ivor returns at the same time as the sofa.

Derry asked to see Ivor at 6 p.m. While they were ensconced, solving a detail of difficulty with Jack Straw, Alastair Campbell rang. Derry will be all over the papers tomorrow. He made a speech in the Reform Club which, Derry says, he thought was private. He compared himself to Cardinal Wolsey. (Cf Ivor on Derry, 8th July.) Do wonder what Alastair Campbell said to Derry.

Ivor produces some papers from his pocket.

'I thought you had better see this.' He has the air of caution of a man holding a match to a thunderflash.

The paper is the planning for the State dinner for Brazil tomorrow. The Royal Party is short of women. There are three unmarried princes. This is solved by arranging for the Lady Richard to bring up the rear of the Royal Procession into dinner, 'escorted by Angus Ogilvy'.

Very much hope nobody I know sees me.

Tuesday, 2nd December

The papers are full of Cardinal Irvine. We are reminded, several times, that Wolsey ended his days in disgrace. Read Churchill on Wolsey: 'for 14 years Wolsey in the King's name was the effective ruler of the realm' but in the end Wolsey made a 'fatal miscalculation' and he was sacrificed to preserve the popularity of the monarchy. After his death a hair shirt was found under his fine linen.

Ivor gets home:

'I've had a row with Derry.'

'What about?'

'Reform of the Lords.' Sigh. 'We had a deal. We don't agree about how to do it so we did agree we would meet tomorrow and put together a memorandum to send to Blair. Then I came into the office today and Lesley waved this bit of paper at me and asked me if I wanted to sit down before I read it.'

'What was it?'

'A memorandum from Derry to Blair on reform of the Lords. I exploded at him.'

'What did you say?'

'That we had a deal that we would write it together and that this is not the way to do business ... I decided I had nothing to lose—if I lose this job there are plenty of other things I can do. He told me to stop hectoring him. I told him I was not hectoring him. I was telling him.'

'He won't have liked it.'

'No. He said he'd try and get hold of the memorandum before it got to Blair. When I put the phone down Lesley was delighted. Delighted. I said perhaps they'd sack me. She said they'd be crazy to do that.'

'Did Derry get hold of the memorandum?'

'He rang me back—said Blair had not seen it and Downing Street had torn it up.'

Monica, William's London Godmother, comes round. Her chicken is roasting in the oven. We are driven to the Palace. The first person we meet is Jack Straw.

'How's the Cardinal?' he asks. I mention that I have been reading Churchill on Wolsey. Detect a glimmer of glee from Jack Straw—don't think he is too fond of Derry. Neither Ivor nor Jack Straw have read Churchill. Tell Ivor I'll mark the page.

We are organised into our places. I process alongside Angus Ogilvy who is kind to me and tells me to take his arm:

'I'm very old-fashioned.'

I am also next to Our Man in Brazil who, Monica told me half an hour ago, worked with her for three months when he was a consul and she was in the Foreign Office. When I tell him this I am not sure he likes it.

The flowers festooning the table are lavish but less smelly than last time. During the speeches ladybirds begin to fly from them. They land on the linen except for one which settles on Robert Fellowes' stiff white collar. His neighbour walks it on to her fingernail and then on to the cloth where they both admire it.

Process once more towards coffee.

Denis Carter finds Ivor: 'About Derry ...' Derry has been bending Denis's ear. Derry is hurt. Very hurt. That Ivor should imagine ... that Ivor could even think ... the very idea that Derry would shaft Ivor.

'Will he do it again?' I ask.

'Not in that way,' says Ivor.

At 11.20 p.m. the Queen Mother, aged 97, is standing firm and chatting like a girl. Draped in silks and shrouded in diamonds, she is a theatrical experience all on her own. Anybody else would look like a Christmas tree.

Discuss Derry's discomfiture when we get home. 'He must know he's made a fool of himself.'

'Yes. As long as he calms down a bit he'll be all right.'

'Cherie looked so thin and tired.'

'She didn't look too good to me. Problems there.'

'The strain must be enormous. Enormous. As for the strain of his job ...'

The Duchess of Grafton, henchwoman to the Queen, who Ivor was next to, told him it was time to get rid of 'those hereditaries', they were 'ridiculous'.

Wednesday, 3rd December

Ivor meets Jim. Jim asks: 'Are they learning?'

'Not quickly enough.'

'Pity.'

Derry, Ivor and Denis meet and put together their memorandum. 'They quite liked my little idea.' Ivor's little idea is that a joint committee of both houses of parliament, briefed to dispose of the hereditaries and to decide what else to do, is put together. The committee will include a 'hand-picked cross-section of political colours' and will make recommendations. If anybody objects to the recommendations afterwards, they can be told they were their own recommendations. They can go quarrelling amongst themselves. 'Brilliant', was Derry's judgement.

Thursday, 4th December

'Something has happened,' Ivor shakes his head, 'something has certainly happened.' At the Freedom of Information Committee today, Derry paused every now and then: 'Is that all right, Ivor? ... What do you think, Ivor? ... Is that all right with you, Ivor?'

'Perhaps he has realised he cannot manage going it alone.'

'I don't know what is going on; I can only tell you what he said.'

'Perhaps he wants you around to blame.'

'I don't mind being responsible for my own opinions.'

Friday, 5th December

Meeting in Clapham for us ALSters. An opportunity to hear what is happening on other sites. A student went berserk with a meat cleaver in the canteen at Norwood last week. Norwood's meeting to object to its own closure was half-hearted. It is like a third world airport: dead greens, disinfectant smells, leaks.

We are brought coffee in cups with Lambeth College's logo on them. Wonder what they cost.

We are confirmed as belonging to the new School of ESOL and Study Support. We have to Map the Basic Skills (show how students need to read and write) of every assignment on every course (of every piece of work every student is set). The effect of this is that we are discovering colleagues who are not able to read and write themselves while teaching their students.

Saturday, 6th December

Ivor is speaking at a lawyers' dinner in Brighton. He asks where to find Churchill on Wolsey.

'I might say something about the Cardinal.'

'Is that wise?'

'I don't see why not.' This is an indication that he sees very well why not.

'If somebody has a tape-recorder ... it only takes one person to repeat you ... think of the embarrassment ... if you make mock of our Lord Chancellor.'

'They might find it funny.'

'Exactly.'

Notice later that, as Ivor leaves the house, Churchill remains behind: 'Don't worry. I won't say anything'

Maybe he was testing—I am often told that I have No Political Instincts.

Monday, 8th December

Meeting at school for eight parents of eight children described by the school as, 'very able'. It is the only meeting I have ever been to where all the parents were there. (The other eight parents will all have been at work.) We are each given a publication by the local education authority titled 'Working With Very Able Children'. Our children are to be put in groups of four for half an hour a week to 'solve problems'. Hide 'Working With Very Able Children' under my coat and sneak it home and upstairs into the wardrobe. Do not know if William is Very Able. Do believe he has expectations and opportunities foisted upon him. Also believe that to be labelled 'very able' at the age of seven can only lead to disappointment.

Ivor is out for the evening. The Privy Council is giving the Queen and Duke of Edinburgh dinner in the Royal Gallery in the Lords. He and Ann Taylor meet them outside and walk them into dinner. Ann did not curtsey. She looked after the Queen, Ivor and the Duke of Edinburgh. The Duke of Edinburgh is in favour of hereditary peers: 'I'd rather they were chosen by God than by the Prime Minister.'

Mrs Thatcher is opposite Ivor. He now thinks this is a mistake. He had refused to have her next to him so she was moved but she butts into all his conversations from opposite; from one side she would have found that more difficult. She shouts across the table (which is narrow) at him and the Duke of Edinburgh; Linda Chalker—Ivor's chosen neighbour, the other side from the Duke—she ignores. Ivor's judgement is: 'She's gone barmy. Bonkers. Over the top. She ignores Tories ... I got 'Oh-Ivor-How-Nice-To-See-You'—Not a word to Linda. Not a word. As soon as she got the Duke of Edinburgh's attention she bellowed 'I am very worried about the price of gold!' He said, 'Oh Yes Um,' and then she told us that if you draw a line north to south, just east of India, you have no religion east of that line.

'Two million Muslims?' said Ivor

'Oh—Indonesian Muslims.'

'Buddhists? Shintoists?' said the Duke of Edinburgh.

Ivor finishes his account: 'And she ran this country for 11 years.'

I guess that Ivor got a certain pleasure processing past some 470 privy councillors who include those who have done their worst for him over 40 years in British politics. Put it to him. 'I have to confess, I did notice David

Owen.'

May remind him of this when I next hear what a failure he has been. Meantime he is noticing people being 'extraordinarily friendly'. Can't think why.

Tuesday, 9th December

Jim Callaghan was sitting on the other side of the Duke of Edinburgh last night and next to Derry. Jim tried to 'have a serious talk' with Derry. 'I told him you catch more flies with honey than with a flyswot.'

Ivor's team continue putting together their piece of paper on Lords' reform. They have got the Cabinet Office on board. (The Cabinet Office is impressed with Damien and Simon who are performing as the whole ministry all on their own.) They have not got Derry on board. He is holding out for a 100% nominated chamber, to be re-nominated every five years.

Begin to see the Duke of Edinburgh's point of view.

'Does anybody else agree with Derry?'

'No. It all depends on Blair.'

'Will you get to see Blair?'

'I am told so.'

Wednesday, 10th December

Jones The Pictures' and Jones The Books' wedding anniversary: 48 years.

There is less teaching this week. Students are beginning to disappear into Christmas.

Revolt is stirring at the lone parents' loss of £6 a week. Nick Brown is low. 'At least you told them there would be a rebellion,' Ivor tells him.

Thursday, 11th December

Revolt is stirred. Ivor is listening to the early morning news.

Rush out of Lambeth College to the school church and arrive as the Christmas service starts. Enjoy it all much more after William has made a success of his solo performance of 'Jingle Bells' on the piano. The singing teacher is silent so the pianist leads the way unmolested, unlike at the Harvest Festival.

When Ivor first told me about the lone parents' loss (Tuesday, 1st July), he was saying it would 'only' save £50million, that it was not worth the fuss it would cause and he did not approve of 'penalising the poorest ... but I'm Old Labour'. In Cabinet today, in his usual seat next to HH, he hears how upset she is about the whole thing.

'Why did she agree to it then?'

'It was all part of the deal she did with Gordon Brown. In exchange for that other things could go through ... she should not have been put in that position.'

'Perhaps she should not have got into that position.'

'I've told her perhaps we could soften it in the Lords ... change some of the legislation ... if she wants to talk to me about it ... Did you know that after April, if you get a job but then lose it and then go back on to benefit, you lose the £6?'

'I did know—it's a disincentive to get a job in the first place.'

'A lot of people don't seem to have realised that Harriet won't last long ... except Blair does seem to have a soft spot for her ... he's extraordinarily loyal to her. She insists on reading everything, dotting every 'i', crossing every 't' ... She can't delegate.'

'She must spend all her time reading.'

'Yes.'

'FF doesn't seem to be much help to her.'

'He's useless. It's the first time he's had to subject his great ideas to civil servants' precision. Anecdotes are no good. Pat Hollis and John Denham are running that ministry.'

Derry and Ivor have finished and agreed their paper for Blair on Lords' reform. 'It's supposed to be in his weekend box. It'll take serious reading.'

'Will he read it?'

'He's going to Luxembourg for the weekend ... there's a rumour that Derry has squared him already.'

'On which side?' Ivor shrugs. He doesn't know.

Hear that Derry will be getting a minder in the spring, 'with no political experience whatsoever,' Ivor notes.

The surveyor's report on our crack arrives. The house could do with 'some redecoration'. Don't see what this has to do with cracks. The surveyor will be in touch about Monitoring the Crack. In the meantime we have a room we cannot use.

Saturday, 13th December

My step-daughter rings, at 3 a.m. Her son was born at 2.15 a.m. They are all fine.

Downing Street rings at 11 a.m. Blair wants to see Ivor at 11 a.m. on Monday.

'But I think Derry's already squared him ... it means breaking with the manifesto.'

'Who else will be there?'

'Derry, Denis, Powell ...'

'Will you let them know you think you've been set up?' Ivor shakes his head.

'If you have been set up—what a waste of time.'

'Yes.'

Sunday, 14th December

Drive to Norfolk to visit The Grandson, Ieuan Richard, and his parents. The baby does not open his eyes. Drive back to London. Have a lunch of awesome disgustingness. Advise you never to go near certain pubs in Norfolk.

Monday, 15th December

Try to make a Bat Costume for the school fancy dress party and competition. My student gown makes body and 'arms' (despite splodges of meals from 1971-74 spattered on it); my grandmother's long thin leather gloves make 'hands'; bat ears are more of a problem.

While waiting to see Blair at 11 this morning, Derry was relishing a quarrel with the Tories.

'The trouble with you, mate,' Ivor told him, 'is that you would regard the Charge of the Light Brigade as a triumph even though it was a bloody mess.' Everybody laughed.

'Including Derry?'

'Oh yes—he can laugh—it's the only way to handle him.'

Once they went in to see Blair, Derry was transformed into near silence and a few questions.

'What was the chemistry like between him and Blair?'

'Formal.'

'Derry didn't talk?'

'No.'

'And did he get his own way?'

'No.'

'Did you get what you wanted?'

'Yes. Entirely. Back to doing it in two stages. Stage One, we'll remove the hereditaries. Stage Two ... there's even talk of setting up a Royal Commission, which is what I wanted five years ago. If the Royal Commission sits for two years and then suggests a nominated chamber ... we'll have had one for two years anyway. I'd like it set up in 1999, to take two years to report, and then its recommendations can be in the manifesto for 2002.'

'And had Blair read your paper?'

'It was scribbled on.'

'Does he understand your difficulties in the Lords?'

'Very well.'

'Did Denis Carter say anything?'

'No. I did nearly all the talking. Derry just hasn't got his head round it. Hasn't got his head round it at all.'

Ivor meets Nick Brown who asks him if he thinks Geoffrey Robinson can survive. (GR has been proposing taxing all of us with savings over £50,000— while he has offshore supplies of several million.) Ivor says he thinks GR can survive but that it is a very bad sign if Nick Brown is asking Ivor for his opinion.

Tuesday, 16th December

The Bat Ears stood up to the fancy dress party.

Tessa Blackstone and Emily Blatch are squaring up to come to blows. Ivor thinks they both lack judgement and either could go over the top.

There is anxiety over the timing of a Government statement on an enquiry into the history of BSE in the UK. Robin Butler says the ex-prime ministers have to be given two days to answer the letters requesting their permission to open up their governments' papers. That takes us to the 19th - William Hague's wedding day. It is felt to be playing foul to overshadow the wedding. That takes us to the time slot before David Blunkett's Education Bill. Nick Brown informs the business managers that David Blunkett would 'go ballistic' if his Education Bill was overshadowed. One solution is to bring BSE forward, announcing it as subject to ex-prime ministers' permission.

Wednesday, 17th December

Back to the fracture clinic. William's plaster is removed and we walk home.

Put up the Christmas tree. It falls over. Put it up again. It falls over. Put it up again. Dance round it.

Ivor has been talking to Pat Hollis. The Treasury has asked HH to make savings of one-and-a-bit-billion on disability benefits. Pat Hollis has found savings of one-and-a-bit-billion on disability benefits. HH has vetoed Pat and has offered savings of over six billion on disability benefits. Pat thinks HH has gone mad. 'She does go her own way,' says Ivor. 'Pat is the only one to have got her head round that ministry.'

Ivor gives Peter Mandelson 'the shock of his life'—The Liberals in The Lords have tabled an amendment softening the effects of the lone parents' loss of £6. Ivor believes half of the Labour Lords will vote with the Liberal Lords.

'Half?!' said Peter.

'Half.' said Ivor. 'And,' said Ivor to me, 'I'm going to tell them that in Cabinet tomorrow. Serve the buggers right.'

Ivor has to see Tessa in the morning. She is trying to see through her Bill without its regulations. 'We objected to the Tories doing that again and again.'

'She's very quiet.'

'She's sinking.'

Thursday, 18th December

Bob-my-Boss tells me a joke that is circulating: Sleeping Beauty, Tom Thumb and Saddam Hussein are arguing: I'm the most beautiful person in the world; I'm the smallest person in the world; I'm the most hated person in the world.

'Let's look in the Guinness Book of Records.' They do so. They find themselves:

'There's Sleeping Beauty! There's Tom Thumb!' Pause. 'Who's Harriet Harman?' And little do they know what is going on and may be yet to come. 'Yes.' I say to Bob, 'Yes, indeed.'

Work is paperwork: registers, records of work, schemes of work, reviews of work, reports of work, summaries of reviews of work, summaries of reports of work ... What about the teaching? Bob tells me it is no longer teaching. It is Guided Learning.

Bob has hold of the Secret Plans for re-building our floor of Lambeth College. He doesn't know why they are secret. All of us in the Study Centre have a look at them. £11 million are being spent re-building across Lambeth College (more than a quarter of HH's savings on Lone Parents). All the walls on our floor are being knocked down and re-built: Study Centre, Library, classrooms, offices, lavatories, corridors. This may be the start of a long story. The work would take months to do. What would we do while it was being done? And afterwards ... (if it happens) ... working across acres of Departure-Lounge-Like carpet ... new computers (100 according to the plan) ... new chairs ... new desks ... needing roller skates. Fewer and fewer classrooms, fewer teachers, a few more of us ALSters: the students will be given their brief and then left to get on with it—told to come to the Study Centre for Support.

Us ALSters will soon be in uniform. A chair, a computer, a desk, space in the Study Centre and one two-hundredth of an ALSter is cheaper than teaching people.

Ivor's message (that he would tell Cabinet of the Labour Lords' lack of enthusiasm for cutting lone parents) got through. He got an instruction from Jonathan Powell not to mention it in Cabinet. Everybody else mentioned it in Cabinet. Clare Short, David Blunkett and others started a call for a Cabinet Away Day where they could Really Talk Things Through.

Nick Brown told Blair of the Labour Lords' shyness at cutting Lone Parents. 'Don't mention it! Don't tell anyone!' said Blair. Nick Brown pointed out that it was no secret; people were working it out for themselves and that people knew that if the Government's Lone Parent Laws are blocked in the Lords they will have to return to the Commons, where the row will be had all over again.

After Cabinet, HH got a chance to talk at Blair. Blair came over to Ivor: 'Go away and sort it out!' (The TUC had been waiting outside to see him for over 30 minutes.) Thereupon, Ivor and Nick Brown got together and decided they would interpret that as the prime-ministerial instruction for Ivor to troubleshoot HH. She has to be led out of the hole she has dug for herself, to the safety of legislation that will get through the Lords without more resistance.

'Did you notice the way He was looking at her in Cabinet?' Nick Brown asked Ivor. They agree that He is fed up to the back teeth with her.

'I like Nick Brown,' said Ivor.' 'He's my kind of bloke. He understands what power's all about.'

'I wonder if Blair knows about HH and the six billion,' I wonder. Ivor blanches. Not something he often does.

'I doubt it.'

'I don't think he'd be very pleased if he did,' I say.

'I told Derry about it. He said 'You're joking!' I said I had it on reliable authority ... of course Pat can't stand HH, can't stand her but ...'

'Maybe the six billion are one of a set of alternatives.'

The other news this evening is that Michael Cocks has put down a question about Derry's refurbishments. Derry has been going around saying his refurbishments were part of the House of Lords' Rolling Scheme of Restoration. Unfortunately they were not. Michael Cocks's question is about whether or not they were. Derry has been grumbling that the answer given will have to be truthful.

'He hasn't been to see me,' says Ivor, hoping that is how things will remain.

Questions have to be answered truthfully, and Ivor does not want the job of 'spelling it out' to Derry.

'I don't want to make an enemy.'

'Who put Michael Cocks up to asking the question?'

'Michael Cocks. That's Michael Cocks.'

'I thought he was a Labour peer.' I get a look which I interpret as 'So What?'.

Friday, 19th December

Ivor sets off for the Lords 'wondering how I'll handle Our Harriet'. He comes back having discussed it with Denis Carter and Pat Hollis. He and Pat agree to meet on 7th January. Ivor tells me that Michael Cocks' question was answered truthfully but he does not think that Michael Cocks has finished with Derry.

Saturday, 20th December

Ivor's cabinet committee on reform of the House of Lords is announced. Ivor did not know the announcement was coming today. *The Times'* man, who was talking to him earlier, is offended that Ivor did not tell him. Journalists tend to assume people (e.g. Ivor) know Everything and find it hard to believe they do not. As if Blair knew about the six billion. Nobody can know Everything.

There is a leak: Blunkett is complaining about welfare cuts. Wonder if the announcement of the reform of the House of Lords was supposed to divert attention from the leak and reassure us of the Government's Radical Intentions.

Monday, 22nd December

The BSE Statement is delayed by the collapse of House of Commons' computers. David Blunkett, no doubt seething in his office, moves into the breach and gets his speech in first after all.

Tuesday, 23rd December

I am 46 today. 'Youth is gone—gone—and will never come back: can't help it,' said Charlotte Bronte when she was 32.

Wednesday, 24th December, Christmas Eve

'A Cabinet Minister's son has been caught supplying cannabis ... his parents took him to the police,' Ivor tells me with my cup of tea.

My mind turns to children too young to be named, old enough to be dealing in cannabis with parents upright (and astute) enough to Do the Right Thing. Mind comes to rest on the Straws.

'Jack Straw' I say.

'Oh poor Jack, I hope not,' says Ivor, not that he would be happier if it was anybody else.

'You'll find out who it is,' I say.

'The tabloids will sniff it out,' says Ivor.

I remember Mrs Jack Straw (not her real name) at Buckingham Palace. When Ivor and Jack plugged themselves into Talking Politics, I turned to talk to her and she said: 'Oh ... are they being boring?' I liked her.

Remember telling Angus Ogilvy that I passed the joint without drawing on it from fear, not moral rectitude.

The sofa leg breaks off.

Monday, 29th December

Christmas was a mixture of festivities and hostilities.

We are at the house and snow has been in the roof, spoilt a ceiling and put out the lights; according to the electrician the snow was 'like icing sugar' and got into his roof too. He put on the lights.

William is victim of local teasing because his Dad is Labour. Local views are not—never have been—Labour.

'Why do they tease me?'

'Because you are seven and you are there.'

'Why don't they tease you? I'll tell them next time I'm not political. If they want to tease they must come and tease you.'

'I don't expect they'll do that.'

'It's not fair. Wouldn't they support Labour if their Dad was Labour?'

It is not fair. And they would support Labour if their Dads had been Labour. As their Dads were not Labour, they do not support Labour. 'This land is Conservative land,' they told William. They also told him Labour were going to ban cattle and sheep and put lions and tigers out to graze.

Tuesday, 30th December

William told local Conservatives that if they wanted to tease, they should tease his Dad, not him.

'Your Dad's too old to know anything.'

We tell William how old Churchill was when he became Prime Minister for the first time and for the second time. We visit the Local Conservatives en masse. There is no teasing. Farm prices (pigs, sheep, cattle) are falling ... further than they fell last year.

A wet gale blows up. So does a dilemma. There is no red wine in the house. There is plenty of red wine in the garage. The garage is 20 yards from the house. The garage door needs two hands to control it in a gale. A torch needs one hand to hold it in the dark. A crate of wine needs two hands to carry it in any circumstances. How much does Ivor want red wine? Not enough to put on wellington boots, waterproofs and plunge into the weather. He shares my white wine.

Wednesday, 31st December

William spends half an hour playing with Local Conservatives' puppies. I spend half an hour talking to local Conservative—to block teasing while allowing puppy-playing.

'Where do you teach, then?' Local Conservative asks me when I go back to work. I tell him.

'It's called Lambeth College. I've been there 20 years.'

'Lots of foreigners, then?'

'Yes.'

'There won't be any English left soon. In 30 years there'll be no English.'

'I'm not English, I suppose, my father's Welsh.'

'Eh?'

'Jones.'

'There's a thought.' Local Conservative has a soft spot for Jones The Books. 'But you were born English.'

'We're Celts really. My mother's Scottish and Welsh ... a bit of English blood ... but we're mainly Celts.' So, I would guess, is the Local Conservative - driven west by the Romans and the Vikings.

We go home before there is further political discussion.

Split my finger breaking twigs for the fire.

Storm, forecast for the last three days, reveals itself with cloudless sky and not a twig stirring. Nor a blade of grass. Nor a mouse. The poison, left down since October, has not been touched.

'Dad! ... Dad! ... Daaaaad!' I hear.

'Has Dad got the radio blaring?' I ask.

'Not blaring,' voice of resignation, 'Blairing.'

Ivor and I settle in to wait for 1998 and survey 1997 and its accidents and triumphs.

Thursday, 1st January 1998

No storm. Colder. Sheep huddle round the house. The gorse is flowering.

Discuss Blair's health: how exhausted he looked just before Christmas.

'I hope he'll be all right ... otherwise we will have problems. I'd go for Gordon Brown.'

Explain how I've been trying to tell the history of the Lords without being boring. 'The legs were cut off the Lords in 1910.' The peers threw out Lloyd George's budget despite a convention that the peers never interfered in financial legislation. In the resultant row, Asquith said that he would create 500 peers. The peers retreated with that sword over their heads. That is how things have remained. My great-grandfather, Henry Jones, was, I was told, to be one of the 500. He was cottage born and Professor of Moral Philosophy at the University of Glasgow (Jones The Thinker).

Reading a biography of Kathleen Scott this evening, I find her version of the 1910-11 furore. I also find this complaint: 'How I love my family and how I love being left alone. It is hard to be a sculptor when there are cooks and nurses and political parties in the world. One imagines one might have been a really fine artist if one had been just selfish and slovenly.'

The Media are engrossed in 'The Cabinet Minister's Son' who sold cannabis. We now know the Cabinet Minister is a man. We creep nearer Jack Straw.

Friday, 2nd January

It is Jack Straw.

Saturday, 3rd January

75 mph winds. 100 mph forecast. The track is a river, getting muddier and muddier. We decide to leave today instead of tomorrow for fear of being unable to leave at all. The journey takes seven hours. The car is blown by walls of wind and water.

Sunday, 4th January

The *Sunday Times* say they have received a letter from Derry's solicitors claiming that it is nearly a libel to suggest that Derry's refurbishments were anything other than part of a Rolling Programme of Restoration. Ivor is alarmed. 'He can't ... He can't expect people to lie for him ... Not the clerks to the Lords ... not me.'

Some time later I ask Ivor if he has decided what to do.

'Yes. I'll speak to Black Rod. Get the facts. Speak to Derry. And I'll have a word with Jonathan Powell: "I know he's a friend of Tony's but ... ... I told Derry it would have to go through all the committees. I made him put it on paper. I didn't want anyone saying I had..."'

Monday, 5th January

Lambeth College. By 10 a.m. the Study Centre thermometer has reached 58F. Go out and buy biscuits under torrents of rain and a borrowed umbrella.

Tuesday, 6th January

Ivor asks Black Rod for 'a piece of paper' with the facts on Derry's Dwelling.

Wednesday, 7th January

Ivor goes to see Joan Lestor in St George's Hospital, Tooting, with her broken hip. They have worked together since 1955. She is friendly but won't support the Government on lone parents. Ivor did not expect otherwise.

Ivor, Damien, Denis Carter and Pat Hollis discuss what to do about lone parents in the Lords. The two concessions they mull over are:

1. exempting those with pre-school children, and
2. giving £10 a week (i.e. more than £6) to lone parents from monies collected by the Child Support Agency, all of which was going to the Treasury.

The problem is only 30% of lone parents have named the absent parent to the CSA in the first place. Ivor & Co believe they might get lone parents through the Lords with these changes. Pat Hollis shows Ivor a letter from HH to Blair in which she refuses to make any changes. Ivor writes a letter to Blair proposing the changes. Pat Hollis takes it back to the Department. There is a flurry from HH's political advisers: Is it wise to write to the Prime Minister? Is it wise to commit yourself in writing? (Ivor is not supposed to know of HH's letter to the Prime Minister.) Ivor arranges to meet HH after tomorrow's cabinet. If all does not go well he will send the letter to Blair.

HH's political advisers also said they were 'very keen' to get the legislation through the Lords. They could not risk it returning to the Commons. Acording to Ivor 'The three junior ministers in that Department get together and run it. HH spends as much time working on the Department's new logo as on anything else. FF is stratospheric.'

HH, however, is 'very sympathetic' to Pat Hollis's tragedy. Her husband has a brain tumour and is dying. She will be taking Wednesdays off in order to go home to Norfolk late on Tuesdays and back to London early on Thursdays. She will run much of the Department from the train to and from Norfolk.

Ivor has his piece of paper from Black Rod. In May, soon after the election, Derry talked to the Clerk of the Works. The Clerk of the Works talked to Black Rod. Black Rod talked to Ivor. Derry's requests started to go through all the committees.

SPRING TERM 1998

Thursday, 8th January

See revised plan for rebuilding our floor of Lambeth College. Put together a list of practical problems: where will the air come from? Why are there no lavatories? Should the student coffee bar be next to the Quiet Area? Why does the staffroom have no door?

Ivor saw HH. She insisted that, after the budget (which comes before lone parents reach the House of Lords), lone parents will look different: the budget will put a new perspective on things. Ivor will wait until after the budget. 'Whose support does she have?'

'Gordon Brown's.'

'Anybody else?'

'Blair isn't prepared to have a bloody great row with her.'

Ivor saw Peter Mandelson: 'Three things—two work, one embarrassing.'

What is in Tony's mind about the Reform of the House of Lords? Peter doesn't know but will find out. Lone Parents are not going to go away. He can see that. He asks: 'What's the embarrassing thing?'

'The Lord Chancellor's wallpaper.' Peter does not laugh. He does take notes. Ivor is very embarrassed. He doesn't want to go and see Tony about it. (Peter agrees.) He doesn't want to go muttering behind people's backs. (Peter Mandelson, agrees.) But ... the Lord Chancellor is going around saying his refurbishments were started off by the previous government. They were not.

Peter will have a word with Tony. Ivor will have a word with Derry.

'I'll have to spell it out to him,' says Ivor, 'he's dug himself into a hole and he must shut up about the whole thing or he will dig himself in deeper.'

My back is Going Wrong.

Friday, 9th January

My back has Gone Wrong. Ivor tries to take me to the doctors' in the car. I cannot get into the car. Scuff 150 yards to doctor who says, 'You should not have come. You should have got one of us to come to you.' Stand throughout consultation. Cannot risk trying to sit down. Scuff home. Scuff to physiotherapists. It is not a slipped disc. It is a pelvic problem. I must spend two weeks 'resting' and 'moving'.

Start learning to 'rest' and 'move'.

Robin Cook's love life is overflowing.

'Puritanical British,' says Ivor.

'Not puritanical, prurient,' say I.

'That's worse,' says Ivor, 'that's interest without commitment.'

Calls from Jones The Pictures and from Switzerland. My uncle is weak and getting weaker.

Saturday, 10th January

'Rest' and 'move'.

Sunday, 11th January

'Rest' and 'move'. Can't read a newspaper: can't hold it up.

Monday, 12th January

Ivor spoke to Derry about his wallpaper. Derry is hurt. Very Hurt. (Again.) That Ivor, of all people, should believe such a Black Lie. A Black Lie. Of course he had never said his wallpaper was part of the previous government's rolling programme. That was a Black Lie.

Ivor is Very Sorry that Derry is Hurt. But it is Ivor's job to tell Derry what is being put about: 'Nobody else will tell you. It's my job to tell you.'

Ivor is upset by a visit—from Brian Morris who was dumped by New Labour in May. He doesn't know if it's a coincidence, but his bone marrow problem which was in remission until then, has surged back. Brian will be away for six months. He has to live in a bubble in a hospital. He manages to joke that he does not have much hair to lose.

Tuesday, 13th January

I continue to 'rest' and 'move'. People tell me of the wonders of a hot bath. I am sure they are right—if I could get into one. Ivor helps me to wash before disappearing into a BBC Radio van in the street to talk about Reform of the

Lords. He then takes William to school.

It will be my treat to watch and listen to the newses through the day. When you are crippled, such sweets entice you from moment to moment. It is not easy to lie on the floor, seeing a great many things that need to be done, and being unable to do them. Some people live like this all the time.

The new Cabinet Committee had its first meeting today: 'A disappointing meeting. Nick Brown said nothing. Peter Mandelson said he wanted a wholly nominated chamber and then left to deal with a problem with the Dome. Jack Straw was abroad. Derry says we need more heavyweights. He thinks he's the only heavyweight on it.'

'But nobody else wants a wholly nominated chamber—not even Derry.'

'True. But I've only just managed to get him off that. When Peter went, I told him at least his problem was finite.'

'At the end of the meeting, Ivor got what he wanted: 'They've agreed that I can 'tickle' Cranborne'. There has been gossip that the Tories want to agree to the demise of the hereditary peerage

'If they do,' says Derry, 'it'll be the diplomatic coup of the decade.'

Wednesday, 14th January

Manage to stand in the bath.

Cock Robin and Cookie Nookie still feature. Blair defends him in the Commons: 'If this goes on too long,' says Ivor, 'he may have to go.'

Thursday, 15th January

Ivor has a meeting at 8.15 a.m chaired by Derry. It's the Business Managers: they have to decide the contents of the Queen's Speech next October and plenty of ministers will be pushing to get their business included. John Prescott has a lot he wants to get in.

Before he goes Ivor washes my hair. Len and Florence take William to school.

Physiotherapist's husband rings: she has flu. Can I go to her partner? Her partner is in W1. How can I get to W1? I can't. Walk to the doctors' to get referred to the St Thomas's physiotherapists. I have not walked so far (150 yards) for seven days.

Notice I have sticky hair.

Walk to St Thomas's. The root of my problem is the sacroiliac joint: 'It was probably a good thing. A warning.'

Ivor has a meeting of the Chequers' trustees. How do they pay for the roof?

Chequers has a plate: Charles II English Delft. It has sat in a cupboard for years. At sale it might reach £156,000. The Prime Minister would prefer it to go to the Victoria and Albert Museum. What if they offered £110,000? Do the trustees have the right to 'lose' £40,000? And what about the publicity?

Mo is given a House Thump in cabinet: 'The agreement has not got anything like the press it deserves ... to get all that lot to agree ...'

After Cabinet Ivor sees the new Robin Butler - Richard Wilson. Richard Wilson talks of the importance of the Lords to this Government. (The Lords defeated the London Referendum Bill earlier this week.) Richard Wilson observes that ministers have still to realise the difficulties the Lords can cause them. He talks of 'your place in history'.

'Does he mean you or the Government?'

'I wasn't quite sure.'

HH is upset: after her and Ivor's meeting (easing off the lone parents with £10 a week from the CSA and leaving out pre-school children) Ivor went back to his office and dictated a piece of paper detailing what he and HH had agreed. He sent her a copy, keeping one for himself. 'You've put it on paper! What if there's a leak! We agreed!'

'Harriet, in all my years I have learnt that if two people are in a room and say they've agreed something and there is no note of it ...'

He thinks the truth of the matter is that HH has not cleared the agreement with the Treasury; Gordon Brown does not know of any agreement.

'How can she function if she cannot put anything on paper? Can't rely on a piece of paper between you and her?'

'She'll be all right when these welfare reforms are up and running. The mistake was in bringing the lone parents in at the beginning: they should have been part of the Budget package.'

Ivor has not sent a copy of the note to Blair. HH was appeased by this.

The Budget will be on 17th March.

'Do you know what will be in it?'

' ——' Difficult to convey the combination of 'yes' / 'no'/ ' I can't tell you' in Ivor's answer which is in sounds but not in words. He follows the sounds with 'Pat Hollis is doing a lot of work on the Child Support Agency ... those fathers.'

The stickiness of my hair effects a seaweed wig: the only thing to do is ask Ivor to wash it again. Water and potion are poured on to my head. There is no lather. More potion is poured on. No lather. More potion. Ivor reads the label of the pot of potion: ' This is conditioner.' We start again. This time he uses shampoo—I think my complaints at Ivor's label-reading powers are restrained and moderate in the circumstances.

Friday, 16th January

We have a quarrel: 'You do nothing ... nothing ... but sit there and give orders ... as if you ruled the world.' That is Ivor talking to me.

'Huh.' (This is me talking to Ivor.) 'I thought it was you that ruled the world.'

A spouse with A Back does not fit into anybody's scheme of things. Sympathy gets stretched. The owner of The Back, spending a day under sea-weed (and with The Back) feels cheated by fate and entitled to make the occasional demand.

Today, free of seaweed, prospects improve and I return to Roy Jenkins's 'A Life at the Centre'. George Eliot, via Mr Vincy, might turn that around: 'The Centre of a Life'.

Politics and public life may be at the centre of Roy Jenkins's life—but are they The Centre? Politicians cringe at 'philosophy'. When I wondered if the next Queen's Speech, announcing the end of the hereditary peers to the hereditary peers, might include a 'philosophical sentence', Ivor looked at me as if I were bonkers. Roy Jenkins tells us he got 'the lowest mark in general philosophy of any undergraduate of [his] college who got a First since the Modern Greats School was established in 1924.' Maybe the 'analytical rigour' he says he lacks would be a handicap to a Man of Action: if you pin yourself under your microscope you cannot live your life. Hamlet put it better:

> ... the native hue of resolution
> is sicklied o'er with the pale cast of thought,
> And enterprises of great pith and moment
> With this regard their current turn awry,
> And lose the name of action ...

or

> Some craven scruple
> Of thinking too precisely on the event ...

Roy Jenkins explains himself: 'I had come to regard the Palace of Westminster ... as the centre of national life ... I believed that the measured development of the welfare state and of a planned framework for the economy enhanced civilisation.' He describes himself becoming cynical only after 40 years.

'You don't think it through,' said Paddy Ashdown; it's fun 'for a while' said Lord Carrington.

> *what is a man,*
> *If his chief good and marker of his time*
> *Be but to sleep and feed? a beast no more.*
> *Sure he that hath made us with such large discourse,*
> *Looking before and after, gave us not*
> *That capability and god-like reason*
> *To fust in unus'd ...*

We tread our lines between 'bestial oblivion' and 'craven scruple' and Roy Jenkins believes his own 'lack of ruthless resolution' stopped him moving on – 'the question of how much I was truly at ease with power. It is not a thought which I suspect much troubled the minds of the great determined leaders of history.'

The assumption is still that Napoleon, Lloyd George and Churchill had power. If Churchill (to take the last example) had not been helped by the Japanese bombing Pearl Harbour, by the Americans joining the war and by there being such snows in Russia—Churchill could have ended his days shot and bombed out as happened to Hitler instead. The Allies might not have won that war. Churchill controlled neither the Japanese nor the Americans nor the weather.

2.40 p.m. My cousin rings me. Her father, my uncle, died two hours ago.

Saturday, 17th January
Much time on the telephone.

It is cheaper to go to Switzerland for the weekend than for the funeral alone.

I shall aim for a wheelchair at the airport.

Put my argument that Roy Jenkins seems to think that Churchill, Napoleon and Lloyd George had power beyond power: cite Japan, America and Russian weather: 'It's how Churchill dealt with those things that counts,' says Ivor.

'But if Germany had invaded and slaughtered him—he could not have "dealt" with anything.'

Ivor recognises that we are not immortal—but within that constraint we have scope.

Monday, 19th January

Back is half better. Jones The Pictures urges against Switzerland.

Our family had been all births since my grandmother died ten years ago. Ten births and no deaths in ten years.

Ivor gets home for an hour for dinner. He has seen Cranborne:

'We need to talk.'

'Yes.'

'Can we have lunch with Denis and Tommy?' (Carter and Strathclyde.)

'Yes.'

'Where? We need to be discreet.'

'Come to me.' Cranborne has a house in Chelsea.

'They are desperate to talk,' Ivor tells me.

'They want to be involved?'

'Yes.'

'They think they might get a better deal if they're involved?'

'Yes. And they might - if they want 2/3 elected, 1/3 nominated. There are people who want a wholly nominated chamber.'

'Who?'

'Mandelson.'

'He's only one person.'

'I get a lot of letters ... I don't think Blair wants a nominated chamber. He wants a good settlement.' 'So the hereditaries might agree to their own demise ...'

'Yes. Then my problems really start.'

'?'

'I'll have to make sure Derry doesn't take the credit.'

'How will you do that?'

'There can be some leaking. But there are some people who want a bitter battle.'

'Why does lunch have to be discreet?'

'We don't want journalists to get to hear of it.'

'Why not?'

'The Tories might have trouble with their own side. But, possibly, Cranborne wants a settlement.'

Ivor goes back to the House for a vote. He is home again about midnight:

'Derry's still sitting on the woolsack. He's been there since 2.29.'

'That's nearly ten hours!'

'He got an hour off for dinner. It's what he's paid for.'

'He can't be very happy.'

'It's his Bill. Janet Young is getting waspish. She made a crack about the Cardinal.'

'Did people laugh?'

'Oh yes.'

'Including on your side?'

'There were some giggles. He's not liked ...'

'What did he do?'

'Sat there looking thunderous.' I laugh. Think better of it.

'Poor Derry.'

There he is: sitting on the woolsack: the pinnacle of his ambition. And he is being laughed at. He must wonder what the hell he is doing in his breeches and tights with his (no doubt hot) bottom on the red cloth. Where can he go? What can he aim for?

Tuesday, 20th January

Walk to the doctors'. I ought to take two more weeks off work.

Wednesday, 21st January

The notice of my uncle's death arrives with A.C. Swinburne on the top:

> *From too much love of living,*
> *From hope and fear set free,*
> *We thank with brief thanksgiving*
> *Whatever gods may be*
> *That no man lives for ever*
> *That dead men rise up never;*
> *That even the weariest river*
> *Winds somewhere safe to sea.*

A joke and not a joke. My favourite obituary is in *The Guardian*: 'The Civil Servant with the European Dream'. He is described as the main architect of Britain's entry into Europe. John Robinson was his name.

My friend Lynnette, who I met in Turkey and who has been teaching in Chile, arrives to swap notes on backs. Hers is ahead of mine: she has travelled across South London carrying home-made brownies all by herself.

Ivor had his lunch with the Tories and his dinner with the Liberals: 'We have eaten for England today,' Denis said to him. They arrived at Cranborne's house in Chelsea and there, playing outside with a Newfoundland, was Denise-The-Driver. She must have tired of driving John Prescott up and down to Hull. She must have had another offer she couldn't refuse. She has left the Government car service and is working for Cranborne. We must have been correct in our assumptions back in May.

A Philippino maid opened the front door, told them Lord Cranborne was upstairs, and upstairs they went to find Strathclyde too. There was a piano that was played, a guitar against the wall, aristocratic scruff. The Philippino served the four of them lunch: egg mayonnaise; cold pheasant and salad; tarte aux pommes. They all agreed that if they could not agree then nobody could agree. They agreed that they wanted to agree a 2/3 elected, 1/3 nominated House of Lords and the end of the hereditary peerage.

'Cranborne has a sense of history,' says Ivor, 'he wants to see the House of Lords into the 21st century ... he's a Cecil; if we can settle the House of Lords that'll be quite something for the Blair Government. Lloyd George didn't do it. Macmillan didn't do it.'

Ivor cannot go any further without the go-ahead from Blair.

'Did you say that to them?'

'Oh yes.' And when he got back to the House he put on paper what had been said and agreed. 'Simon seems delighted. Delighted. But he is such a good civil servant you can never be sure. Every now and then he says things like "oh, this is a bit political for me," and works harder. He and Lesley and Damien are loving it and working so hard.'

'They're being a whole department all on their own.'

'That's it.'

'And they are writing history.'

'Exactly.'

'It could all go wrong.'

'Yes. Derry didn't believe it. Didn't believe it. Said Blair wouldn't decide anything. Would say it was Difficult and file it away and Think About It.'

'That tells us how Blair deals with Derry ... says he'll think about what Derry says ... it doesn't tell us anything about how Blair will behave to you over this.'

'I'm not sure. Derry was complaining. We'll put in an urgent request to see Blair tomorrow. Then I should see him on Monday. He may think he'll have problems with the parliamentary party. People who want a nominated chamber.'

'He ought to agree.'

'I think so ... but Derry wasn't sure. After he'd gone I said to the others: if this works, our problems will really start.'

'?'

'?'

"We'll have to stop the Lord Chancellor taking the credit for it. There were roars of laughter." (Ivor is pleased with this joke – he tried it out on me a few days ago.)

Dinner with the Liberals (Bill Rodgers and John Harris) was in the Reform Club. It did not go so well.

'They say that they cannot agree if they do not know what we are doing. Which is reasonable.'

'And you don't know what you are doing.'

'We can't say that. But that's always the problem between opposition and government.'

We worked out that the combined ages of Bill, John, Ivor and Denis were 269 years.

Along with settling the Contents of the House of Lords, they have to consider its Powers. That is where the House of Commons may get uneasy: it won't want to see itself undermined/overtaken/overshadowed.

There was a general meeting about House of Lords Works. Ivor sees the word 'china' on a list. He asks what the Lord Chancellor has spent on china. There is an embarrassed silence. Nobody will answer him.

Later in the day he gets a note: we are not sure of the precise amount, but it is in excess of TEN THOUSAND POUNDS (the capitals belong to this diary – not to the House of Lords' note).

It is Pugin china, a dinner service—only about 20 settings. What about the cutlery?—wonders Ivor. He thinks it is the price of the curtains and carpets and Pugin sofas that will really cause embarrassment.

The mind does boggle. Especially a mind like mine that buys plastic disposable cutlery and washes it and re-uses it when demand gets heavy.

Thursday, 22nd January

Fly to Geneva.

Friday, 23rd January

Drive to my uncle's funeral. Jones The Pictures has brought snowdrops and daffodils; I have brought all our forsythia. Ivor spoke in French; Jones The

Books and my cousin spoke in English.

The children ran round and round at the lunch—in a mixture of French and English and Nepali. There was a special ice-cream for them: 'sans alcohol'.

Saturday, 24th January

To Chamonix and the top of Mont Blanc - 'the highest mountain in Europe' we said.

Monday, 26th January

Go back to work. Faint. Come home.

Black Rod told Ivor he thought the £10,000 on china might include the cutlery.

The press are full of New Labour's 'snouts in the trough'. But for Derry, nobody would be noticing anything. He started it.

'Nobody's going to say that,' said Ivor '... you know what he did today - he told Downing Street about my meeting with Cranborne.'

'He'll be taking the credit.'

'I won't let him do that.'

There is a row between Frank Dobson and Gordon Brown. Frank wants to offer the Health Service staff 3.85% (ish). Gordon wants to offer the Health Service staff 2.5% (ish)—in phases. Ivor thinks Gordon will win.

Tuesday, 27th January

Jonathan Powell spoke to Ivor. Tony is 'warm' about Ivor's deal with Cranborne. They will meet next week.

'So Derry's wrong,' I say.

'I think he should like it ... it's common sense.'

'It'll save time, hassle and money.'

'It would have been a good row though.'

'A ridiculous one.'

The main reason for Jonathan Powell's phone call, however, was the Scrutiny Committee. The Scrutiny Committee is 'rather an important little committee', housing one peer from each of the biggest parties: Cledwyn Hughes (who chairs it), Francis Pym and George Thomson. Every time anybody is proposed as a new peer, all the information on them is dug out (M15, M16) and goes to the Scrutiny Committee. Nobody can be a new peer until they have been scrutinised by the Committee which declares they can be a new peer. Over the past few years I have heard of a few people whom the Committee has declared cannot be new peers.

The problem with the Scrutiny Committee is that the combined age of the members is nearly 240 years. Cledwyn is 81. The tactful way to retire him is to retire all of them. It is proposed that Brenda Dean (60ish) takes over. William Hague would choose the new Francis Pym, Paddy Ashdown a new George Thomson.

Ivor talks to Cledwyn.

'There's not much to it,' says Cledwyn, 'I don't know what Brenda Dean can do that I can't.'

Ivor has a chat with Margaret Jay about her father Jim Callaghan: 'The problem with him was that he would say—oh, you know far more about that than me—you go away and sort it out—and you'd know he was watching you.'

'Perhaps he meant it.'

'Do you really think so?'

'Yes I do.' He felt his lack of formal education.

'He was a good prime minister,' says Ivor, 'a much underrated man.'

Wednesday, 28th January

Tomorrow's Cabinet meeting is going to discuss cabinet ministers' pay. Ivor is planning to stick up for himself. He earns less than any of them. Less than Derry's political adviser. He writes a letter to John Prescott saying this. Ivor has been trying to do something about Lords' ministers pay too. Blair has let it be known 'not in writing' that it is 'between a rock and a hard place'.

'That's what he's paid for. Difficult decisions. If it was easy it wouldn't be in front of him.'

Thursday, 29th January

Read Roddy Doyle and Roy Jenkins. Prefer the latter.

Today's cabinet meeting starts with Blair and Cook on Iraq: it is DAN-GEROUS: the Iraqis have great stocks of nerve gas and enough power to reach Israel; the Israelis have nuclear weapons.

If the Iraqis nerve-gas Israel, the Israelis could 'nuke Baghdad'. The Americans and the British are agitated. The French are holding back—the Iraqis owe them a lot of money. The Russians are holding back—they regard the Iraqis as clients.

Then they go through state sector pay rises. Then they turn to welfare reform.

Friday, 30th January

Engineers and workmen arrive to diagnose our crack. They find more cracks. They drill holes to see what we are built on. I can see sand and rock. It is difficult to avoid this being translated into mud on the carpet. I make tea and coffee. Several times. They have driven from Maidstone and Folkstone. Folkstone drinks coffees, Maidstone drinks teas. Folkstone does not take sugar, Maidstone does. Folkstone does not drill. He measures. Maidstone digs and drills.

Monday, 2nd February

The Chair Man comes for the sofa. Again.

Return to work. Do not faint. Feel like a sandcastle who knows the tide is coming.

The tide does not come today.

Tuesday, 3rd February

Chevening has raised its head. Its trustees have let it be known (to a tabloid) they cannot treat Robin Cook's girlfriend as if she was Robin Cook's wife. Ivor rang Captain Husband who cannot think who had been talking to the press. Ivor could.

The trustees have advertised for Captain Husband's successor. They have interviewed three candidates and have chosen a Colonel. Lesley rang Captain Husband. The Colonel has not been offered the job. Ivor is arranging for Robin Cook to meet the Colonel before he is offered the job.

Lambeth College is beginning to talk about talking about this year's Staffing Review. (Jargon for which jobs are safe this year.)

Have now managed two days' work. The sandcastle sensation dominates.

Ivor's day was 'pre-Blair, Blair, post-Blair.'

Pre-Blair, the Team (Lesley, Damien, Simon) briefed Ivor for the meeting to get 'the prime-ministerial chop' on the agreement with the Tories on the all-in-one House of Lords Reform. They put together all the things they could think of that might be raised. Derry was dubious: He won't like x. He won't like y. Derry did not think Ivor would get what he wanted. Simon was not political.

At one o'clock there were Blair, Jonathan Powell, Richard Wilson, Blair's constitutional adviser, a constitutional civil servant, Ivor, Denis and Derry.

They took half an hour. Ivor got everything he wanted: he summed it up to Blair at the end: 'Let me be quite clear: it is your *avis favourable* that I go ahead as far as I can to agree with the Tories an all-in-one reform of the House of Lords: the removal of the hereditary peers and a 2/3 elected, 1/3 nominated chamber?'

'Yes,' said Blair.

They also agreed they could not have three-way talks with the Liberals and that they must be careful not to be outflanked by the Opposition—Blair does not trust them.

They agreed they would introduce the end of the hereditary peers in the Queen's Speech in October if the agreement came to nothing.

'We also touched on the powers of a reformed chamber. We certainly don't want to give it any more. There are bound to be more difficulties with an elected chamber because it will have democratic credibility.'

'Does Blair mind that?'

'He's surrounded by people who are warning him about it but I think he has a wider vision.'

'He can see further than the end of his own nose?'

'He sees it as part of the constitutional reforms of this Government - by the next election the Constitution will have been transformed.'

'Is he pleased?'

'Yes.'

'Are they surprised?'

'Yes. The transfer will be very difficult. I reckon the first elections will be in 2003. There are lots and lots of nuts and bolts to work out. Blair said certain people should be nominated automatically - the head of the BMA, for example. Anyway, I've got the go-ahead. We agreed the Cabinet Committee should continue.'

'In fact it's redundant?'

'Yes—but there will be detailed legislation. And Blair said he would tell cabinet—and his cabinet committee with the Liberals. It'll leak.'

'Does that matter?'

'No—if I was being mischievous I'd get one of the lobby correspondents to ask Alastair Campbell a question at the morning meeting.'

Post-Blair there was jubilation. And they began to work out the next moves. Ivor thinks he will Have a Word with Cranborne this week. And with Bill Rodgers—not that he would tell BR of his discussions with Cranborne. Then they will have to formalise it.

'Will you continue taking lunch off Cranborne?'

'I don't think so.'

'You could ask them to lunch here.'

'I don't think I can compete with Cranborne in the lunch stakes.'

Ivor also needs to get it clear that Cranborne has the go-ahead from Hague.

'How will you know that?'

'I won't—but he would be left looking a fool if he says he's got it and it turns out he hasn't.' Ivor is pleased. 'I got the timing of it right. They were asking me if I had started negotiating with the Tories last October ... that was much too soon.'

Ivor is turning his mind to numbers. Once the hereditaries are gone, there will be 500 life peers. And he wants 600 in all: 200 nominated, 400 elected.

'They die at the rate of 20 a year. Then we could exclude people on the grounds of non-attendance. We could have a voluntary retirement age of 75 ... there are lots of details to work out.'

'And Cranborne wants to be part of all these decisions.'

'He does. I asked Damien to put together a piece of paper with all of them on it - he said "When do you want it?"—I said "Tomorrow"—and he went a bit white.'

'I bet he did.'

'He's worked most of it out already.'

'So you've got until October.'

'The summer really. There's detailed legislation to work out. That's plenty of time.'

'A big piece of history.'

'I don't think history is static ... I hope you're, writing it all down?'

'There hasn't been much recently.'

'I can't think of anything I haven't told you ... Frank Dobson and David Blunkett are impregnable.'

We discuss cabinet shuffles: 'I don't think there'll be one,' I say, 'he knows the problems he's got ... shuffling will mean different problems.'

'I think you're right—though I think he wants to get rid of Clare Short. She is TACTLESS.'

'He'll leave it until spring 99.'

'He'll have to do it about then - the point comes when those knocking on the door to be let in have to be let in ... Helen Liddell.'

'And then he'd leave it again until the election?'

'There's a lot to be said for some new faces just before the election. About a year before.'

'It looks as if you could be left where you are for the whole of the five years.'

'I'll have to take it day by day.'

'Perhaps you'll be left until 2003—the elections.'

'Oh not that long.'

We also discuss Blair's system of working: 'He'll have to change some of the people round him,' say I.

'Yes. That'll happen. Some of them are not very good. The way he works it' Ivor describes a pyramid with his arms, 'all the decisions have to go up—it's very hierarchical—to him. He can't keep it like that.'

'He'll need allies.'

'The time will come—he won't be able to avoid the Cabinet... We've not agreed formally in Cabinet to attack Iraq. And if Iraq is attacked without Cabinet agreement there will be complaints. Private complaints, but complaints.'

'Perhaps he wants to work on his own. Without allies.'

'I certainly got the impression that our Derry does not have the ear of the Prime Minister. It's entirely his own fault. He went at it like a bull at a gate. Blair is keeping his distance.'

'He must be disappointed.'

'He won't sack him.'

'That's not the same as not being disappointed—he'll be hurt too. He'll feel Derry has let him down.'

'He could be right.'

Wednesday, 4th February

William has red and sticky eyes. GP prescribes 1. salt and water 2. substance in a tube.

My back is bearing up. Tide is hovering.

The Chair Man returns the sofa: 'Fourth time lucky,' he says.

Ivor has had 'a difficult day'. The Liberals know something is going on. Downing Street does not want to upset them. (Blair does not want to upset Paddy Ashdown.) The Liberals will have to be included. How to include them?

Thursday, 5th February

My noisiest group in Lambeth College complain about the teacher who taught them when I was dealing with my back. I tell them: 'You've complained about me often enough. You think I am too strict. And I won't accept that you can't do the work.'

Garcia, noisiest member of the noisiest group, informs us he will earn his living as a Porn Star. I inform group that porn stars earn peanuts.

Start group on their next piece of work: to describe how to make or mend something. I give examples: a recipe, a puncture, a hairstyle. 'What about sexual intercourse?' asks Garcia (of course). Inform him that reproduction would be fine but he would have to use Biological Language. When Garcia starts to talk about 'vaginal mucus' (apropos the drinking of milk, I think) I am deaf. But when he asks if anal intercourse is dangerous I say any unprotected sex is dangerous.

'He's had too much dope, man don't listen to him,' the rest of the group advise. At the end of the afternoon Garcia is still on the ceiling.

Ivor is late while I am learning from the newses that Derry has caused a rumpus by advocating Privacy Laws to gag the Press. The Press are up in arms. Downing Street has slapped Derry down: the Prime Minister is not in favour of privacy laws. Tell Ivor, when he gets home,

'Derry is a loose cannon, getting looser.'

'He went barmy on Day One,' says Ivor.

'The next thing is he'll muck up your agreement on the Lords.'

'He doesn't have the power ... It was his meeting this morning on devolution ... we just went round and round and round.' Ivor shakes his head. 'Since I shouted at him down the phone I've had no problem with him at all.'

Ivor was late because of a vote: 'For the first time in my life I found myself in the same voting lobby as Mrs Thatcher. I told her it must be a first.'

'As a man of honour,' she said, without humour, 'am I in the right place?' He told her she was. And that was the truth.

Friday, 6th February

I have finished a week back at work without collapse.

Headlines on Derry's Dressing Down are bigger than on the Blairs in the US. Downing Street will not be pleased.

I am missing having a dog. Ivor says he will agree to our having one when he leaves the Cabinet. I am not convinced that will be soon enough.

Ivor and Denis's next meeting with Cranborne and Strathclyde is fixed for Monday.

Chevening has been on the phone to Lesley all day: 'We've never had a Lord Privy Seal showing so much interest.' Captain Husband's problem is that he has promised his job to the Colonel without having the authority to do so. He and his band are agitated at having Robin Cook and Ivor meet him. They want to have the meeting now.

'The Foreign Secretary is abroad running a war,' they are told. They have to wait.

Go and meet Ivor for lunch at the House:

'Derry's got a dreadful press. Dreadful.' As soon as I get into Ivor's office he scatters the papers before me. 'Damien's taking bets that he'll be gone by Christmas. He thinks he'll resign.'

'Resign?'

'Yes. He may announce he's sick of it and throw in the towel. Blair won't get rid of him.'

'He might have to if this goes on ...'

'He may remove him from all the politics and leave him being Lord Chancellor.'

'He'd be very isolated. He'd hate it.'

'That's why Damien thinks he'll resign.'

'Has he been talking to anyone?'

'No. It's just Damien.'

I look at the papers:

'What would Derry do instead?'

'Be a law lord.'

'This is pretty humiliating for him. He must feel terrrible. Hurt. Misunderstood. Furious.'

'I wonder how he gets on with Cherie Blair,' wonders Ivor.

'Um. That's the key to what happens next ... the only vibe that I picked up when they were talking together at that Palace dinner was that she was very hurt.'

'She would be. He's let them down badly.'

We eat in the peers' dining room. Discuss (surprise, surprise) Derry (in mutters).

'His staff can't be very happy,' I state The Obvious.

'I wouldn't like to be one of them today.'

'They'll all be reading their newspapers under their desks,' say I.

'It's very gloomy whenever you go in there. Long faces ...' Ivor adds that this is not alleviated by a collection of Heads. Derry has borrowed ancient philosophers' Heads from Scottish museums. They loom down on the proceedings.

By the time we get to coffee and the room overlooking the river, Ivor is saying Gareth Williams would be a good Lord Chancellor. And if John Smith—who would also have made Derry Lord Chancellor—was Prime Minister, none of this would have happened:

'He'd have sat on him. Right from the start. He was never his pupil. He was his contemporary. As soon as I'd heard about the wallpaper I'd have rung John up—he'd have had Derry in and put a stop to it.'

'Why couldn't you have rung Blair?'

'I was closer to John.'

Michael Cocks comes in. He's just joining us when Charles Williams comes in too. He is shaking and separates Ivor to another table for some time.

Michael Cocks talks of Derry's 'lack of experience'. When Ivor returns, Michael Cocks suggests starting a rumour that Derry has taken commission on the wallpaper: 'The thing is wallpaper makes sense to most people. They've all gone out and bought three or four rolls. They know what it costs.'

After Michael Cocks has gone ('his great enemy is Benn') I learn that Jane Williams is ill.

'Poor Charles.'

'Poor Charles.'

'He'll be distraught.'

'He is.'

We look out at the river.

'He told me Prescott is trying to bring him into the Government because he doesn't think much of Helene Hayman.'

'I don't believe that ... Michael Cocks told me he thought Prescott was doing well "because he doesn't pretend to be more than he is" ... I suppose that will have been a dig at Derry.'

'He can't stand Derry. Derry's never been elected to anything. Michael Cocks was Government Chief Whip when we didn't have a majority in the Commons.'

When I get William from school I manage to start arranging more maths for him.

Ivor would like Simon to take a note of his Monday meeting with Cranborne and Strathclyde. And he would like to get a signed agreement from the meeting. He is not sure Cranborne will wear the presence of Simon or the signing of an agreement. He is also trying to work out how to include the Liberals.

Sunday, 8th February

Derry's problems are spread all over the newspapers.

Monday, 9th February

Pat Hollis has a message from Norfolk. She has to go. Helene Hayman sees her into her car. She has to decide if her husband should have antibiotics.

'At least she's being driven,' says Ivor.

'She'll try and work in the car.'

'She won't do much.'

Ivor and Denis meet Cranborne and Strathclyde. The meeting is too sensitive for Simon to be there or to take a note. Cranborne is 'having trouble with his party'. He is not sure he can get Hague to agree. And as for the shadow cabinet ... 'There'll be a bloody great row.'

Reluctantly, Ivor gives Cranborne a piece of paper detailing the outline of a possible agreement. Cranborne promises that only Hague will see it. Ivor makes it clear that the piece of paper is his thoughts, not the Government's.

'We will abolish the hereditaries if we don't get an agreement,' said Ivor.

'Yes,' said Cranborne, 'you've said that before.'

'You're getting a picture,' say I 'of what a mess the Tories are in.'

'Yes,' says Ivor.

'Who would argue against it in the shadow cabinet?'

'Oh, people like Howard—he'd rather lose than concede.'

'Howard and Cranborne can't have much in common.'

'Nothing at all.'

Ask Ivor if he has seen Derry today:

'In the distance. He saw me and fled.'

Tuesday, 10th February

Visit the physiotherapist. Very much hope it is for the last time.

Ivor hears that his piece of paper has reached Hague. He hasn't heard any more.

John Prescott displays his radical transport plans. He wants a national body to run them. Cars will pay for city centres.

Tessa has upset Nick Brown. She went off and organised a PPS for herself from the Commons without his knowledge. Now everybody else wants one too.

'I don't see why she should need one,' says Ivor. 'I gather Nick Brown went ballistic.'

Wednesday, 11th February

My cousin's baby has been born in Switzerland. A little girl. The eleventh birth: Fiona Audrey Victoria.

Ivor learns that Hague is putting the plans to Ancram (the Tories' constitution person) and Howard.

'Why Howard?'

'It's not quite clear ... perhaps he is the most powerful man.'

Thursday, 12th February

The Cabinet go over Iraq. It looks as if 'we' will attack at the end of next week.

'People asked a few questions.'

'Did anybody protest?'

'Clare asked a few questions.'

The Lords' reform Cabinet Committee met: 'Peter Mandelson is very suspicious. He doesn't like it. Everyone else is OK. Peter says "It'll end in tears."'

The House of Lords wished the Eldest Peer a happy hundredth birthday. Ivor led the tributes. The Eldest Peer slept throughout, wrapped in a blanket in a wheelchair.

'I *nearly* laughed.'

Denis Carter rings late in the evening. He thinks the agreement is leaking.

Friday, 13th February

It is not leaking.

Saturday, 14th February

The Eldest Peer has died in his sleep.

We are at the house and in the sun. The warmest February day since records began. We sit outside and blink. Part of the garage roof has blown off.

Monday, 16th February

Start to drive back to London at leisure. Stop halfway and Ivor rings his office. There has been more on the Lord Chancellor's refurbishments in the media. There are rumours that the Lord Chancellor will be making a statement in the House at 2.30. Ivor tells his office he will be back by 1.45. Ivor's office tell him he ought to be back earlier than that.

I had forgotten how quick Ivor could be.

We arrive to a house in which the heating has gone off. Ivor goes to the office while William and I wait for our friend Mark to solve the heating. We are still waiting when Ivor comes back from the office.

'Derry is being "economical". "Economical". He's even economised to the Prime Minister.' In answer to the rising number of queries about the Lord Chancellor's refurbishments, Downing Street has been defending Derry with words that are removed from the facts. The reason for this is that Downing Street does not know the facts.

Mark comes and solves the heating.

I learn from Ivor that Black Rod, Michael Davies, Mr Good and AN Other are clear about the facts: Derry said he wanted his refurbishments. So they did as they were told and set them going. A question has been put to the House about the contents of the refurbishments and the cause of them. The answer has to be written tonight. Simon Burton sits down with Black Rod, Michael Davies et al to find a form of words for the answer. They find a form of words. They put them to the Lord Chancellor who won't accept them. Simon Burton et al find another form of words and, at about 8 p.m., Simon rings Ivor with them. Ivor does not like them all that much but says OK. At about 9 p.m. Simon rings again. The Lord Chancellor won't accept those words either. Black Rod, Michael Davies et al have refused to budge from their idea of the facts. Derry has refused to budge from his idea of the facts. (Black Rod & Co know Derry started it. Derry—solo—says it was a pre-arranged part of a rolling programme of restoration.)

'No!' says Ivor to Simon. 'Really? ... In that case I need all the details of all the meetings. And I need them tomorrow.'

'The diaries?' says Simon.

'The diaries,' says Ivor.

Earlier in the day, Black Rod had told Ivor that he and Michael Davies had decided that Derry had persuaded himself he was telling the truth.

'That's very charitable of them,' I say, 'when Derry is trying to bully them all into covering for him.'

'I'm afraid he is,' says Ivor.

'Will Black Rod be bullied?'

'Only so far as he sees fit ... I've told him I want him to keep to the facts.'

(Black Rod is General Sir Edward Jones KCB CBE, ex-Deputy Commander of NATO and has a mind of his own.)

'He can't think much of Derry,' say I.

'I should think his views are unprintable. He's a soldier. A man's word is his word ... He reminded me of what I said when he first came to see me about this in May.'

'What did you say?'

'That it would be a disaster ... And I have had other hysterics to deal with today: Liz Symons weeping at Denis ... about "what people will think" about somebody else answering "her" question. So I had to ring her. And she sobbed and wept at me. I told her not to be silly. Denis and I agreed it was an extraordinary way to behave ... She's been leader of a big union.'

Tuesday, 17th February

Ivor rings. The pieces of paper are beginning to appear. The Killer is an internal memo dated 4th May ... the Sunday after the election.

'A copy of that piece of paper is with him ... well with his office now.'

'It must be like sitting waiting for a volcano to explode.'

William and I catch a bus to Hamleys. He spends his pocket money on a shield, breastplate, sword and visor. Other people may have more need of them than he does.

Early afternoon I hear Dennis Skinner in the House of Commons making a point about the Lord Chancellor's lack of political skill: buying beds at £8,000 while denying legal aid. (In fact the beds were £23,000: £8,000 each and they had Puginised headboards.) The Lord Chancellor's PPS says that the refurbishments are a matter for the House of Lords. I ring Ivor to see what is happening.

'The shit's really hit the fan here. I've been talking to Alastair Campbell and I've got to talk to Jonathan Powell. Derry will be very angry. But there's a press briefing for 4 o'clock and Downing Street are getting wider and wider of the mark.'

When Ivor gets home I hear of the Killer Memo: it is an internal Lords memo to Ken Cregeen from Patrick South and dated 4 May 1997, three days after the election. It is headed Refurbishment of the Lord Chancellor's Residence and says first that The Lord Chancellor made it clear that he regards the refurbishment of the residence as an absolute priority. Mr Cregeen is meeting the Parliamentary Works Officer on Tuesday (6 May) to discuss taking the refurbishment forward ...

Secondly it summarises the situation: the residence will require complete redecoration and refurbishment ... The Lord Chancellor made it clear that he and Lady Irvine should make the final decision on all aspects of the refurbishment ...

On and on it goes until, eighteenthly, The Lord Chancellor and Lady Irvine would like a regular supply of flowers and would therefore like to meet a florist to discuss their requirements.

Another meeting is planned for the 13th ... The Lord Chancellor would like the clock from the Prime Minister's Common's office. The Lord Chancellor likes the look of the Leader of the Lords' (Ivor's) desk and chair (Ivor was interested to note)!

By the 26th June the Lord Chancellor is showing impatience. He writes to Black Rod at length: his art contacts are providing art loans; the public will be admitted to view; ... 'Neither my wife or family will have any need to live in the residence ...'

Ivor tells me Black Rod and Michael Davies have mutinied: they will not countenance Downing Street dealing with House of Lords matters. They came to see Ivor and said so. Ivor told them 'Fair enough.' Nor will they countenance departing from the facts in answer to questions ... the Lord Chancellor, having been reminded of the facts by the appearance of The Killer Memo, has agreed to Simon et al's form of words.

This is the point at which Ivor has had to get involved. After the form of words was agreed with Derry—and included in paragraph 4—Derry said he had sent it to Downing Street. Ivor spoke to Alastair Campbell to get Downing Street back on the mark.

'Notice particularly paragraph 4,' said Ivor to Alastair.

'What?' said Alastair

'Paragraph 4 ...'

Alastair Campbell's copy had no paragraph 4:

'What a Fucking Mess,' he said. He is trying to talk about Iraq and Northern Ireland and all he gets are questions about the Lord Chancellor's Refurbishments for which the Lord Chancellor is providing him with idio-syncratic information—to put it mildly.

Alastair Campbell said he would get on to Jonathan Powell.

Jonathan Powell got on to Ivor.

'Paragraph 4 is the important one,' said Ivor to Jonathan Powell.

'Paragraph 4?' Jonathan Powell did not have paragraph 4 either. 'I wonder what happened to paragraph 4?' said Jonathan Powell.

'I wonder,' said Ivor. Ivor sent Jonathan Powell paragraph 4.

'There's not much the matter with paragraph 4' said Jonathan Powell.

'Will Derry know Jonathan Powell has got paragraph 4?' I ask.

'He will now. I expect he'll blame the typist.'

Ivor also told Alastair Campbell and Jonathan Powell of the Killer Memo of May 4th—and advised them to give the full facts (of—eg—price of beds)—to prevent the drip drip drip of it all coming out slowly, thereby doing more damage—not to mention the fact that in Ivor's view, all this evasion is wrong.

Ivor is tired, disappointed, ashamed and hurt. This is not what he came into government for, nor is it the kind of government he wants to be part of.

'It's dishonourable. Dishonourable. We have wasted two days on the Lord Chancellor's bloody wallpaper.'

'What must Black Rod think!'

'He's appalled. Appalled. When I saw him last he said "we've come a long way to meet you."'

'I said "not me."'

'"Sorry" he said "not you. That was a mistake. Not a Freudian Mistake. A mistake."'

'He's a nice man, I could trust him but I'm afraid he lumps me in with the whole lot of them.'

'Politicians you mean.'

'Yes.'

There has been no news from Cranborne on The Agreement. But the Tories have announced that Hague is making a big speech on the constitution soon.

'Perhaps he'll put it in there to circumvent the objectors,' I wonder.

Wednesday, 18th February

Ivor has been asked to go to Korea next week. A president is being installed and Robin Cook can't go because of Iraq. It'll be the first time since January 1985 (when Margaret Thatcher sacked him from Brussels) that he will have done an official trip. After 13 years lying fallow he want to go. Hope this will sustain him through two 12 hour flights.

Thursday, 19th February

Cabinet is hoping there will be a settlement on Iraq. Some of the Arab governments are saying that Saddam Hussain will concede.

Blair says, through Jonathan Powell, that Ivor has to talk to the Liberals (Bill Rodgers and Bob Maclennan) about reform of the Lords: 'I won't tell them about my talks with Cranborne ... but I'm going to have to join the joint cabinet committee with the Liberals.' (That will be the fourteenth.)

Derry and Ivor were elbow to elbow for one meeting today. They avoided a look or a word for the entire length.

'The trouble is he knows I disapprove of him.'

'And you didn't say anything to him? You let him suffer?'

'That's right.'

Prescott was not silent: he and Ivor and others were gathered outside the Lord Chancellor's office, waiting to be allowed in for another meeting, and Prescott made clear his disapproval. Once inside, Prescott addressed everyone—and the wallpaper

'Well! I don't think this is worth £1,000 an inch!'

Derry tried to laugh along with the rest.

Mandelson, meanwhile, is concerned that the Government is about to be wrong-footed by the Tories on House of Lords Reform: that Hague will claim the leading role as his own in a Constitutional speech next Tuesday. Can Ivor find a form of words for a press briefing for the weekend which the Government can refer to in the event of a Tory attempt at a takeover?

Ivor finds a form of words.

The man from the insurance company comes to put sensors in our walls to measure for cracks. The monitoring has begun. It will continue every eight weeks for 12 months. It may 'only' be that our extension is falling off our house. As long as the house is not falling off the extension ...

Ivor comes home with a gadget. Ivor and gadgets do not mix.

'I've got a bleeper ... the office want to be able to contact me while we're driving tomorrow ... in case Peter Mandelson wants to talk to me about the briefing for the weekend.'

'Do you know how to work it?'

'I think so.'

Friday, 20th February.

Drive down to the house accompanied by the bleeper. It bleeps as we reach the point of the journey furthest from a telephone: 'Please ring Lesley ASAP'

'What about a car phone?' I wonder.

'They did mention that.'

Half an hour later, at the house, Ivor rings Lesley.

'Damien is worried,' says Ivor, 'he doesn't want me in Korea when Hague makes his great speech ... Ann Taylor has said she will handle it ... Damien's ringing me back ... I can't organise my diary on the basis of what might happen next Thursday.'

'When's Hague's speech?'

'Tuesday.'

'That's not Thursday.'

'It would rumble on ... I could be back by Thursday. Let's see what Cranborne says; I'm meeting him on Monday afternoon. I'll talk to Ann on Monday too. But I can't cancel Korea on Monday afternoon. The Foreign Office would be furious.' The plane is at 9 o'clock that evening.

Damien rings back. Ivor tells him: 'Ann and Denis and you could manage it between you.'

Ivor tells me: 'I don't want Derry involved. For lots of reasons.'

'I can see why Damien's worried ... he can see a great steamroller obliterating your molehill of an agreement.'

Ivor says nothing.

Saturday, 21st February

The Roof Man comes to look at the roof-free sections of the garage.

The Scottish Art Establishment is provoked to protest. How is it the Lord Chancellor can borrow pictures when the Scottish Art galleries are saying they cannot afford loan exhibitions?

'The Lord Chancellor,' *Radio 4* booms through the house, 'is fast out-running Saddam Hussein as the tabloids' bogey man.'

Ivor is more and more miserable. More and more discredit is flowing over New Labour.

'Terry Boston was saying to me "What will happen when the rest of it leaks?"'

'It's beginning to look as if it will ... over the next six months.'

'I told Alastair Campbell to tell the press everything all at once to stop this. He clearly doesn't want to.'

'Maybe it'll all come out in that Lords' committee. The members will surely start asking questions ... and somebody somewhere who knows will be living with somebody somewhere who tells.'

'You may be right.'

Our woodpeckers are out and about. Do not want to go back to London. And as for Korea ...

Monday, 23rd February

It looks as if Saddam Hussein is lying down quietly.

The Lord Chancellor is not lying down quietly: he has issued a statement saying his refurbishments were a decision of the House. 'Is anybody going to do anything about it?' Ivor asked Black Rod. 'No,' said Black Rod. 'It would demean the House of Lords to get involved in a slanging match with the Lord

Chancellor.'

'I'm ashamed of Derry,' says Ivor. 'Ashamed.'

Ivor had his meeting with Cranborne. All goes well with the Agreement. Cranborne would like a piece of paper from the Government. Ivor cannot manage that.

At 7.25 p.m. Ivor leaves for Korea. At 7.40 p.m. William realises that Ivor has taken his briefcase and in his briefcase is William's bookmark.

I realise that Robin Cook could have gone to Korea after all. Try to make a substitute bookmark. Am told I have failed.

Tuesday, 24th February

Substitute bookmark still subject to criticism. It is, I notice, in use.

9.30 p.m. Phone call from Korea. Enquire after bookmark. Can hear sounds of rummaging in briefcase. The bookmark is fine.

Wednesday, 25th February

Inform William of well-being of bookmark.

My 9 a.m. students want to understand Iraq. I go along to the library to photocopy yesterday's *Times*. Am confronted by today's *Times*. The whole of Derry's impatient letter to Black Rod is printed verbatim. The only discrepancy with my records is the date. Derry wrote to Black Rod on 26th June. *The Times* dates the letter the 1st July. This will be because the top of the letter, including the date, will have been cut off the copy given to *The Times*. The top will have been cut off to conceal which copy was copied. Each one has been initialled to an individual and leaving the initials intact would have narrowed the hunt for the mole.

If 'they' have that letter 'they' might have the Killer Memo of 4th May. I think 'they' would have leaked it if 'they'd' had it. Unless 'they' were the Lord Chancellor. The letter and Princess Margaret's stroke push the Dome Launch to an obscure corner of the front page.

Imagine the atmosphere in the Lord Chancellor's Office today! Hope they all have a sense of humour and can duck behind the philosophers' heads.

Decide to apply for tickets to visit the Lord Chancellor's Residence when it is open to the public. Ring the Palace of Westminster. Am put through to the Lord Chancellor's Department. Am told to watch the press. Am told 'I do not know any more than you do.' Ring the Palace of Westminster again and ask for Black Rod's Office. Am told tickets are a matter for the Lord Chancellor's Office. Am transferred to the Lord Chancellor's Office. Am told:

'I will put you through to someone who can help you.' I wait.

'Patrick South,' says a Very Tired Voice. (Patrick South is the author of the Killer Memo ... I am Very Sorry for Patrick South. And I shouldn't think he was thanked for doing all that work on a Sunday.)

I explain. There is a pause ...

'I suggest you apply in writing ... Do you know where to write to?'

'The Palace of Westminster?'

'Yes.' I am given the postcode. ...

Ring Oldest Friend in Scotland and ask if I can apply from her address as I can't apply from here. She is amused.

Thursday, 26th February

Halfway through my day at Lambeth College I decide to take a break in the new staffroom. This is not a simple matter: not only is it a long way from anywhere (old one having been replaced by marketing/enterprise suite) but also the Facilities Manager has changed the lock. You cannot get in without a Special Key. Bob-my-Boss has a Special Key. He lends it with the instruction 'You must get your own from the Facilities Manager.' I make my way to the new staffroom with Bob's key. Johnnie-The-Security-Guard is inside playing snooker with his friend. I try to open the door. I fail. I try turning the Special Key the other way. Nothing happens. Johnnie-The-Security-Guard comes to help. He fails too. We discuss the situation through the locked door: 'There's no phone in here,' says Johnnie, 'you'll have to ring the Facilities Manager.' I find the nearest phone. The Facilities Manager does not answer. I go down to Security at the main door. Much hilarity. 'How long shall we leave Johnnie locked in there?'

'Oh!' says Security. 'There's the Facilities Manager!' I approach him and tell him the tale. I laugh. The Facilities Manager does not laugh. I follow the Facilities Manager back to the locked door. The Facilities Manager blames Johnnie (through the door). I laugh more. The Facilities Manager then blames the door. I laugh even more. The Facilities Manager thunders at the lock. It opens.

'I'll have to get a locksmith,' says the Facilities Manager.

'Can I have a key to the door?' I ask. 'I've had to borrow this one.'

'Not now,' says the Facilities Manager and hurries off.

I smoke in the new staff room for five minutes—with the door propped open. Wonder why the Facilities Manager had a new lock put in.

When I get back to the Study Centre and Bob-My-Boss I tell him the story and return his key.

Bob stamps about.

'You know what else the Facilities Manager has done ...'

'?'

'He's changed the lock of the gents. So no one can get in there.'

'?!!'

'When I asked him why he said he had to do it because 'People Like You' kept using it when it wasn't working.'

'So,' I grasp the situation, 'you can't get into the gents and you can't get out of the staffroom ...'

Bob is additionally riled because he has heard that the Facilities Manager is earning more than the rest of us. And his solution to broken gents is to change the lock on the door.

Learn that the closure of the Norwood site has been brought forward to this September. None of us can see how Electronics can be moved in seven months ... because it has to be re-installed somewhere else. On the other hand, five three quarter empty sites will become four half-empty sites ... which must be more sensible.

Ivor gets back from Korea with the bookmark.

'Did you get back to anything? Could you have stayed in Korea for another day?'

'I could—all I got back to was Derry's wallpaper.'

Ivor is worried. He is not often worried: 'I don't think Blair knows the facts ... I told Alastair Campbell about 4th May' (the Killer Memo), I told Jonathan Powell ... and I talked to Mandelson.'

'Perhaps they've not told Blair ... he's like the cuckolded husband—everybody knows except him.'

'The trouble is it's my responsibility.'

'Then you'll have to tell him, on his own.'

'Nobody likes the candid friend.'

'You're not a friend. You're a colleague. He might not like you for telling him, but he should respect you. Unless he's a smaller man than I think he is.'

'I could lose my job ... I'll have to decide.'

The Times' leader today was on Derry's lack of 'candour'. And Blair was asked in an interview if he had confidence in his Lord Chancellor. 'Of course I do,' said Blair. What else can he say? He has to say that or to sack him. There is no half way.

Friday, 27th February

Pat Hollis's husband died last night. She was on the train back to Norfolk. The train was late. He died moments before she got home.

Chevening bubbles on. Ivor and Robin Cook have been told the Colonel has been appointed. Captain Husband 'could not wait any longer'. Ivor and Robin are seeing the Colonel on Monday afternoon. Ivor has written Captain Husband 'a stiff letter'.

Derry is to appear in front of the Commons Select Committee on Public Administration. The Committee cannot see how the Freedom of Information Act, the European Rights Bill and new privacy laws can fit together. They think the Lord Chancellor may be able to help. The Committee is chaired by Rhodri Morgan, who was selected for a Welsh seat ahead of Ivor and walks past our front door on his way to the Commons. Ivor rings Rhodri.

'If,' says Ivor, 'people start asking Derry about his refurbishments you must call Black Rod too. You must not just accept what Derry tells you.'

Rhodri says they are not supposed to hear Derry on refurbishments as they are House of Lords' business. But Rhodri gets the point. 'If they did ask Derry anything,' says Ivor, 'and he lied, that's a capital offence. If he's got any sense, he'd say he wasn't there to answer questions about that.'

'It looks,' say I, 'as if he's going to get away with it.'

'Not if I can help it,' says Ivor. 'I do not approve. He has behaved dishonourably. He has tried to shift the blame on to the officers of the House. He shouldn't get away with it. He's supposed to be head of the judiciary ... if he was anybody else, Blair would see it that way too.'

He has found Black Rod and told him that if the committee gets into the issue of refurbishment, Rhodri might have to call him. 'But what can I say!' says Black Rod.

'The facts,' says Ivor.

The *Today Programme* got hold of Ivor on his private line. They thought he was his secretary at first. Ivor's office is concerned to know how they got hold of the number. Ivor tells Today he cannot appear on their programme: 'They want to ask me about Derry. I can dodge the question. I can bluff. Or I can drop Derry in the shit. I don't mind dropping him in the shit. He deserves it. But it's a bit blatant.'

Another builder comes. We have to have the outside of this house re-painted, despite the cracks. The nine-year-old paint has peeled back to the timber. We are beginning to look like a house that is waiting to be boarded up. He did our doctor neighbour's six years ago and it still looks healthy. (He also did their electrics and left them with a live wall—he will not be doing our electrics.)

4 p.m. Ivor leaves for Sainsbury's.

5.30 p.m. Simon Burton rings. Can he have a quick word? I explain Ivor is at Sainsbury's. I will tell him when he returns. Expect that will be this evening.

6 p.m. Ivor returns – he likes Sainsbury's; it makes a change from the House of Lords. He has a mass of bags. They stay in the car while he rings Simon. Gareth Williams has Broken the Rules. Jeffrey Archer has started a debate: females should inherit the throne if they are born before males. Gareth Williams, speaking for the Government, has told the House that the Queen agrees with Jeffrey Archer and the Government agrees with the Queen. Unfortunately, Simon has been told, it is Against the Rules to use the Queen in an argument. The fact that Robert Fellowes has written the words that Gareth Williams speaks is not the point.

'Oh,' says Ivor, 'we'll have to say we'll look at it. And if Gareth has broken the rules he'll have to apologise. He'll do it very well.'

Saturday, 28th February

Go to Cats. I don't think I will be going again. I cannot say the same for William and Ivor.

Sunday, 1st March, St David's Day

We have a great bunch of daffodils in the kitchen, in bud when we were given them yesterday and in flower today, smelling of daffodils.

Watch vanloads of police heading for the Countryside March. I am in favour of The Countryside—whatever that means—but I am not in favour of hunting and the hunts have organised the march. Our local Conservatives, as rural as it is possible to be, are not in favour of hunting either. It damages hedges, fences and fields and frightens animals: last time the hunt came near us, two cows lost their calves. The Countryside is no more united than The Government or The Middleclasses or The Greeks or any other generalisation.

Monday, 2nd March

Bob-My-Boss tells me the latest on the Facilities Manager. He has decided to change the lock on the main door to the car park. A special lock is not good enough. He wants swipe cards. They will cost £3,000. (There is nothing the matter with the lock—at the moment.) I tell Bob I have no special key, despite my request.

The Clerks to the Lords say Gareth Williams has not broken the rules. Emily Blatch continued to insist that he had. Ivor felt he got the better of Emily Blatch (he is not her number one fan) with the help of the clerks.

Tuesday, 3rd March

I apply in writing for a special key. The Facilities Manager is not in today. He may not be in tomorrow.

Derry comes up in front of Rhodri's committee. He is asked about his wallpaper. He talks and talks. Can see Rhodri looking Rhodriish in the background. Ask Ivor if he saw it.

'A few seconds. Economical sod.'

The Cabinet Committee on the Reform of the Lords is at loggerheads. Peter Mandelson, the one-time lone voice, has been joined by Jack Straw and Nick Brown. Jack Straw is adamant: he wants a nominated chamber. Nick Brown joins him: he sees an elected Lords 'making mischief'.

'We have to go back to the Prime Minister,' says Ivor.

'So it may all fall apart.'

'It may ... though he'll be sensitive about U-turns.'

'The others are being very short-sighted.'

'I think so ... we'll have to see—Ann Taylor is sitting on the fence.'

And Damien is Very Angry. So angry that he Said Something to Jack Straw - political advisers are not supposed to speak out of turn to ministers.

Wednesday, 4th March

No special key for me today.

Get interim report on our cracks. Our extension and our house may be subsiding. We have a leaky drain and our soil is soft. In the meantime they will continue to monitor.

Now Derry is beginning to wobble on House of Lords' Reform: maybe they should be going for a wholly-nominated chamber after all.

'It'll be interesting,' I say, 'to see if Blair stands firm. If you see eye to eye. It will be quite a test.'

'Yes,' says Ivor, 'it will be a test. He's got the whole of the Commons ranged against him.'

Damien has been going round all day looking Very Hurt.

Ivor discovered, two days ago, that Derry has called a meeting for 7.45 a.m. tomorrow. I wonder at what point they will all stop trooping in at whatever time Derry says: 6 a.m.? 5 a.m.? 4 a.m.? Ivor investigates. The meeting is now

8.15 a.m. Why then? They look at Derry's diary. He has another meeting at 9.30 a.m. The first meeting should only take half an hour, says Ivor. He does not see the point.

Thursday, 5th March

12.15 a.m. We are asleep. The phone rings. I answer it with thoughts of death for I know of no births due.

'Damien here. I'm sorry to ring you so late. But there's something important splashed all over tomorrow's papers which Ivor ought to know about.'

'What's the time? What's the time?' asks Ivor. I have no idea. I give Ivor the phone as if Damien was the speaking clock. Ivor listens.

Cranborne has leaked the molehill-of-an-agreement.

'He wanted all this secrecy,' says Ivor and goes back to sleep.

7.30 a.m. Alastair Campbell rings:

'Hello, Ivor. How are you? I didn't ring you last night because it was so late...'

They agree that the two 'secret' meetings with Cranborne were Informal Soundings. Alastair Campbell wants to know for his morning briefing—thinks the leaking is a Tory plot to 'get Derry' for lying in front of Rhodri in Tuesday's committee. (Derry was asked if there had been Discussions about House of Lords' reform—and he said there had not.)

7.40 a.m. Today rings. Will Ivor go on Today with Cranborne? He will not - because the burden of Damien's pre-dawn call was to catch him before Today to advise him against going on.

7.50 a.m. We listen to Cranborne on Today.

'So much for the Honourable Party,' says Ivor.

'I should think that's the end of your agreement,' say I, 'he's blown it—you'll have to abolish him too.'

'It's difficult to see,' says Ivor, 'how it can be rescued now.' Cranborne is saying the Agreement is breaking down because the Government can't agree. It could be that the Tories can't agree and this is Cranborne's last stand against his Very Awkward Squad.

Get to Lambeth College. No Special Key. Meet the Facilities Manager on the stairs. Ask him for my own Special Key. He will leave one at Security for me. Some hours later I go to Security. No Special. Key. Security rings the Facilities Manager. 'Give her one.' Security gives me my own Special Key.

3 p.m. Catch Ivor and Cranborne on television. My favourite moment is when Ivor says they could offer Cranborne a life peerage instead of

abolishing him. Cranborne, with a white carnation, insists the hereditary peers are the only independents left. Ivor agrees that some of them do believe that.

4.15 p.m. sit outside William's piano lesson and write this. It pours. Think of roof-free garage at the house.

'A much better day than yesterday,' says Ivor when he gets home. 'And I got my special key,' say I.

In today's Cabinet Meeting Blair instructed Ivor: 'I want you to flush them out ... go as far as you can to get an agreement with the Tories on House of Lords' Reform.'

Better still, later in the day, Ivor got a message from Blair's constitution person in Downing Street confirming the prime ministerial instruction in detail. Lesley was so pleased she punched the air. Damien stopped looking Very Hurt. Simon was not political.

'So,' said I, 'you and Blair do see eye to eye.'

'So it seems,' said Ivor, 'and I don't think he's too worried about what's in the agreement as long as there is an agreement.'

'Who else,' I wonder, ''round that cabinet table can see ahead to ten, fifteen years from now when there is no more New Labour and they need a democratic second chamber ... even if they can't see that the country needs one—apart from you and Blair?'

'Gordon Brown, Prescott,' says Ivor.

'Is that all?'

'The more I see of Prescott the more I like him. He's genuine. He's a goodie.'

Rhodri's committee is restive: has the Lord Chancellor lied to them about the House of Lords? Rhodri is writing to the Lord Chancellor for clarification.

'I have spent the day defending Derry,' says Ivor—the irony being that Ivor told Rhodri not to believe Derry automatically on wallpaper, not the Lords. Rhodri's suspicions, once alerted, do not discriminate.

The loggerheaded Cabinet Committee (on reform) is redundant. Ivor is deciding what will be done with it.

At 5.30 p.m. Ivor 'had it out' with Cranborne. Cranborne told him all about how it was that he did not leak their meetings. Ivor listened.

'After all,' said Cranborne, 'we can't work together if we can't trust each other.' Ivor continued to listen. He thinks they are 'just' on speaking terms, and it 'may' be possible to rescue 'something'.

Jim Callaghan is worried about Ivor. He tells him: 'You're out on your own.'

'I've got the Prime Minister's support,' Ivor tells Jim. Jim did not know that.

Nonetheless, Ivor's exposure concerns him: 'Watch your back.'

Peter Mandelson continues to sound his warnings: the Tories are out to get you. (Peter Mandelson does not trust the Tories.)

When Ivor went into the guest room today he met with complaints: 'Why didn't you tell us about all this at Tuesday's Meeting?' (There had been a meeting of Labour Peers on Tuesday to discuss Lords' Reform.)

'Come on!' said Ivor, 'I can't hold secret meetings in public!'

Tell Ivor that the work he is doing is Not For Now. It is For The Future. (Approve of myself.) Ivor listens.

Friday, 6th March

Bob-My-Boss's birthday. Buy him a gingerbread man and put it on his desk.

Don't do much else. Lambeth College is too quiet.

Sunday, 8th March

Papers full of Government plans to reform the Lords. Ivor does not know anything about these plans and does not recognise what is being said. Derry is congratulated for leading the way and getting it right. Ivor says he will do some briefing so papers stop getting it wrong.

'Then again, I probably won't bother. As usual.'

Go and see Flubber. It flies and it is rubber, hence flubber. I don't think I shall be going to see it again. It is green.

Monday, 9th March

Sun.

Alarm at Lambeth College: news of which jobs are going is filtering through as people are called in to see The Power. The Throne is putting in an appearance later. The English Teachers (of whom I was one until I took my year's unpaid leave) are called in. I think there are nine of them. 4.5 of them have to go. All of them can apply for the remaining 4.5 jobs. Among them are my oldest friends in the business. I ring them up to show solidarity. Also among them are the people whose work I preserved three years ago, with difficulty, when The Power wanted me to do all of it myself. They shared my work while I was on a year's unpaid leave and they kept it to themselves when I returned. I am not ringing them up to show solidarity. Nor am I naming them here, which I think is very nice of me—but They Know Who They Are.

A better person than me might be one hundred per cent sorry for them. I am some percentage glad that they are learning what it feels like.

Pat Hollis came back to work today. She says she wants lots and lots of work.

Ivor got a note from Downing Street. Blair wants the loggerheaded Committee (on Lords' Reform) to stop discussing policy. He wants it to start discussing tactics. But 'I don't want to take instructions from that lot on my tactics ... some of the buggers want to see the whole thing fall apart.'

'I'm sure Blair thinks you can work out a way to deal with that,' say I.

Ivor told Derry what he had been told by Blair. Derry did not know.

'There you are!' say I. 'That's how Blair's dealing with Derry. He's getting sidelined ... How many cabinet committees is he left chairing now?'

'Well the two devolution ones are winding down, there's not much left there.'

'Your reform one has been taken over by Blair—what else?'

'There's the one that decides Government business—that's really administrative - but powerful.'

'I bet that Derry is given no new cabinet committees to chair and that is how Blair will deal with Derry ... leave him to slide back into being Lord Chancellor and talking to judges.'

'It's hard for him,' says Ivor.

'For Blair you mean?'

'Yes. It's hard.'

In the course of the day Ivor and Prescott et al had a meeting with Derry who kept them waiting in his outer office for twenty minutes. 'Prescott was furious'. Can't imagine he was soothed by the philosophers' heads.

Towards the end of the day Ivor and Denis had another meeting with Cranborne and Strathclyde.

'Cranborne keeps going on about wanting a piece of paper from the Government for the Shadow Cabinet. He wants an options paper. I told him he didn't want an options paper, he wanted Preferences. But in the end he said he wanted "just headings". And I asked him what he meant by indirectly-elected peers ... and he meant nominated by the Scottish Parliament and the Welsh Assembly.'

'What about England?'

'Good question—he muttered about 'making up' constituencies ... but he really hasn't thought it through. I told him we were under pressure of time ... he knows that.'

'You know,' I said, 'I still think he may have leaked it all because he couldn't get any support.'

'It hasn't done him much good.'

'Yes it has—he's started getting leader writers arguing his case.'

'That's true ... And you know what he said today for the first time?'

'He agreed to the end of the hereditary peers.'

Tuesday, 10th March

Bob-My-Boss has done some sums on Lambeth College's financial position. He thinks it's worse than we thought it was. I will ask my question at Lambeth College's Financial Controller's meeting tomorrow morning.

Ivor had an unsatisfactory day: the messages coming through from Downing Street are getting blurred; one message contradicted another message.

'It looks as if Blair is changing his mind,' he said.

'Could it be that these people round him, who don't want your agreement, are twisting the message?'

'Yes.'

Denis Carter lost his temper at the twisted messages: 'Tactics! Tactics! All he thinks about are tactics! He's got no policy at all!'

Damien said:

'And do you know, I was offered promotion and double my salary in my old job last Friday ... and I turned it down for this!'

'Quite right too,' said Lesley, 'this is much more fun.'

Ivor continues to believe Blair wants Any Agreement rather than No Agreement.

'And I'm not one hundred per cent sure Cranborne isn't just playing games.'

'Doesn't he want to go on until he can say it's you who's broken the agreement?'

'Of course. And I am trying to manoeuvre him so that I can say exactly the same thing about him. That's the game. Then we abolish the hereditary peers and Cranborne can change his mind and fight for them all over again.'

Wednesday, 11th March

Lambeth College's Financial Controller puts us in the picture: our funds are shrinking year by year. I ask my question:

'Assuming this continues, how many staff will we have to lose by 2000?'

'80.'

'Eight 0?'

'Eight 0.' There is silence. 'That's just arithmetic.'

I also hope, out loud, that plans to borrow 7-11 million, partly against the sale of sites, to refurbish the three remaining sites, will not blow up what is left of Lambeth College.

The Financial Controller agrees: some monies will not be borrowed until other sites have been sold: 'My neck is on the line.'

There is a chill in the air.

The Financial Controller also made it clear that when The Throne appeared in front of the select committee in the House of Commons, the MPs ('Labour MPs') did not warm to The Throne's special pleading for inner London colleges. They have their colleges in their constituencies which say they are being bled dry by inner city colleges getting preferential treatment. And Margaret Hodge made it known that she favoured the merger of the inner London colleges.

Ivor's day was not much better: 'Blair's wobbling. I'm not getting clear messages. He seems to be changing his mind. And I'm negotiating with Cranborne with two hands tied behind my back: one is fighting my own people; the other has no policy.'

He met Derry to sort out tomorrow's meeting of the loggerheaded Committee:

'He's pathetic. Pathetic. You know how he wanted to get rid of the hereditaries and leave it at that—he wrote that letter to Blair behind my back and I had a row with him—now he wants two thirds/one third.'

Thursday, 12th March

Driving back from Lambeth College, I see swathes of smoke blowing across the river from Westminster. I drive slower and slower, along with everyone else, and stare. The swathes are not coming from the Palace of Westminster. Ivor is safe. Drive a lot further before I am sure they are not coming from William's school. Roads around are closed and filled with fire-engines. It looks as if it is an empty building.

Ivor is late.

At the loggerheaded Committee, while they were talking, Jack Straw drafted a letter of what he thought Ivor ought to write for Cranborne. It is a set of questions. Not options. Not preferences. Not headings. Later in the day, Ivor met a civil servant who was passing on this letter for Blair's clearance as if it was Ivor's. Ivor had to intervene, get it back to his office and draft it himself.

He then saw the minutes of the loggerheaded Committee. He thought someone had been tampering with them. He had to sort that out.

'The real problem is that Blair's constitutional adviser—Pat MacFadden—doesn't want a reformed chamber. He just wants to get rid of the hereditaries ... this does not look good for the future ... if Blair insists on making all the decisions himself.' Then the people round him pervert the decisions as they pass them down the line, pervert the advice, questions and information coming back up the line. There is a game called Chinese Whispers—but in that the only perversions are mistakes.

'You'll have to stick to Blair's instruction to you in Cabinet ... that was in public ... To Flush Them Out.'

Ivor knows this. It is difficult with all the perverters in-between.

In the midst of straightening the twists, Ivor exclaimed: 'Why do I bother?'

'Because,' said Simon, ' you think some of these people have been here for much too long.'

Ivor has heard that Derry's driver is not happy. The car pool is driving Derry in shifts. There is an early shift and a late shift.

Ring Oldest Friend. There is no reply to my letter requesting tickets to view the Lord Chancellor's Residence.

Friday, 13th March

I remember the Dunblane children.

Ivor is off early to see Derry: 'I have to work with him.' And Ivor hears Derry on Blair and the loggerheaded Committee: 'I'm fucking sick of this. The fucking Prime Minister won't make any decisions.'

Jack Straw is fighting an elected second chamber; he is trying to shaft Ivor:

'If it came to a battle between me and Jack Straw, I'd lose ... he's much more powerful in this Government than me.'

Saturday and Sunday, 14th & 15th March

We visit The Grandson, Ieuan Richard, aged three months, and Gwen, aged 91. Then we went to the Duxford Air Museum. That would be interesting if you were interested in aeroplanes.

Monday, 16th March

Ivor sets off for his day without optimism:

'With Jack Straw, Nick Brown, Peter Mandelson and Pat MacFadden ranged against me, I'm not going to get very far.'

'Doesn't Jack Straw throw his weight around a bit?'

'Yes. And people remember.'

Oldest Friend rings. A letter addressed to Ms Armstrong has arrived from the Lord Chancellor's Office. Shall she open it? She opens it. The Lord Chancellor's Residence will be open for two mornings a week. Details are yet to be arranged. Shall she send it on to me or bring it with her when they make their Southern Trek later this month? She'll bring it with her. (She checks that I will own up to being Ms Armstrong should she be pursued by Officialdom.) Oldest Friend asks me to get hold of *What's On* in London for their southern sojourn.

Tuesday, 17th March

Lambeth College's Union meets in the Brixton Centre. Norman is there and speaks. There are many people I have worked among (on and off) for 23 years. We look older.

There is nothing the Union can do. People will be made redundant. Meet one colleague from the olden days: 'I'm 51. You get tired. I might go.' The Union recommends we 'look hard' at early retirement offers because another 40 are destined to go next year and 40 more the year after.

'But Lambeth needs English teachers!' says someone. Lambeth does. But they are not employed in Lambeth College.

Wednesday, 18th March

My Oldest Friend's husband telephones from Scotland.

She walked her elder daughter to the corner to wait for the school bus this morning. She was walking home to her younger children, along an Aberdeenshire lane, when a neighbour drove by with a drum of fuel on a trailer. The trailer came off and hit her. She was killed immediately.

Friday, 20th March

The funeral will be on Tuesday.

Simon and Lesley rearrange Lords' business so Ivor can come with me.

Sunday, 22nd March

The funeral will not be on Tuesday. The police are unable to release her body.

Monday, 23rd March

Ivor asks the Lord Advocate for the name of the best personal injury lawyer in Scotland and tells him that her body has been withheld and the funeral postponed. The Lord Advocate has the procurator fiscal's report by mid-morning.

The funeral will be on Wednesday at 2pm. Oldest Friend's husband says British Airways will have to put on an extra flight.

Tuesday, 24th March

Send spring flowers from William, anemones from Ivor and me.

Wednesday, 25th March

I am asked to read:

'Lord you have made so many things! How wisely you made them all! The earth is filled with your creatures. There is the ocean, large and wide where countless creatures live, large and small alike. The ships sail on it and in it plays Leviathan, the sea monster ...'

Her brother gives the address and finishes by saying that the larks have been soaring higher and singing sweeter here than ever before.

Her husband says he will be a mother and a father: 'so when you see me going around here in a dress ...'

I drop my bag at the graveside and am left scrabbling among the grass-clippings and in the wind for keys and peppermints and driving licence and handkerchief. How she would have laughed.

Thursday, 26th March

There don't seem to be many jokes left in the world.

SUMMER TERM 1999

Thursday, 2nd April

At last Thursday's Cabinet, Blair remarked that it was the little things that were going wrong. The big things were going right: 'It's the signals that matter. Not the policy.'

'Very revealing,' said Ivor to me, 'I don't expect he'd see it that way if you put it to him. But very revealing.'

Ivor has an early morning—with Gordon Brown. Frank Dobson has put in a colossus of a bid for money and has justified all expenditure in detail.

'Why,' wonders Ivor, 'in some areas are 80% of impacted wisdom teeth removed in a day—while in other areas only 30% are? I can't imagine the teeth in one area are so different from the teeth in another area.'

Cranborne has been swirling around accusing Blair of acting like Al Capone and threatening all hereditary peers with no life peerages.

'He's not serious,' says Ivor, 'he's fighting to the death for the hereditaries.' And Ivor met Brian Griffiths, a Tory life peer, in passing: 'You should know,' Brian Griffiths told him, 'Cranborne has got his own agenda. He has not got the support of the life peers. We think that what you are trying to do with the Lords is Absolutely Right.'

(Ivor has always described Brian Griffiths as A Nice Man. This started in 1970 when Ivor, the Official Labour Candidate, lost to the Unofficial Labour Candidate in Blythe, Northumberland. Brian Griffiths was the Tory Candidate and found my younger stepson weeping at his father's defeat. Brian comforted and reassured. Ivor has not forgotten. Neither has my younger stepson.)

'Perhaps,' I consider, 'Cranborne & Co are just beginning to believe that they really are going to be unseated.'

'Perhaps they are.'

Monday, 6th April

My Oldest Friend's children aged 7, 11 and 14 are here with their father. They brought with them the letter to me from the Lord Chancellor's Office.

The Cabinet Committee on public expenditure grilled Dobson for two hours.

'Poor thing,' said I.

'No,' says Ivor. 'His demands are extraordinary.'

Tuesday, 7th April

My Oldest Friend's family fly home to Aberdeenshire. We miss them.

The loggerheaded Committee had its best meeting ever: 'I think I got everything I wanted,' said Ivor. 'We agreed that negotiations with Cranborne had collapsed.'

'But if that's happened—and you're not getting an all-in-one reform—the others don't feel the House of Commons is threatened any more.'

'True. They don't. But they did agree to a whole lot of things.'

'Including an elected chamber?'

'Partially elected, anyway ... and a nominations committee.'

'Why the change?'

'I'm talking to them more about what I'm doing. I spent a long time on the phone to Peter before the meeting.
'

Wednesday, 8th April

Terry Boston startled the Lords by mounting a defence of the Lord Chancellor's wallpaper. The matter had just subsided.

'I am going to ask him,' says Ivor, 'why he did it. Nobody knew he was going to.'

Ivor's office likes the idea that he and Denis take their staff out to dinner. 'The civil servants and the political advisers can speak frankly to each other,' said Simon.

'It seems a happy team,' said Ivor.

'Very happy,' said Simon.

Easter

Helen of the Treasury's father dies. We spend Good Friday driving to North Wales (two hours not moving round Birmingham). We stay with our Joneses in Bangor.

'Grandad's nose and Grandad's clothes,' says William. He is taken to the Roman Fort and they pick bluebells overlooking the water where Jones The Books, Jones The Doctor and Jones The Thinker sailed—after the latter had left his village a few miles inland.

William's cousins' grandfather also came from a few miles inland. His funeral is in Welsh. He is buried among snow and sun and daffodils in the shadow of Snowdon. It is as lovely as the Scottish hillside where my Oldest Friend was buried two weeks ago.

We drive south to Ivor's family. On Easter Day we find Ivor's childhood home and the hut where the pigs were kept during the war. We are offered a visit to the graveyard and the family plots.

'No,' I say at once. No more graveyards for a while, please.

We drive back to London and get a hamster.

Friday, 17th April

We visit The Grandson, Ieuan Richard. He is growing as he is supposed to grow.

Pass the British Library on our way back from the station. 'Is that place open yet?' wonders Ivor.

Monday, 20th April

Back to Lambeth College. My colleagues are to be interviewed for their redundancies this week and next.

My Stockwell cousin rings the doorbell. His father died on Saturday morning. Lambeth looked after his father so well he may vote Labour. His father came with flowers when William was born. We remember my grandmother's house in Surrey.

Derry opens his residence to some of the press. Ivor went to look in - had to leave for a vote—and was so angry that he couldn't go back.

Tuesday, 21st April

Word process this to 7th of April, including 18th March.

Seas of sorrow all around. My Oldest Friend's death. If she had had her three score years and ten, there would have been less pain.

Find a jaded colleague: 'It's my own fault.' She had been at the opening of the British Library   galleries last night. The whole place is being used by academics as a model of how not to plan a project. Jaded Colleague says the design is unmistakeably 1970s. They had to rip out the computers because they had gone out of date before the place opened, then they had to re-wire it. She has been told that the only structure of comparable cost was the Channel Tunnel.

Ivor is busier than he thought he would be: it's Public Expenditure's (PX's) time for Jack Straw tomorrow. The plan was that Alistair Darling and Ivor would Do The Police and Alistair Darling and Derry would Do The Prisons. A message has come through late in the day: Gordon says could Ivor do the prisons too? Ivor does not know what has happened to Derry, but he does know he has a lot of extra reading and not much time.

Find the diary written by my Oldest Friend over five weeks in Summer 1971(?). We were together at the house and a while later she typed me a copy. I had not noticed before how she headed it:

CIDER WITH JANET
TRANSLATED FROM THE ORIGINAL BY THE AUTHOR
WITH ALL ERRORS INCLUDED

SUMMER 71 (?)

Tue 29th June ...

and off she goes. I read the 60 sides several times.

Wednesday, 22nd April

PX cross-examines Jack Straw for two hours: 'The problem,' says Ivor, 'is that Jack is in favour of putting people in prison.'

'Is anybody else?'

'No ... except I don't know what Derry thinks about prison.'

'He's probably waiting for the Prime Minister to make a decision.'

'In that case he'll wait forever ... anyway, Jack wants ten new prisons ... £100 million. He is Jack The Lad ... he's very wily is Jack ... when his back's against the wall he starts talking about "the politics of the next election" ... we got it out of him that his bottom line is that he wants to go into the next election with the same numbers in the police force as there were at the last election.'

'OK?'

'Well ... the expense! And we got Jack to agree that new prisons would be private prisons—prison staff in private prisons get £15,000 and the others get £19, 000 ... so they are much more expensive.'

'What I'm not clear about,' I put my head round what I've been listening to, 'is whether your PX Committee says A can have the money—and do what they like with it—or A can have the money for a specific purpose only.'

'They have money already—they are bidding for extra money.'

The next time PX gives Jack a hearing, they have agreed they will 'nail him'.

'How many times do you see each person?'

'As many times as we need to—twice certainly.'

'The next PX is going to be Very Amusing: George Robertson has Upset the Treasury; he saved £95million on the quiet - AND DID NOT TELL THE TREASURY. (He thought he could pocket those £95million for defence.) Then the Treasury found out: 'I have never read anything like the Treasury brief for this next meeting,' says Ivor. 'It is vitriolic ... he has really upset the Treasury ... the officials, that is.'

'Silly of him.'

'Very'

'He must realise it.'

'Yes ... but he won't have seen the Treasury briefing we've got.' Ivor shakes his head. 'The trouble is you can't really cross-examine them—there isn't time.'

'So,' I get a grip, 'you have to make twelve assumptions per question and they can stall on the preceeding eleven.'

According to Jonathan Powell there will be no reshuffle 'before the summer'. He has written to Ivor saying so because Ivor has written to him saying that before there is any shuffling he should see Blair to tell him about Lords' ministers', performances.

Thursday, 23rd April

Ivor was telling Cabinet of next week's business in the Lords (as he always does): they may have to sit all night over the Amsterdam Bill because they have four Lords who are insisting on talking and talking ... 'but one of them —Peter Shore—is in hospital.'

'Where?' asks Frank Dobson. Cabinet belly-laughter at the picture of Peter Shore war-pathed by Frank Dobson (and his hospitals). And Ivor took Bertie Denham's advice (to make it clear that the Lords is Very Very Difficult: the vote lives on a knife edge) and told Cabinet that the Government may lose a vote tonight.

Then George Robertson faced PX: 'We gave him a bashing ... Derry tried to get something out of him but got nowhere ... when I saw him later he muttered that George was a Good Witness.' (Ivor says he did get something out of George Robertson.)

The Lords' vote was 64 to 65. The Government won by one. Ivor can announce his triumph in next week's Cabinet.

Friday, 24th April

Denis Carter has 'gone ballistic': last night there were eighteen government ministers in the Lords (most scheduled to whoop it up at a fund-raising dinner in the Hilton) and four government ministers out of town (with Denis Carter's permission). After 7 p.m. Denis Carter informed all eighteen that they could not leave until after the vote. One government minister ignored Denis Carter: Derry Irvine. His excuse? He's a Cabinet minister.

Denis Carter wrote Derry Irvine a Strong Letter: How can we expect Labour Peers to stay and vote if the Lord Chancellor does a bunk? Ivor expects Derry will say his staff never gave him the message.

The news of Derry's departure is leaked. I ask how.

'Well Damien is looking very pleased with himself.'

When the press came back to enquire into the matter, Derry asked Denis to put out a statement saying Denis had given Derry a Special Dispensation. Denis's ballistics crescendoed. He did no such thing.

'Derry is learning how difficult it is in politics without friends,' say I.

'I'm not sure - he's got one friend left.'

'The Prime Minister.'

'Yes.'

Derry has also caused upset by telling the Welsh Assembly that he thought their plans for equality were illegal. And he has talked to the Daily Telegraph who have said Derry will reduce the number of Church of England seats in the Lords.

'I don't know what he's been saying—or where he got it from,' says Ivor.

'Don't worry,' said Damien, as Ivor started to leave, 'they'll get him in the end.' (This immediately confirms my suspicions that Derry will outlast Ivor in this Government!)

I end my day at my grandmother's first cousin's funeral in West Norwood. A soprano sings Faure for us. No more funerals please.

Saturday, 25th April

Ivor is occupied by the Treasury's reading of David Blunkett's submission to PX. The Further Education paragraphs are of special interest to me—that is where Lambeth College belongs. Ivor has been asked to focus on it as his special subject for PX purposes. Ivor is surprised by the chaos of David Blunkett's submission. There are contradictions: in one paragraph more money is needed to give students more human attention; in another paragraph more money is needed to buy computers so students can work on their own with less human attention—which is cheaper in the long run. He reads the sections on schools with less care—but if the schools are all going to be so good (all problems having been solved with money) what will there be for Lambeth College et al to do? Discuss these findings.

'It's only a bid,' says Ivor, 'and Blunkett's got the Prime Minister on his side.'

Monday, 27th April

Emergency Union meeting at Lambeth College as The Throne has not agreed to all union demands on redundancies. I cannot go since I have William with me as his school holiday is in progress.

Ivor does not think he is flavour of the day with David Blunkett; he informed PX (not David Blunkett) 'my poor wife' has worked in FE for years so he has plenty of anecdotal information. When David Blunkett appeared Ivor enquired what role FE would fulfil when the schools were improved.'

'He didn't seem to have any answer to that. Gordon Brown liked it.' They did not get on to the doubling up of computers and human attention.

'Would you like,' Ivor asked me, 'to talk to David Blunkett about FE?'

'I don't think I can,' I have a gut reaction. 'I really don't think it would be professional.'

But the Government does need to get its head round FE and decide what it wants to do with it. Mixed messages will send the colleges into faster and more contradictory (and more expensive) spins within and among themselves. The single clear proposal I found was that there should be 100 mergers of colleges.

Tuesday, 28th April

Cherie Blair is going to write a diary and put it on the internet. I don't think it will be like this one.

Ivor gets home peeved: 'I had a good day until I was given the list of 18 new peers - no Scots, no Welsh, very few women.'

'Wasn't it discussed with you at all?'

'Not at all.'

'Amazing really. And plain rude.'

'I don't think it's deliberate. They just don't think.'

'I suppose they don't think it matters because you'll get rid of the hereditaries soon.'

'I need people with which to get rid of the hereditaries ... the Tories can hold that up for about a year.'

Just as Ivor thinks he is getting somewhere—wham!

Ivor has to go back to the Lords after we have eaten because of the all-night indulgence ('it's Stoddart')—on Amsterdam. He finds Simon, Lesley, Chris, Damien and Fiona playing monopoly in his outer office.

'Did they have to be there?'

'Oh no.'

'Had they eaten?'

'Damien had been out for some food.'

And when Ivor left after midnight Chris and Damien were still there 'battling it out.' Chris was talking of a draw. But Damien wanted to go on to the end. They both had money and property.

Wednesday, 29th April

The Head of Art and Design, his boss and a hairdresser drove to Plymouth and back yesterday to look at Plymouth's FE college. It was nothing like Lambeth. 96% of the students finish their courses; there is a florists and a restaurant in the foyer where we have security guards; they work a 48 week year; the budget is devolved to departments and there are plans to devolve it further ... if that is David Blunkett's idea of how FE is everywhere ...

I have found two poems for my funeral: John Donne's 'Death be not Proud' and Blake's 'The Fly':

> *Little fly*
> *Thy summer's play*
> *My thoughtless hand*

Has brushed away

Am not I
A fly like thee?
Or art not thou
A man like me?

For I dance
And drink and sing:
Till some blind hand
Shall brush my wing.

If thought is life
And strength and breath:
And the want
Of thought is death;

Then am I
A happy fly,
If I live,
Or if I die.

Damien conceded the Monopoly to Chris at 12.30 this morning.

Nick Brown told Denis Carter, who then told Ivor, that when he saw Tony he said that if a cabinet minister in the Commons had disobeyed his instruction to stay and vote (as Derry had in the Lords) Nick would have gone straight to the Prime Minister and told him he should sack him.

'So Blair must be getting the message that Derry Irvine is a problem—even if that's not precisely what Nick Brown said to him.'

'Oh, yes. But there's nothing he can do. The problem is Derry doesn't care. And now he has upset the whole of the Bar by naming the legal aid people who are earning most. He didn't do much legal aid but my goodness he was coining it. He's a bloody disaster—if he can't get on with the Bar he'll be a very bad Lord Chancellor.'

The Lord Chancellor wanted to invite the New Labour MPs to see his wallpaper.

'You'll have to invite the Labour peers first,' Denis told him.

'Who'll pay for it?' asked the Lord Chancellor.

'You will,' said Denis.

Denis has also told Downing Street that it's time Number 10 entertained the Labour peers and their partners - (none of us have had a look in). Maybe I will get to see the wallpaper one day.

'You'll never have seen so much money spent on so little,' says Ivor.

Ivor spent time today with Peter Mandelson. He's discovered things go smoother if he gets Peter Mandelson on board first. Ivor explained why reform of the Lords should, after the end of the hereditary peers, be in the hands of a Royal Commission rather than a joint committee. The logger-headed Committee wants a joint committee because they are under the impression that there would be more Labour control. But on a joint committee there could only be nine Labour members, out of 20. The logger-headed committee have not worked this out for themselves. Peter Mandelson says Blair wants to go down in history as the man who sorted out the second chamber for the 21st century. Mandelson agrees that Ivor should give *The Times* an interview telling of his disappointment with Cranborne & Co: they are not behaving as if they are serious, they keep finding objections and if they want to waste time, the Government is not going to play along with them. They have to 'bite the bullet' or the Government will go it alone. Ivor tells *The Times* this and *The Times* agrees not to publish until Friday.

'Perhaps that's what Cranborne's waiting for—waiting for you to talk to him through the newspapers.'

'Peter's view is that we should get in there first.'

Thursday, 30th April

Bob-my-Boss emerges from days of meetings with the Union and with Management. It looks as if no redundancies will be necessary after all.

Ivor is pleased with his loggerheaded Committee: he and Peter Mandelson want a Royal Commission; everybody else wants a joint committee of both houses: 'We have a firm disagreement' and Blair may have to decide 'though he won't want to.'

'Why are you pleased then?'

The loggerheaded Committee agreed to:

1. no retirement age for peers; there is no such thing in the Commons and none of the loggerheaded Committee want to be thrown out on account of their own ages;
2. no attendance requirement: how could you police it?

PX met Margaret Beckett: 'I didn't have to do my brutal questioning bit ... what she's asking for is sensible.'

David Blunkett is asking for more money for more classroom assistants.

The Lords—'it was packed'—debated the reform of the introduction ceremony. The Government won. 'You've never heard such nonsense' from some of the Tories. 'You'd think we were reforming the Queen—and the nation would crumble ...' if new peers don't doff their borrowed hats three times to the Lord Chancellor.

David Blunkett announces Beacon Schools. Turn of the century language is upon us: 'fast-track', 'ballistic', 'spin-doctor', 'road rage', 'beacon'; moving on from second half of the 20th century language: 'access', 'lone parent', 'racism'. All words that will date and become fixed in an era.

Friday, 1st May

It is cold. It has been the wettest April since 1818. The skies have been crying too.

Derry's car is off the road. Its driver said it skidded on oil in Stratford and hit the kerb and staved in its front side.

'That's his story and he's sticking to, it,' says John.

Ivor is disappointed by the lack of position given to his *Times* interview. He thinks *The Times* night editor decided it wasn't news after the political editor had gone home.

The Duke of Norfolk and Ivor meet in the House of Lords' car park: 'You've got to decide what you are going to do,' about Lords' reform.' Says the Duke of Norfolk.

'He's right,' says Ivor.

The Reeses give us supper to mark the anniversary of the election last year. Also there are the Denis Carters and the John Morrises. There are two anecdotes which cause most mirth: When the news came through, in the middle of the night, that Turkey was invading Cyprus, Callaghan, the Foreign Secretary, was asleep in his bed in Kennington. He had to get into the Foreign Office immediately. His driver was asleep in his bed a long way away and would have to go and get the car, which was even further away, before he could go and pick Jim up and take him to King Charles Street. There was no time to spare. Jim took himself out into the Kennington Road determined to hitch a lift from whatever came first. And first came a milk float. The driver allowed himself to be commandeered and drove Jim over the river amongst the milk.

'I've never dared ask Jim about that,' said Ivor.

'In case it's not true,' said Colleen Rees.

'I got it from his political advisor.'

The second anecdote came from the horse's mouth—Merlyn Rees's. It was the Queen's Jubilee and there was a ceremonial service in St Paul's Cathedral. Idi Amin of Uganda was the Bad Guy of the Moment and the Government was afraid that he would present himself in London for the festivities. Early in the morning, before the St Paul's service, a message came through that an unidentified aircraft was flying in the direction of London under the name U1. An emergency meeting was called for 6 a.m., chaired by Jim Callaghan, then Prime Minister. Merlyn, the Home Secretary, had to go too. He dressed himself up in his St Paul's Cathedral splendour and arrived to join the senior service personnel and the senior spies at the meeting. Time passed, U1 advanced and Contingencies were set up. The time of the service approached. Jim had to go to St Paul's. He told Merlyn to stay. So, in his finery, Merlyn over saw the emergency for the rest of the morning and Colleen went to St Paul's on her own. Eventually all was revealed: U1 was not Uganda 1; it was an Air Lingus trial flight.

'How did you find out?' Ivor asked.

'The Irish told us ... the Irish have always been very helpful.'

'What was Merlyn supposed to do?' John Morris wondered.

'Make the decisions, I suppose,' I said.

'What would they have done if Amin had landed at Heathrow?' Ivor wondered on the way home. 'I suppose there wouldn't have been a car.'

'Or the lift would have got stuck. Or the M4 would have been jammed up,' said I.

There was general agreement over supper that Blair is stopping talking to Derry and talking more to Roy Jenkins and 'Jim doesn't like it'.

Sunday, 3rd May

It is cold. Cold. Cold. Even joggers are wearing jerseys.

Tuesday 5th May

Emily Blatch started to make a statement in the Lords at a time when the rules did not allow for a statement. She said if she was not allowed to proceed she would walk out. She was not allowed to proceed. She walked out.

Then came her amendment. Somebody else struggled through it for her. Then she walked in.

'In a shadow cabinet,' said Jim to Ivor later, 'a long time ago,' when Attlee was Leader of the Opposition, 'there was a discussion about the shadow cabinet walking out of something. Clem said that the problem with walking out was that you had to walk back in again.'

'So,' said Ivor to me, 'Emily Blatch looked rather silly.'

Ivor's struggle today was to stay on top of EMU. Blair does not decide precisely what to say in the Commons until nearly the last moment. This means Ivor has to get to grips with all the background 'in case', for his parallel statement in the Lords.

Cranborne gives a press conference at which he says he could mess up Government business—if he wanted to. He compares himself to 'a rat in a trap' who will bite if it is not given a way out. I cannot help but think he has not thought this metaphor through.

Waiting in my car for William to finish school I watch a magpie making its way down the pavement. Every now and then it attacks the wall alongside. Then it eats the seeds blown from the saplings planted in the street.

Our friend Mark comes and fixes a leak in our heating.

Wednesday, 6th May

Start attending colleague's class to learn how a computer works and how to use it. All it is is on or off and '0' is 'on' and '1' is 'off'. Everything else follows from there.

Ivor replied to Cranborne's threats by saying that the Government would bring in Lords-quelling procedures which have been used twice this century.

Ivor grumbled to Jim about the eighteen new peers who will not all be there to help him get Government business through the Lords. This is because the people Jim wants to be peers are not being made peers.

'Have you been to see him?' asked Jim.

'No,' said Ivor.

'Why not? Why don't you go and see him? Tell him you need peers who will work. Thump the table at him.'

'Jim,' said Ivor, 'at 65 I am the oldest member of the Cabinet.'

'Ah,' said Jim, 'I see ... he'd be crazy to get rid of you.'

Ivor was at the same meeting as Derry today. Everything proposed, Derry was not happy with. Derry would not accept Ivor's 'form of words'. An adverb was changed. Derry accepted them.

'I have never seen anyone so insecure. It's extraordinary. He has to prove himself a hundred times an hour.'

Ivor's chief trouble today is that the Lords has to see through the legislation for the Northern Ireland Assembly and Jim Molyneux has added an amendment: nobody may sit in the Northern Ireland assembly who is a member of an organisation which has not renounced violence and handed over its weaponry. ('He's got a point,' I say.)

If this amendment is carried, it will have to go to the Commons, who have already passed the Northern Ireland Assembly legislation—without the amendment. The amendment in the Commons would light all sorts of fires. 'Imagine Ian Paisley,' says Ivor.

The Tories are not sure they want to vote for Jim Molyneux's amendment. However, they are sure they want to out vote the Government on the social security legislation which is the same evening and for which they have called in all their voters.

'Tommy has suggested we have the social security vote first and then he can send everybody home ... he'd be embarrassed to defeat the Government on Northern Ireland.'

'But he can't control his voters.'

'He can't.'

'Nick Brown wouldn't be very happy if that came over to the Commons.'

'He'd be distinctly unhappy.'

PX tomorrow is for Chris Smith. He wants to make all museums free. It would cost £50 million. Ivor would prefer them free for children, students and OAPs but not for 'rich tourists' and the rest of us. 'I'd prefer to spend the money on the performing arts.'

I am supposed to be sitting outside a polling station at eight o'clock tomorrow morning for my friend Liz (who takes us to the opera) who is standing in the local elections a little way from here. She tells me her New Labour Members may be members but they are not workers and she needs help. And those who do present themselves are would-be politicians who do nothing except talk. They are not going to get far. She complains more that local Liberals occupy themselves with rubbish collection and pigeon shit while some local residents have housing not much better than the pigeons.

Liz is looking after five polling stations by herself. I go to bed without knowing where I am to be at 8 a.m. tomorrow.

Thursday, 7th May
I find all I need on the doormat at seven o'clock and get down to Lawn Lane polling station 55 minutes later. I am joined by the Liberal candidate. No Tories have been seen by the time Liz takes over from me over an hour later.

The day is complicated by the fact that William's school is a polling station so he has no school - Ivor takes him to friends in the morning—while Lambeth College is not a polling station so I have to work. William has to come too for the afternoon.

I do a further two hours at Henry Fawcett polling station at the end of the day. I am harangued by one voter: 'Are you Old Labour or New Labour?'

'Neither.' I smile my politest smile. Only William's presence in my voting booth - outside Liz's patch—prevented me from voting Green.

'But Tony Blair says you are.'

'I don't feel I have to decide.' I go on smiling.

'She's only writing down numbers,' says William.

Chris Smith - 'his budget is tiny. Only a billion'—does not care for Ivor's proposal to make some people pay for museums. He is doing his costings 'reluctantly'.

Next week there are three PXs: they are looking at John Prescott's 'enormous portfolio'. Ivor is enjoying it: 'I was very impressed by the Treasury document I saw today. It takes an over-view of all the PXs and calculates the effects on the economy of the different proposals: if you want to encourage A you do B; if you want to encourage C you do D and so on.'

'The one I've been least impressed with so far is David Blunkett,' said Ivor.

'I told you I was surprised by the chaos.'

'Gordon has got a great deal of money tucked away.'

I, who spent half an hour in Lambeth College today in an impromptu meeting with students' attempts to write spread out in front of us, tell Ivor the money must go on the schools.

'I don't want to pay more to bad teachers,' he says.

'What about the rest of us?' I say.

My colleagues and I had agreed our students' work showed a reading age of six years. In effect everything had gone wrong, or stopped going at all, when they were six.

'If we pay all teachers £1,000 a year more' Ivor starts to do the sums.

'£1,000 is nothing. You should be talking £10,000.'

'How can we get rid of bad teachers? The unions wouldn't have it. How long can we afford to have them out on strike?'

'Still, you've got to make the profession competitive—it won't take five minutes; it'll take years—so jobs are difficult to get and people want to hold on to them. Upgrade the entry qualifications. Nobody with less than a second class degree, like has been done at the Bar.'

Ivor apologised to Cranborne for the humiliation of Emily Blatch being disallowed her statement last Tuesday: 'But what could I do?'

'Absolutely right,' said Cranborne, 'I've no complaints at all. I've read Hansard. No complaints at all about the way you handled it. Emily arrived here in a state—she'd been driving for six hours or something.'

'Her problem,' said Ivor, 'is she still thinks she's in government and has got the whole of the civil service behind her. She can't cope with being in opposition. Can't cope at all.'

He and Cranborne did an interview on the BBC World Service.

'Cranborne has started calling the Government an elective dictatorship. I told him it's a phrase we hadn't heard for eighteen years, since they were last in opposition. It's what the Tories always call a Labour Government.'

Cabinet were told to expect losses of 200-400 council seats in these local elections.

'We did spectacularly well in 1994. We even won Croydon.'

The social security legislation has got through the Lords with one amendment.

'That's a great tribute to Pat Hollis. She has done very well indeed. Remember the lone parents.'

Jim having been told that Kenneth Morgan, his candidate for a peerage, is not to be given one comes in to see Ivor: 'I've written to the Prime Minister. I've told him I want him to look at it personally.'

'Does he know there's a convention that a peerage proposed by an ex-prime minister is accepted?'

Ivor mutters something about Jonathan Powell.

'Powell! Powell! Who is this Powell? I wouldn't even recognise him so I could cut him!'

'Jim,' says Ivor to me, 'does not approve of the way Number 10 is run.' He doesn't approve at all. 'These anonymous, unelected, unaccountable people.' He shakes his head. In the meantime he has rung Jonathan Powell and enquired if he knew of the convention that Jim knows of.

'I think,' says Ivor, 'Jim does blame me for not thumping the table at Blair.'

'Well why don't you?' Ivor shakes his head. 'What,' I persevere, 'would you go and thump the table about?'

'I don't mind about the trivia.'

'What is not trivia?'

'I suppose if the Prime Minister decided to stop at the hereditaries - and not reform the Lords beyond that—then I'd go and thump the table. But I'd have to be prepared to put my job on the line to do that.'

'He's not going to do that.' That seems to me to be clear.

'He's keeping his cards very close to his chest.'

'He's told you.'

'Reform of the Lords is not at the top of his agenda. He's got Northern Ireland. The Middle East. He doesn't focus. Though he said in Cabinet we need to get rid of the label of the biggest quango ever and reform the nominations procedure.'

'There you are, then.'

'I may yet get the two thirds elected one third nominated. We'll see.'

Ivor had to cancel a meeting with Robin Cook. Cook's diary secretary is not pleased.

'Denis wouldn't let me go.'

'What were you meeting about?'

'Chevening and the UN.'

'What about Chevening?'

'I don't know.'

'What about the UN?'

'I don't think he's taking it seriously enough.'

Friday 8th May

The Government has lost about 200 seats. Liz did not win.

William regales us with impersonations of some of Ivor's colleagues. He limps. He squints. He shakes. He fumbles.

'They're all old and deaf and blind,' he says. I tell him that you can work in the Lords until you die so it is 'a graveyard waiting room.'

'That's exactly what it is,' says Ivor. Hailsham 'has not been seen since Christmas'. Yet Brian Morris is due to come back from his bubble in June.

We set off for school, for Lambeth College and for the Lords.

Ivor sends a consultation document to the Cabinet Office's constitution office. Some time later he receives a deputation which includes Pat MacFadden. Damien suspects a plot.

'Damien can smell a plot a mile off.'

The deputation says it needs to do as the Prime Minister says and quell the accusation of creating the Biggest-ever Quango in the Lords. They have put together 'about 50' ideas of how to do so. 'All daft,' says Ivor, 'but it takes time.'

Ivor receives a deputation from David Hacking who once had lunch at the next table to ours, with his son who could inherit. We were with our son who could not inherit - and not only because he is not the eldest son. David intends to Cross the Floor of the House, from the Tories to Labour.

Ivor asks if he can wait until he has spoken to Downing Street. That suits David Hacking who has not spoken to Cranborne. Ivor thinks David Hacking feels this may help his chances of staying in the place by being translated into a Life Peer from a Hereditary Peer.

'I didn't discourage him from thinking that.'

'Will it help?'

'It might do.'

Saturday, 9th May

Robin Cook is in trouble again. Were there or were there not British contributions to Sierra Leone's internal troubles? Did or did not Robin Cook know about them? What should and should not have happened?

Sunday, 10th May

I have read Bridget Jones's Diary. Like other fictional diaries and letters—I think of Diary of a Nobody and Daddy-Long-Legs—the whole is a story with a beginning, a middle and an end. A Real Life diary cannot begin and end; it can only start and stop; live and die. I once asked a wise old doctor what he found the hardest part of his job.

'The unsatisfactoriness of endings' he said.

If you look for endings in life you will be disappointed. Endings exist in Art: edges frame pictures; words contain poems; notes hold music; the mind—and language—circumscribe ideas. The point may be that Art can transcend the constraints of its container. Life cannot.

Monday, 11th May

Bob-my-Boss says the rescue of jobs is not confirmed but that 'it should be all right'.

Bob has arranged for me to meet my first New Deal student. New Deal is a New Plan: anybody aged 16-24 who has been unemployed for over six months has to do one of several things if they want to go on getting benefit. One is to come to college. The appointment is for twelve o'clock. I wait until 12.45 and then give up. How can I help somebody who is not there?

Alastair Campbell wants to speak to David Hacking. Where can he contact him? A message is left for him to ring Ivor. He rings while we are having supper.

'Alastair Campbell would like to talk to you if that's all right. Where can he contact you?' David Hacking gives his home number. '

'By the way,' Ivor goes on, 'I've not told anybody except the Chief Whip. He knows.'

David Hacking says he's not told anybody at all.

'Except his wife,' I suppose, says Ivor to me.

We return to our supper.

Tuesday, 12th May

John, Ivor's driver, rings. He's not well. He's got a tumour. He's arranged for another driver to pick Ivor up this morning.

The Study Centre is hot and airless. The sun shines outside.

Suddenly remember being told that a cabinet once had a meeting at which it agreed that if one of them, or one of their families, were taken hostage the remainder of the cabinet would not be blackmailed. Must ask Ivor if this agreement has been repeated with this cabinet. I would like to know.

Ivor gets back to eat but will have to go off again to vote. He has had a busy day.

'My first meeting, with Ann Taylor, took 50 minutes. It should've taken ten.'

When he got back to his room there was Andrew overflowing with his latest inside story. Back in October it was his old friend high up in the DHSS. This time his Private Secretary in the Cabinet Office is 'very close to' Richard Wilson, the new Robin Butler.

The inside story is that there is going to be a Cabinet reshuffle next Thursday week: Gavin Strang and David Clark are Out; HH is Down (but not Out); Peter Mandelson is In.

They speculate that HH will be Minister for Women.

'Harriet's had it,' says Ivor, 'they'll have to have a Minister for Transport.'

'Perhaps Harriet will be given that.'

'Can you imagine John Prescott putting up with Harriet?'

'He might not have any choice.'

'It's his ministry.'

Reflect on Andrew's Latest and conclude it does not add up.

'Would Helen Liddell come in?'

'Or Stephen Byers ... there are lots of them knocking at the door.'

'Jonathan Powell told you there'd be no reshuffle before the summer.'

'Perhaps he meant no reshuffle in the Lords ... Anyway I'm seeing Peter Mandelson tomorrow. I shall ask him.'

'That'll be interesting ... will you be alone with him?'

'That's why I can ask him ... I'll get a reaction ... Andrew got terribly worried when I said I'd ask Peter—said it'd get 'his man' into 'terrible trouble'. I told him I wasn't daft. He's still afraid it'll get back to him.' By whom I understand Andrew himself. 'I'm also going to tell Peter Mandelson that I DO NOT WANT TO RETIRE ... despite anything he hears,' that Other People may be Putting About.

Alastair Campbell has decided the news of David Hacking should come out next Tuesday. They've agreed it'll be handled by the Lords.

'Does David Hacking know any of this?'

'I'll have a word with him tomorrow.'

They all live on tenterhooks: Who knows? Who doesn't know? What is there to know? Who's about to be sacked? Who's about to get a job? Ivor has never felt safe since he was the Labour candidate in Kensington in 1959. He lost. He has lost since. And he has been sacked twice by Margaret Thatcher. He now wonders when he will be sacked by Blair. David Hacking must be wondering if he is being sacked by New Labour before he has even joined.

One of Blair's new peers came to see Ivor today. He's 33 and runs Planet 54—a name to be taken literally as far as I am concerned.

'That is not serious politics,' says Ivor, 'they do not take the Lords seriously ... they want media attention and a few ex-MPs "to keep Ivor happy".'

'Imagine Blair 30 years from now, in the second chamber himself, and living among his mistakes,' I say, 'he'll see the problems he gave you then.'

I ask if the Cabinet has discussed one of its number being kidnapped. It has not.

It has been so hot I have had to water the pots in the backyard.

Wednesday, 13th May

The pots are happier. It is still hot. The laburnum is out on our roundabout.

The painter who came to estimate our painting never came back. Another painter came and he is returning. We are going to be painted.

Ivor saw Peter Mandelson who said: 'There was talk of a reshuffle but I don't think Tony's got time.' Blair has to visit 15 European countries over a few days. He will do three a day. No time for shuffling.

On hearing of Ivor's disinclination to retire, Peter Mandelson says: 'In all the talk of reshuffling, your name has not been mentioned.'

Ivor believes him.

They also discussed how 12 European prime ministers were kept hanging around in Birmingham with nothing to do. 'Tony was badly advised,' says

Peter Mandelson. His irritation with other advisers shows. Advisers are afraid of falling out of favour too. 'Somebody should have thought of it,' says Ivor.

The two of them then walked down to a meeting of the Parliamentary Labour Party which Blair came to talk to. The PLP tackled him on reform of the Lords. Was it definitely going to be in the Queen's Speech? Blair 'more or less' said yes. He also mentioned the Government's success in getting legislation through the Lords where there is no majority 'unlike here'.

Derry is starting to try and get rid of his robes, his breeches and his tights. Another Lord Chancellor, with a less abrasive first year behind him, might have more support. He is also proposing to abolish the Bar, allowing solicitors to appear in court as barristers do.

'The Bar will be furious,' says Ivor.

'Is it just a crazy plan?'

'No ... it's following on from Mackay.'

Ivor is preparing for his loggerheaded Committee tomorrow. Jack Straw is not 'on board':

'I'm going to have a word with Our Jack.'

Thursday, 14th May

Ivor gets up early to read papers for today's PX: John Prescott. I don't think Ivor has got up early to read papers since the Government came in to power. He did it all the time when he was in court. 'Being a barrister is very useful.'

The Study Centre is over 80 degrees Fahrenheit and as I get hotter my temper gets shorter and as the students get hotter they get slower and more restless. None of this is conducive to work.

Bob-My-Boss, suffering under the same conditions, chooses this afternoon to point out rings burnt on 'my new table' by coffee mugs. He brings my fellow ALSters in to show us all while I am working at the table in question. I am not sure whether this is because he thinks I have been abusing his table or so that he can make his point more tactfully by including everybody in his admonishments.'

I greet his complaints with, 'Oh yes ... oh dear ... especially in the sunlight ...' while fellow ALSters are saying, 'I can't see them.'

Bob says he'll bring in beer mats. I suggest Study Centre Coasters. Nobody smiles. Bob leaves us.

'Petty! Bob's being petty!' fellow ALSters dismiss the matter.

Ivor got all but one thing he wanted from his loggerheaded Committee. (Jack Straw was away.) Ivor wants them to publish their Green Paper in July.

Everybody else wants to publish in October.

'You chaired that meeting very well,' he said to Derry afterwards.

'Did I?'

'Yes. I got everything I wanted except for one thing. And,' he continued to me, 'he did chair it well. I have no problem with him now. I have to butter him up. I need him.'

PX saw John Prescott with Hilary Armstrong and Gavin Strang. Gavin Strang is responsible for transport - today. Ivor had read the papers for the meeting with his eyebrows rising. Gavin Strang was suggesting 10 major new road schemes and 22 minor ones. And he was suggesting Vast Tram Plans to be followed by more Vast Tram Plans. The price would be in billions.

'Ten major new road schemes?!' said Ivor to John Prescott.

'What?!' said John Prescott. 'What road schemes?!! That hasn't been agreed. I didn't know that was in the papers!' Gavin Strang shrank.

'Trams … ?' said Ivor.

'What trams?!!' said John Prescott. 'That hasn't been agreed. I didn't know that was in the papers!' Gavin Strang shrank further. He was turned to. He muttered about bringing the roads back to the standards of the Tories' earlier plans.

'Hadn't he cleared it all beforehand?' I am amazed. Ivor shakes his head.

'Hadn't Prescott read his papers?' I am continuing to be amazed.

'His empire is vast. He can't read everything.'

'Hasn't Gavin Strang got the personality to get through to Prescott?'

Ivor shakes his head: 'Gavin Strang will be having a bad evening. A bad evening. You have to stand up to Prescott. I've got a lot of time for John. Ever since 1972 we went to the Sudan together. Until then I thought he was another militant seaman—and he thought I was so right-wing … We get on now.'

I imagine Gavin Strang's crushed evening. He will, if he knows about it, be glad Blair hasn't got time for next Thursday's shuffle.

Friday, 15th May

It is hotter than ever. The lobelia in the backyard is coming into flower. The pink geraniums are fading. The fuchsia flowers' tips are showing. The jasmine is expanding.

We're going to La Traviata at the Albert Hall this evening. We have Chevening seats. Ivor had been Chairman of the trustees for a year before he discovered Chevening had Albert Hall seats.

I don't expect Captain Husband will choose tonight to take his friends to the opera.

When Ivor was leaving William at school this morning, Charlie-The-Caretaker told him: 'Your boss is coming here on Tuesday.'

'!' said Ivor. He knew nothing of this. He set enquiries in motion. Blair will not have time - if Ireland and G8 stop him shuffling they will also stop him visiting schools. But David Blunkett and HH will be there.

'Do they know you have a child in the school?'

'Harriet does now. Fiona told her. Blair knows too, if he took it on board.'

Some of the school staff are uneasy with the Downing Street connection which exists because of the school's proximity to government offices. The last time children from the school were invited to something the school was asked, without subtlety, to send a mixed bag of children. Some staff took offence: they resent their children providing New Labour Backdrop. One of them told me so.

Outside the Albert Hall we meet a local family we know. Its members include two colleagues of Ivor's. Of one of them, Ivor says 'I see him around in Downing Street. I'm not sure what he actually does.'

Inside the Albert Hall we see the consultant who operated on Ivor 18 months ago. He does not see us.

'I'll ask him how he enjoyed La Traviata at my next appointment.'

We do not see Captain Husband.

We both enjoy La Traviata. I am struck by the 'satisfactoriness' of the ending. Violetta's death is A Creation; Real Life Death cannot be A Creation.

Sunday, 17th May

Drive to Wiltshire to visit Denis Carter's farm. There are 3,300 sows and their piglets so, we reckon, 30,000 pigs. And 500 cows. And 4,000 acres. Are they millionaires? We think they must be. Some of the pigs live out in the fields with hummock-like huts. Some of them live in 'Pig Units'. These include the Longest Pig Hut in England. It is Factory Farming. The pigs are in iron pens. They cannot move. There is no bedding. They sell 50,000 pigs a year. Before we saw the 'Pig Units' Denis told us he was not 'happy' with them. They are illegal from the end of the year. I describe our Local Conservative taking a piglet into her kitchen at tea-time to sew up its torn ear. 'None of that here!' says Denis's farming partner with a laugh which has nothing to do with being funny.

We are treated to Sunday lunch of roast lamb with four puddings and wine.

'I've learnt about cruelty to pigs,' says William on the way home.

Monday, 18th May

The Study Centre is hotter.

Charlie-The-Caretaker, reddening in the heat outside the school gate, tells me HH and David Blunkett will be there at 8.30 tomorrow morning.

Ivor comes back hot too. The result of all this heat is that we quarrel. The result of the quarrel is that we do not speak. The result of not speaking is that the Government may have melted away for all I know.

Tuesday, 19th May

According to the radio by the bed, the Government stands.

The school playground is awash with cameras. I snoop. HH is holding forth while children flit round her. The Singing Teacher swats them off. No sign of David Blunkett or his dog.

The school rings. Homework Club is cancelled. I ring Sara and we all picnic in the park. It is cooler in the breeze under the trees.

Ivor gets back to eat but has to go again to vote. He has had his ears tested. Right ear fine. Left ear not fine. His left ear will be supplied with an aid.

'Damien will be pleased,' Lesley tells him.

'Why?'

'He sits on your left.'

'What happened to David Hacking's floor-crossing?' I remember to ask.

'He doesn't want to do it today. His mother's ill. But Denis has seen him and he's filled in the form to join the Labour Party.'

Wednesday, 20th May

Ivor gets back from voting at a quarter to three in the morning.

I take William to school.

It is supposed to be cooler today. I haven't noticed. I expect the weather will change in time for our holiday next week.

Bob-my-Boss has got a perforated eardrum. He is deaf in one ear too.

Ivor has had a letter from Blair agreeing that he should take his pay rise. The Lords, it can be argued, is not the Commons. 'The Prime Minister would prefer there to be no publicity.'

While I am having supper with my friend Jenny of the British Council, and her friend Ann of the Foreign Office, in Pimlico the bulk of the heat is broken by lightning and rain.

Thursday, 21st May

Ivor was not at PX's meeting for Robin Cook: 'Just as well - I'd be on the side of the Foreign Office.' Today they have Clare Short and Jack Cunningham. For Clare's session, 'I'm doing debt—Alistair Darling hands us our subjects.'

I learn that when the Lords was working until dawn Ivor opened his office, his balcony and his drinks cupboard to his peers.

'Did anyone else stay late?'

'Simon and Damien stayed.'

'Was Derry there?'

'Of course not. He's much too grand.'

At Clare Short's PX meeting she dealt with Derry by being rude: 'If you listened to me ...' and

'If you heard what I said you might understand ...' and 'If you let me finish ...'

Derry asked another question.

Clare did not answer.

Derry asked it again.

Clare did not answer.

Derry asked it again.

'I'm waiting for the supplementary,' said Clare.

'I enjoyed it,' says Ivor. 'I like Clare. She can be a pain, but I like her.'

John Prescott chaired the Cabinet Meeting today for the second time in this Government. All went well. Blair was not there because he was working on Ireland. HH and Ivor communicated on paper. She had 'been impressed' by the school. 'Is your child boy or girl?' she asked him and 'Where will he go next?'

'Good question' wrote Ivor, 'on which I am firmly silent.'

'Are you Roman Catholic?'

We are not.

At the Privy Council meeting earlier this week the Queen told Ivor she hoped there would be no trouble when the Japanese Emperor was over next week. 'He is,' she said, 'very, very hard work.'

Ivor's day ended in farce. He had to go to Moss Bros to hire his white tie and tails for the State Banquet for the Japanese. He was driven up to Covent

Garden, entered the shop and was given his ticket to mark his place in the queue. He got to the head of the queue and was stepping in to take his turn when his driver dashed in with a mobile phone: Come Back At Once. There Is A Vote. Ivor dropped his ticket and fled. Back at the House: 'How long have I got?'

'Three minutes.'

He did not have three minutes. He missed the vote. 'Will there be another vote?'

'No.'

He set off for Moss Bros once more. They had rounded Trafalgar Square and were in front of the National Gallery when the mobile phone rang again. Come Back. There's A Vote. He came back and voted.

They set off for Moss Bros for the third time. They arrived and Ivor got another ticket. He got to the head of the queue picked up his white tie and tails. He took them back to the House.

Fiona appeared with a cup of tea and a doughnut: 'You look as if you could do with some carbohydrate.'

Damien spied the Moss Bros bag. Ivor muttered about 'what A Trial a white tie was. What A Bloody Nuisance. What A waste of Time.'

'At least the Government pays for it,' said Damien.

'?!' said Ivor. He has always paid for it himself.

'I'll check,' said Damien. Lesley was back immediately.

'Of course the Government pays.' Ivor found his receipt.

Friday, 22nd May

We get to the house and admire the garage roof.

Ivor listens to reports of the voting in Ireland.

The May blossom is out. We can count the hawthorns down the valley.

Saturday, 23rd May

Ireland has voted to have its own assembly.

'They're all hemmed in to a democratic structure,' say I.

'What do you think was the point of it all?' says Ivor. 'Mo has done very well.'

'She had a lot going for her.'

'Yes.'

'Her age, her sex, her education, her type ... and her brain tumour.'

'Paisley will be exposing that as a plot soon ... It'll be interesting to see how

David Trimble handles it ... he's got to have No-Voters with him in the chamber.'

'He's never been part of violence has he?'

'No, I don't think any of the Unionist politicians have.'

'Mo will know that.'

'She has no illusions about any of them.'

I learn that Ivor had a letter last week telling him that his Security Risk Rating has risen from Liqht to Moderate.

The wind here has risen from Light to Moderate too. I ask Ivor what he is going to do.

'I suppose I should look under the car a bit more ... I don't want the police crawling all over the place.'

We walk to our wood.

Monday, 25th May

There is a bird which trills with the same tone as the telephone. When we are sitting outside with our cups or glasses of this and that we think the telephone is ringing. We nip in to answer it to find it silent. The bird is continuing to trill. I cannot identify it but I know that a bird with a sense of humour could have a lot of fun.

William has found two ways of getting Ivor to nip at his nippiest:

'Number 10's on the phone' and 'Blair is making a statement.'

Number 10 was on the phone on Friday. Ivor did not nip because he thought it was a prank.

It was Fiona—'I don't know why she came through Number 10' - to say Lady Richard is to Process with the Royal Party into the State Banquet tomorrow. 'I thought she'd want to know.'

The Royal Party remains short of women. I'll be with the Duke of Gloucester: 'I think he's an architect,' says Ivor.

Tuesday, 26th May

We catch the train to London to go to the dinner, feed the hamster and the gerbils, and to make sure the painters painting us are all right. We find Peter Samuel's numberplate on the doormat. There are three phone calls from the Government Car Service to get a car organised to take us to the dinner. (It must be at least a mile.) The Car Service is in turmoil: John has gone into hospital today; Barry (Clare Short's driver) has had a heart attack, aged 42. Ivor starts his Moss Bros routine late enough to fluster himself. The phone calls, which punctuate the routine, fluster him further. Then buttons begin bursting off his rented waistcoat across the kitchen and into the painters' debris.

'I shall be Having A Word with Moss Bros.'

None of us—me, Ivor, William, Monica—can find one of the buttons.

'You'll have to go without it.' (Me.)

'I can't.' (Ivor.)

At 7.50 p.m. he goes without it. And with a driver who has been brought out of retirement.

At 8.05 p.m. we are standing waiting to go in to have our first drink (I wouldn't like to call it anything so crude as queuing) and I put my hand to my head to find my hair is wet from its wash in honour of the occasion.

I am processed into dinner by the Duke of Gloucester who, like Angus Ogilvy last time, is kind to me. I also sit next to Prince Michael of Kent and feel like a member of the audience who has taken the door on to the stage by mistake. It was Gloucester in King Lear who had his eyes put out—'vile jelly!'; we have strawberry mousse for pudding, no jelly. I ask this Gloucester about his architecture: 'I'm a retired architect. People don't want a duke as an architect.'

'Everybody has their prejudices. Couldn't you practise under another name?'

'I tried as Richard Gloucester but...'

I describe our houseful of paint. He asks about our wallpaper. I laugh (oh Derry!) and tell him I have never put wallpaper on a wall in my life.

I admire the Queen Mother (aged 97 and three-quarters) at the end of the table: 'How does she do it?—all those operations, all those bereavements.'

'She doesn't think about it—she doesn't think "Oh, no, I've got to sit next to the Archbishop of Canterbury again!"'

Prince Michael of Kent asks me what I know of Japan. I tell him that all I know is restricted to my great-uncle's imprisonment and forced labour on the Railway Line during the war, my family's refusal to buy Japanese goods and my own discomfort at finding myself at this dinner.

'A lot of people here would feel like that if you asked them.' I ask him if he's been to Japan. He has; three times. He adds 'I am going to Siberia on Monday.' I laugh ... 'Yes that's quite a good line, isn't it.'

He is brushing up his Russian. I tell him the only Russian I know is, that 'Ladybird' translates as 'God's little cow'. He translates it.

The Duke of Gloucester processes me out of dinner towards coffee. I look at a domed ceiling and wonder if it is mock-Palladian. It isn't, I am told, because Palladio was the man who worked out proportion so a ceiling is either Palladian or it isn't. It can't be mock-Palladian. The ceiling is neo-classical. (It is also ugly with podgy cherubs disporting themselves round the rim.)

'The ladies are supposed to separate.'

I am pointed to a further room where about five of them are starting on their coffee—'but it doesn't usually work'—we see Cherie Blair and two other ladies chatting by the men and not moving into the further room: I make a little joke: 'I don't think it would work with New Labour!' and move on as I have been bidden.

Princess Alexandra is looking after me: 'Would you like some coffee? It won't keep you awake.' The Queen Mother is standing firm on her new hip. The Queen comes over to us. She says of her mother, 'pretty good isn't it?' to which I say that it makes me want to kneel down. I think the Queen misunderstands me—thinking I am making some anti-curtseying crack—for she blows her mouth out in a raspberry. I try and put this right by muttering 'an example to us all'.

I see the Queen Mother taking to a chair and my observation tells me she is having to make an even bigger effort than she did last time I saw her at work here. She is hurting.

Wednesday, 27th May

The painters are installed, the gerbils and the hamster are fed and we catch the train back to the house.

Our gate is swinging wide. It has been lifted off its latch by about 150 sheep who have invaded our field. They have been so successful that the latch has disappeared. Our field is rich in grass (the land outside our field is not) and the sheep have feasted so fully that they have had diarrhoea over the French cricket pitch, the rugby pitch, the swing-ball pitch, the baseball pitch, the scratch-ball pitch, the football pitch and, most particularly, the spot where we sit with our cups and glasses of this and that, the path from the gate to our house and the front and back door steps. I herd the sheep out of the gate while Ivor rescues a lamb that has trapped its head in wire by the pussy willow.

William empties the car and unpacks the shopping until Ivor discovers he has also trodden lakes of sheep shit into the house and across the carpet. Ivor scrubs the carpet. I, having herded the sheep out, try to sheep-proof the gate which means inventing a latch. I use a chain and a miniature stake.

The Local Conservative comes over the hill to check on his cattle in the field opposite. He is especially concerned to check on Sam, his bull, who is the successor of Francis who choked to death on a potato. Sam is content. We eye the Grey Bull in the field next to ours. William describes how they have been roaring at each other.

'They don't usually fight,' says our Local Conservative. He is thinking of going to Australia.

Throughout the evening, the sheep who have now bloated themselves into inactivity heave at the gate. I watch them and feel smug.

Thursday, 28th May

5.10 a.m. I am less smug. It is light. There is a cacophony, a hullabaloo. There are thumps and bleats. Some of the bleats are gutteral, some of the bleats are pitched 'gimlet-like' (as Ivor puts it later).

Sheep have massed, swarmed and are marauding.

The thumps are sheep resting their blown bellies against our walls. The bleats are sheep who have lost each other between the washing line and the japonica.

I cannot pretend it is not happening. I have no more chance of continuing to sleep than I have of flying. I get out of bed and put on my boots and Ivor's coat and head into the dawn sunlight and about 150 sheep. It is beautiful.

The gate is as wide as it ever was.

I herd once more.

I spy Ivor's head (he cannot be wearing his coat) appearing from odd corners. Then disappearing – so he does not deter the sheep from leaving the field. I think it is called Moral Support.

I create another latch. The night's sleep is over.

Two walkers appear: can they use our telephone? The National Trust have found them camping and told them they cannot camp where they are. They have to move. I hear them describe me to the person they are asking to come and pick them up. I had never thought of myself as 'a dear old farmer lady' before. It is the 'old' that stings.

Coming back from taking William to ride I can see that my sheep-proofing is holding. Sam, however, is less sanguine. He is standing at his gate bellowing and pawing the mud. The Grey Bull is doing the same thing at his hedge. He is also jumping up and down. The earth shakes.

I ring the bulls' owners: I do not wish to watch the beginnings of rampage, let alone combat, without passing on responsibility for failing to do anything about it.

Roger comes down in his all-purpose vehicle. The bulls calm down. 'If they get out and start fighting ... I wouldn't do anything about it if I were you.'

I certainly wouldn't, I agree.

Ivor wonders if our car would be all right.

Two crows and three hawks fight over their space in the sky. The hawks dive at the crows. The crows pester the hawks.

By evening, a sheep has settled down to die by the stream.

Friday, 29th May

The dying sheep is not quite dead. Her lamb keeps her company.

The next time I see her the crows are taking out her eyes. Her lamb has wandered away with other sheep.

Saturday, 30th May

I go the Annual General Meeting of our local preservation association. We hear that the Government gives more money to 'opera in London' than it does to all of the national parks put together. Politicians and Planners are the twin evils to our association. Our mantra is that our national parks should be 'wild and free forever'. Ivor wishes he had been a fly on the wall.

A thunderstorm. Our wires are hit and the telephone leaps in the air with a crack and a flash of blue. I unplug it and our television. Then we discover we have lost our electricity.

Within two hours the Sir Galahads of SWEB hove over the horizon in an orange all-purpose vehicle.

'You all right?'

'Yes. And pleased to see you.'

'The lightning struck the transformer. We'll have you back on soon.'

Half an hour later the kettle is boiling and over tea and ginger biscuits we learn of the virtues of SWEB.

Sunday, 31st May

We have to leave for London.

We find plenty of evidence of painting. We also find that, in order to paint, the freezer has been unplugged. It has not been plugged in again. Its contents are wet and wilting. We throw them out.

Our living conditions are rudimentary. Ivor thinks they would be improved if we had milk and bread and cheese.

Monday, 1st June

The painters are sorry about the freezer.

Lambeth College is a refuge from dust and ladders and disorder.

Get a note telling us that this year's ballot on whether or not to strike over redundancies has been won by Norman & Co—by four votes. I wonder if we will strike.

Read that Lambeth College is planning to 'update' its IT equipment. What will it do with the 'outdated' equipment? Lambeth College has hundreds of machines. William's school has about two and a half. I expect I will feel I have to do something about this.

Visit the school to enquire if they want secondhand IT stuff.

Ivor rings to say he may be home in fifteen minutes and have to go back to vote or he may be home in an hour and not have to go back to vote.

Ivor rings to say he is coming 'now'. He will have to go back again.

We perch in the kitchen with pasta.

Lesley rings to say The Whip is Off. No more votes.

Ivor changes out of his suit. He dozes.

Simon rings to say The Whip is On.

'What! ... I'll have to change ...' Ivor runs into his suit and tie and shoes and out of the front door.

Ivor rings: 'I missed it ... there may be more ... you'd better go to bed.'

Tuesday, 2nd June

Ivor tells me he got back at one o'clock this morning.

The painter wants to pay us for the food lost from the freezer. In the middle of the day I have a brainwave: why doesn't he paint the bathroom instead? It would be worth more to us than it would, cost him. I ring Ivor and put it to him. 'Good idea.' While I plod on at Lambeth College he is Getting On Top of the Paperwork.

When I get home the painter likes my brainwave too.

When Ivor gets home I hear Derry is 'at it again'. One of the statues he has borrowed for his residence he has found is too big. He wants to move it to his entrance. He says it needs a new plinth. That will be £10,000. And he is not happy with his lighting. Of course there was no electricity in Pugin's day but antique lights at £4,000 would ease the situation.

'It'll bring the whole thing back on to the front pages,' says Ivor.

'You'll have to say something to him.'

'I'm not supposed to know about it.'

'Derry can't have learnt anything.'

'And he's got a spin doctor all of his own and he didn't know anything about it.'

'Who told him?' Pause.

'Oh, someone who knows him better than me rang him up and he said "What?? ... What!!"'

'Aha ... so that way you may be able to bring Derry under control.'

Ivor changes the subject.

'I'm seeing him tomorrow and I've got to tell him people won't wear him taking off his wig.'

'What about the breeches and tights?'

'He might just get away with that. But I've discovered he gets extra allowance for presiding over the House.'

Poor Derry! He rises to these illustrious heights to find himself tied to a woolsack, buttoned into breeches and topped with a wig. And when he has the wrong lights and is short of a plinth somebody tells.

Maybe Damien is right and Derry will throw off his restraints and GO.

'They're all going mad,' Ivor continues. Donald Dewar says a Scottish gallery has had a good idea and would like a portrait of the Cabinet. It will cost £100,000. 'Donald ought to know better.'

'It's amazing what vanity causes people to do.' I shake my head as if it had never had a vain thought in it.

'Do you know, the Foreign Office got on to me to say that because I am going to Manila and Vietnam and it will be hot, I should get a lightweight suit made and they will pay for it.'

Ivor is going to Manila and Vietnam next week. Lady Richard was invited too. It is one of the rarest of moments: I wish I was Lady Richard and could go.

I wonder how many suits the Foreign Office has paid for over the years. They must have begun paying when politicians stopped being men of independent means.

Wednesday, 3rd June

I spend part of the day putting myself in the middle of A Situation. As I suspected, I am beginning to regret it already. As I have said, Lambeth College is getting rid of 'outdated software and old machines' and buying at 'least 440 'better' computers. At the same time William's school limps along with nearly no machines of any kind. It cannot afford to buy one 'better' one.

What is Lambeth College doing with its 'outdated software and old machines'?

I ring the man who 'leads for the College on curriculum IT issues'. He tells me to ring the Head of Information Services.

He tells me that what they do with them is a decision for Senior Management.

'Who is Senior Management?'

'The Finance Director.'

I ring the Finance Director.

Yes. He has spoken to 'the lawyers'. Institutions that sign disclaimers can take over Lambeth College's 'old machines'.

I ring the school. They cannot believe me. They consult their part-time music-teacher-cum-accountant-cum-computer-buff. Yes.

I ring the Head of Information Services: 'I spoke to the Finance Director and he says they can go to the school if the school signs a disclaimer.'

'It may be easier for us to give them all to one dealer ... how many does the school want?'

I understand the Head of Information Services to be saying that it is easier to hand over many rather than few.

'50, 60?'

'Oh, I thought you only wanted about six.'

'Oh, no ... and it's not me, it's the school ... I'll ring the school and confirm a number.'

I ring the school: 'I know it sounds mad but it's easier for the College to hand over more rather than less ... I mention fifty ... how many can you take?'

The school goes away to consult. I ring back. The part-time music-teacher-cum-accountant-cum-computer-buff says they can take fifty. I ring the Head of Information Services: 'Fifty please.'

'Let me have the details.'

Two days ago we had a letter from the Throne of Lambeth College: although we have not had to lose staff compulsorily this year (so many are going voluntarily), 'simple arithmetic' tells us we will have to lose about eighty next year. The implied plea is Please Go. Even I can see that we are being replaced by at least 440 'better' computers.

The painters proceed apace. We are eating standing up as our seats are being painted and our table is under wraps.

In the evening we go to an 'At Home' given by Princess Alexandra and Angus Ogilvy. Ivor and Angus Ogilvy have forged a Working Link: 'The Prince's Trust: 'It's a good scheme,' says Ivor, 'it gives small sums of money, sometimes quite large sums of money, to start young people in their own business. Most of the businesses take off.'

Angus Ogilvy has used Ivor to connect the Trust to the New Labour Government. He found Ivor and said We Don't Know Any Labour People ... Help!

'One thing us minor royals can do,' he told Ivor,' is raise money for good causes.'

Ivor is asked to the At Home to reinforce the Working Link. Angus Ogilvy had a good meeting with the Treasury this morning.

'Do you need to see Alistair Darling?' asks Ivor.

'Not at the moment.'

'Let me know when you do.'

As we are standing over our supper at the end of the day Ivor wonders how I can write up the At Home. 'I know. It'll be difficult to do it all without being silly.'

This is because although the At Home was for bankers and politicians (all but about four of the Old Tory Wet Establishment, not one from the Shadow Cabinet), it was peppered with people I regard as frauds. They spent their time circulating and smiling and kissing rather than talking. Among them was one plus husband, I have known since I was a child. I had to introduce myself twice. I think they stopped seeing my parents years ago. Jones The Pictures and Jones The Books are not Circulators nor Smilers nor Kissers. And they are Talkers.

Apart from those politicians and bankers peppered with frauds was a smattering of War-horses: grand old aristocratic females, no doubt widows, Landed Ships of State in disastrous silk Frocks who did not give A Damn. They have a splendour all of their own.

I think our hosts know what surrounds them.

Still standing, we discuss the fraud plus husband from my childhood.

'I don't think they were pleased to see me. She didn't say a word to me. He was very uncomfortable.'

'Yes?' said Ivor, 'he felt intruded upon ... found out ... you know too much about him. You know he's basically a fraud. And he can't stand me.'

'Why not?'

'I don't know. But it's mutual.'

'I told him you'd told me he didn't speak much in the House and asked if that was his policy and he said he made set pieces.'

'I hadn't noticed.'

Ivor did not see Derry today. 'I waited for him for an hour.'

But Ivor did have lunch with a journalist, and they discussed who were the successes of the Cabinet.

'We agreed entirely. He said Derry had become a figure of fun and the only way for that to be put right would be for him to stay silent for five years.'

Thursday, 4th June

I send the school's details to Lambeth College's Head of Information Services. I wonder if he is going to change his mind about giving machinery away and mention money. There is a rumour that Lambeth College has gone hundreds of thousands of pounds over budget in its plans to rebuild parts of itself to fit in the parts that are being moved from other parts. Plans have to be redrawn. What will happen if we are not ready for the beginning of term in September? Not to worry! We will rent portacabins and put them in the car park.

My mind boggles.

I remember to go to the ladies before I go home. Both of our bathrooms are wreathed in wet paint as rewards for my foresight.

Ivor gets home to eat between votes: 'I am very pleased with my little committee.'

'Which?' I can't be sure this is the loggerheaded Committee. It must be less loggerheaded.

'Reform. They are all moving away from a joint committee of both Houses towards a Royal Commission which is what I've wanted all along.'

'Was Jack Straw there?'

'Oh yes, it was a proper meeting. They have stopped having their knee-jerk reactions and have started thinking about it.'

'What's made the difference?'

'My paper. I submitted a paper explaining how complicated the numbers were in a joint committee—how it wouldn't guarantee a government majority—and they've read it properly and thought about it. It'll have to go to Blair for a decision but we can give it a gentle steer towards a Royal Commission.'

'How long would a Royal Commission sit for?'

'18 months. Two years.'

'It'd all take ages ... what's the timetable?'

'We'd get it through the Lords in 99. Perhaps 2000 if the Tories block it. The Royal Commission could sit until 2002. The Government would give evidence to it. Then the Government would decide what it wanted to do with the recommendations. That would be after the next election. I have always said it would take six years.'

'I've never heard you say that before.'

'I say it in every speech I make.'

'I don't hear your speeches. I live with you ... it really is a huge reform – much bigger than all those assemblies.'

'Yes. It is. Much bigger.'

We continue eating pasta. We won't be having pasta for a long time after the painters have finished.

'Did you see Derry about his wig?'

'Yes. I did. Three times. All he could think about all day was his bloody wig. I told him I thought I could get him out of his breeches but not his wig.'

'Why not?' said Derry.

'You're not the most popular person in the House.'

'Why not?'

'Your wallpaper.'

'The House behaved very badly over that. The House failed to take responsibility for that. It was initiated by Tom Legge.'(TL was Derry's senior civil servant at the time.)

'Derry!'

'Don't you believe me?'

'Derry – I've seen the papers.'

'Don't you believe me?'

'Don't push me, Derry.'

'Do you believe me?'

'No!'

'How could you ...'

'And if Tom Legge did suggest it, you should have thought about it. Your antennae should have told you, advised you not to do it ... Denis advised you not to do it ... And,' Ivor says he looked Derry straight in the eye, 'there had better not be any more expenditure.'

'No,' said Derry, 'there isn't—except bookshelves for the office.'

'No!' say I, 'Unless his spin doctor's spoken to him and he's dropped the lights and the plinth.'

'I've seen the papers,' Ivor shakes his head.

'Doesn't he realise you must know?'

'He's *twp*,' Ivor shakes his head again, 'that's what he is. He's *twp*' Ivor speaks Welsh in extremis.

Derry tried another tack with his wig: 'The Prime Minister is very keen on it.'

'In that case I'll go and see the Prime Minister.' Derry backed off.

Ivor does not believe Blair spends his time thinking about Derry's wig.

Then I learn that Ivor has left the 'fucking' thises and the 'fucking' thats out of the dialogue: relayed cold with our domestic pasta they would be resoundingly shaming.

'Derry's a bully ... a bully ... you just have to stand up to him . . . that was how it went ... two cabinet ministers f-ing and blinding at each other.'

Friday, 5th June

The painting should be finished today.

I work on this at work.

Ivor is making a speech on reform on Monday. He is not saying anything he has not said before, and not much more than was in the manifesto.

'The difference is that Downing Street is puffing it ... some people still don't believe it's going to happen.'

He sent a copy of the speech to Downing Street and a copy to Peter Mandelson for approval. Peter Mandelson came back: it should be 'more magisterial'. Ivor says what he thinks he should say and tolerates the ritual of seeking approval.

I tell Ivor I am pleased with how I have Written Up last Wednesday's At Home: 'I think I've solved it by not using names ... I've put the people into categories ... lists of names are boring.' Ivor listens. 'They were politicians, bankers, frauds – and old aristocrats.'

'I saw one of those ... She's rather splendid.'

'I've described the politicians as mostly Old Tory Wets.'

'Oh no—you can't describe all the Tories like that!' He names exceptions.

'All right then. How can I describe them?'

'The failed politicians of the 1980s.'

'They're not failed! Or only in the sense that all politicians fail in the end.' Ivor makes an expression which I understand as disagreement.

'All right then—who's not a failed politician?'

'Blair.'

'He's not had time to fail yet.'

'He may resign. Though most of them can't let go.'

'D'you want to read my diary—just the At Home bit?'

'No.'

There is silence. 'Oh,' I say.

'Maybe in the summer when I'm feeling stronger but the thought of it makes me ...'

Ivor mimes falling into a pit without a bottom.

'I suppose it could embarrass the Government.'

'It certainly would. What you should do is walk away from me now and sell it. You'd make money and it would be the end of my career.'

'Then the diary would stop too. I don't want to do that! I suppose it'll make less money in ten years' time. Do you think people will still be interested?'

'Oh, yes. I think people will still be interested.'

Saturday, 6th June

We clean. Every now and then Damien rings up about Ivor's appearance on ITV's news this evening.

Monday, 8th June

We did not get so far as cleaning the basement floor. The dirt is being carried up through the cleaned house by draughts and our feet.

The painter takes away the ladders and empty pots of paint. There is more cleaning to be done.

I arrive at Lambeth College to find the door from the car park has been taken off.

'What's happening?'

'You're getting swipe cards.'

I remember—back in March—hearing the rumour that £3,000 was going to be spent on swipe cards. I did not realise this also meant getting a new door. I go and get my Personal Swipe Card from security.

Ivor made his speech and said the things he had been saying for months. The rest of his day trundled by. The one stir was that Gordon Brown wants to see him tomorrow and Ivor's office can't find out what he wants to see him about.

'He won't say. It's probably Dorneywood.' Dorneywood is the Government house for the Chancellor which he is not using and John Prescott is. Ivor chairs the trustees.

'It might not be,' say I

'What could it be then?'

'Maybe he wants you on board over some disagreement with Blair; maybe he's seeing every member of PX one by one to sound out their views; maybe he wants you to provide a Heavyweight Political Perspective on what he wants to do with all the money ... health? ... education?'

'At any rate he can't sack me!'

'No. I think he'll be worried. He's got these huge decisions to make quite soon, isn't it?'

'Yes. July. Why should he be worried? He's the Chancellor of the Exchequer!'

'Oh, come on ... you've been around long enough to know that most of those people are driven by anxieties and insecurities ... absolutely haunted by them. Unless they're no good. Or nutters. I should think Gordon Brown lives on his nerves the whole time.'

'True.'

If Gordon Brown knew that Ivor was thinking—with relief—'he can't sack me' he would be astonished.

Tuesday, 9th June

I arrive at work to find the new door in place. It has no lock of any kind and opens when I touch it with my elbow. I stay at work for about an hour. There is nothing to do. Nobody around. When I leave there are three men working on the new door ... talk about locking the stable door after all the horses have bolted. I suppose it will stop the new machinery walking out on its own.

Lesley and Ivor went over to see Gordon Brown and Lesley was not allowed in. Ivor did not see the need to be so Hush Hush. 'I suppose they're afraid of leaks.'

Alistair Darling was there too and for 40 minutes the three of them took an overview of the ministers and their submissions to PX. All the ministers have been heard and it is decision time. They agreed that Frank Dobson and David Blunkett were the most disappointing: making whopping blanket bids claiming they needed more money for everything. No priorities. No organisation. No planning. No alternatives. They agreed that George Robertson had done well - though Gordon Brown is not sympathetic to him. ('There are too many Scots around the place.' said Ivor.) They agreed that John Prescott had done well. And Jack Straw was OK too.

'Now that we have seen all of them we have to look at the gaps,' says Ivor.

'What gaps?'

'Being the puritanical Scot he is, Gordon wants to pay off some of the National Debt before the next election.'

I realise that of the money that Gordon has got 'sloshing about' (Ivor's phrase) he does not want to give it all to ministers to spend.

'We agreed that he'd have to give some to Dobson and Blunkett but he's got to make sure it goes to the right places.'

'I suppose Gordon thinks he runs the country.'

'Well ...' Ivor gives me A Look which I read as 'you could say he does'.

Gordon also told Ivor that he does not want to go through this process again. He wants to make this one last three years. He is making a statement to say so in two days' time.

'He'll do it if he can get away with it. Ministers won't like it.'

The newspapers listened to Ivor's speech yesterday as if he had never spoken before.

Most are on his side.

Denise-The-Driver saw Ivor walking towards her down a corridor. She sniffed and turned away from him. Denise is not on Ivor's side. Sides do seem to be being taken.

Cranborne appears to have Hague over a barrel. 'It'll be interesting to see Hague defending the hereditary peers in the Commons.'

Wednesday, 10th June

The new door at Lambeth College remains lockless.

I spend two hours marking students' work. Six of the 13 students have done what they ought to have done to earn their certificates. I make a copy of my marks and put it in a safe place. I need to keep evidence of the marks that I gave.

A fellow ALSter tells me of the 13 New Deal students he started with and the four that are left:

'You can say what you like about New Deal but you cannot force people to come here. They drift off to whatever other ways they've got of earning money.'

Bob-My-Boss tells me that 'they' were in the Study Centre yesterday afternoon and 'they' plan to knock through the back of the Study Centre into the next classroom over the summer, ready for next term. 'They' will demolish Bob's office in the process. I think Bob is referring to 'them' as 'they' because 'they' include Danny, the Study Centre Supremo, and he does not want to speak ill of his Football Friend and Carousing Crony.

I collude because I want to get to the facts: 'I thought "they" were going to completely rebuild this place next year!'

'"They" are.'

'Then I don't see the point of "them" fiddling about with it now. What a waste of money.'

'Yes.' Bob is glum.

I do not cheer Bob by foreseeing that it will never be ready by next term, that dust will get into the machinery and that none of it will work.

I rush back at midday to meet Ivor for a sandwich while he packs for Manila and Vietnam.

'Gordon was very late for PX this morning. He was seeing Blair on his way. He is going to make this statement tomorrow. And he does want to get into the black on the National Debt. We're coming back from Vietnam a day early. There are some very big PX meetings. And I've got to sort out Liz Symons. I spoke to her this morning. She's in Seattle. I told her to stay there. I've had a good press.'

A photocopy of a cartoon is dropped on to the stairs.

'This has arrived.' I show Ivor a letter telling us our house is not subsiding, though we need a new drain: our leaking drain could give us problems in the future.

'I'm going to have to fight to keep Lords' Reform in the Queen's speech. There's so much legislation for the Northern Ireland assembly that we are going to have to get through.'

Tony and Lesley arrive to drive to Heathrow. Ivor leaves for Manila and Vietnam.

It rains. William and I watch bits of Scotland playing Brazil.

An envelope arrives containing telephone numbers in Manila and Vietnam. I ring Fiona to thank her and as I do so Brazil scores a goal. I can hear the whole of Ivor's office shouting at the office television. The shouting must be echoing down those House of Lords' corridors.

Thursday, 11th June

We get a phone call from Manila. Manila is hot.

Lambeth College's new door opens at the touch of my elbow.

Drift through my 'working' day doing a bit to this. Bob tells me he is opposing 'their' plans to tinker with the Study Centre walls. When I leave three more people are working on the open door.

While William is having his piano lesson I listen to Gordon Brown's statement. I wonder if Ivor knew his plans to sell off government assets.

It is cold.

Friday, 12th June

Sun!

The school playground is sprinkled with children in blue and white. It is a non-uniform day. You pay a pound to school funds and you can wear your own clothes for the day. The children have come in their own uniform: football colours.

I do not go in to Lambeth College. I would have nothing to do except report on the door. Perhaps it will be locked by Monday.

Read the Good Press of Wednesday. *The Independent* says Ivor 'shows every sign of being a genuine reformer'. The Express has a cartoon of a military Ivor aiming a machine gun through a Lords' Reform fence at a turbaned Cranborne who holds a sabre. A military Blair is sitting on the fence.

Ivor has loads of ammunition and Cranborne has a placard: 'Down with the Infidel'.

Saturday, 13th June

Phone call from Manila. Lesley is catching the next flight home. Her mother is dying.

William and I go to Oxford. Helen of the Treasury is Unwell. Homer wants to ride in Nelson's buggy which, long ago, was William's buggy. I bought it in Scotland with my Oldest Friend.

Saturday, 14th June

Back in London and a phone call from Vietnam. Ivor had five hours to kill in Singapore between flights. He met Clare Short doing the same thing. They killed the five hours together over lunch. I am asked who's got a peerage (there are birthday honours out now). I don't know.

William starts Being Ill.

Monday, 15th June

William continues Being Ill. I cannot leave him and go to Lambeth College. I ring Bob and tell him I am working at home. I certainly am.

I start Being Ill.

Tuesday, 16th June

Ivor gets back at dawn. He is Not Very Well. He and William are Not Very Well together while I struggle to work.

The door does not open. I try my swipe card. The door does not open. I try my swipe card. The door does not open. This continues until the door does open.

Meet an Art and Design person: 'They're talking about sacking people and they spend £3,000 on this!'

Bob mentions the fact that the Chair of Governors at Lambeth College has been made a dame. Bob also mentions that the governors are spending a weekend away in a hotel at the expense of Lambeth College. Since they are talking about sacking people and are paying for X thousand square metres of space in central London it seems extraordinary to pay for more square metres for a weekend outside London.

Read that we are offering a new course: Cleaning Science.

When I get home Ivor goes to work. He comes home with snippets of what he's missed. A mouse strolls across the backyard while I hear them. The in-tray was three and a half feet high. The Liz-Symons-Lie-Issue has not died down. David Hacking has crossed the floor. 'There's another coming.'

There is worry that Lords' reform won't be in the Queen's speech—'I don't know what I'd do. I suppose I'd have to resign.'

And Lesley's mother died before she got home.

I tell him of the four from 13 New Deal students. I am told: 'New Deal will be a success. A lot of people have got a lot riding on that. The Government will say it is a success.'

'The Grass Roots will know something different.'

Wednesday, 17th June

The mouse has strolled into the house overnight.

The door at work opens at my second attempt.

Sit and work on my own.

Two architects enter. They have drawings of the Study Centre after it has been tinkered with. I snoop.

'What happens to the sink?'

'Yes. I'll do something about that.'

I buy mouse poison on the way home.

Ivor thinks the Privy Council thinks he is going to be in his job for some time. They have suggested that they pay for him to have white tie and tails made. They think it would be cheaper in the long run than paying for him to hire them each time they're needed.

'I spent an hour with Derry today.'

'On his wig and breeches?'

'No.'

'What then?'

'Next session. It's going to be a very short session. We won't get a Queen's Speech until the end of November ... and the next would be in the October. Derry has got two pieces of legislation he wants to get through—legal aid and the reform of the Bar. I suggested he put one in the first session and one in the second. He didn't think that was a good idea at all. I then made another suggestion—that we combine the sessions and have one long one.'

'And one Queen's Speech?'

'Yes.'

'And?'

'Derry wasn't sure—so none of them supported me—not Ann Taylor—though Nick Brown pricked up his ears. And David Milliband did.'

'They're frightened of Derry.'

'Yes, they seem to be.'

'They think he's got far more power than he has got.'

'I'm not so sure.'

'Were you the only one there who stood up to him today?'

'Yes. Anyway, in the entire meeting nobody suggested delaying reform of the Lords.'

When Simon and Ivor were walking back to Ivor's office, Simon asked what was 'behind' Ivor's suggestion. 'He seems to think there is a plot.'

'But you're only trying to find more time to get more legislation through.'

'Exactly.'

The Express has offered last week's cartoon for £150.

I put down the mouse poison.

Thursday, 18th June

The mouse poison has not been touched.

The door opens at my first swipe!

Learn that the Study Centre was kept open over half-term for New Deal students. Three staff sat waiting for them all day all week. Not one came.

There is a rumour that Lambeth College's chief New Dealer has been sacked.

Ivor rings before he comes home. The Foreign Office has asked him and Lady Richard to fly to Fiji for ten days at the end of the summer. The Foreign Office suggests Lord and Lady Richard have a holiday before or after a Fijiean jamboree.

Can we go?

We play pros and cons.

Prime pro is that we want to go.

Prime con is eight years old.

We decide to discuss it this evening.

This evening comes and the dilemma remains.

24 hours in a plane is a long time for anyone and is too long to impose on an eight-year-old to suit his parents' pleasure. Could we leave him behind? Where? There are not many options. We cannot go.

At PX this morning Alistair Darling led an overview of what they should do with the money.

Ivor said what he believes: that Health and Education were the most disappointing bids and both have to be given money. They cannot be given £4billion each and left to get on with it. They have to decide priorities.

'Did everybody agree?'

'Yes.'

'Why didn't anybody else say it?'

'They've got departments.'

'And they're worried about their jobs, I suppose.'

'Yes. And I am detached. When I said that it was easier for me because I hadn't got a department, there were guffaws. But I won't be popular with Blunkett. We agreed that he and Dobson must each produce a paper with some priorities. They won't be pleased with me.'

The press are occupied by a row between Brown and Beckett, saying cabinet decided for Brown and against Beckett.

'They were sitting together at today's meeting. Things were perfectly pleasant. Relations were fine. It hasn't even been mentioned in cabinet ... there was no cabinet today. Blair's in Strasbourg. Prescott's in Luxembourg.'

PX's other problem is that Social Security is not under its control: it's 'by far the biggest expense. By far. And it's been put in a special little committee under Blair.' Ivor shakes his head.

'Blair can't make all the decisions himself. He can't stay on top of everything,' I say.

'Jim does not approve. He does not approve at all. He doesn't think that is what a Prime Minister should do. He thinks the departments should be left to get on with it and the Prime Minister should watch. The risk is that Blair could burn himself out.'

'The country will get sick of him one day ... he's doing all the PR.'

'Yes. And he's good at it. He's very good at it.'

David Hacking is not getting a warm welcome from the Labour peers: 'At a party meeting Merlyn asked what qualified a Tory peer to join the Labour Party.'

'What did you say?'

'He had to apply.'

'Was Hacking there?'

'No. Margaret Jay is leading 'a little rebellion'. She thinks ministers in the Lords are working too hard. And she's got a point—if they're there until two in the morning and then have a departmental meeting at 8.30. There's her, of course, Tessa Blackstone, Liz Symons, Pat Hollis, Helene Hayman ... though she doesn't seem to mind, she's been in the Commons. None of the others have. The ex-MPs are OK. And the trade unionists are solid as rocks ... we'll have to see if we can do something about it. Jim thinks they're working too hard. And he had a divided cabinet and a minority government for five years. Blair hasn't got the ideological divide.'

'I suppose,' I suppose, 'you lot are held together by wanting to win the next election.'

'And how.'

'I suppose,' I suppose again, 'that a few cracks will show before the next election but nothing much until after it.'

Later in the evening Ivor returns to Blunkett's and Dobson's bids: 'It really wasn't good enough just to ask for more money for everything.'

'I told you how amazed I was by the mess of David Blunkett's.'

'You're not supposed to have seen it.'

'I can't believe,' I really can't believe, 'that cabinet ministers' partners never see cabinet papers.'

'If you're not careful, it-' by which Ivor means this diary, 'will have to be vetted by Richard Wilson.'

I give a queen-like raspberry.

'This is nothing to do with him. I'm just astonished that it hasn't been done before.'

Ivor brings home cabinet papers about twice a year—as a matter of policy to protect home from work. But cabinet papers must be spread about many cabinet ministers' homes much of the time. And cabinet ministers' partners have eyes and minds of their own. Given that any person's job is part of any person's life, it must be a sad and peculiar partnership that does not share it.

Ivor is kept abreast of Lambeth College. He reads whatever I think would interest him.

the Lords and the Commons—women and men. Marianne and Fiona were tugging for the Lords' women. They won on two tugs—'even though the Commons cheated'. Lesley and Simon—and Ivor—were there to cheer.

Ivor is continuing to try and pacify Margaret Jay.

The problem of cramming legislation in before the summer recess is swelling: 'Blair wants to get landmines through. The only way we can do that is to leave out the minimum wage. Blair has told the House of Commons it won't be sitting in August ... we may be sitting in August.' I stiffen. 'But not for long.'

Tuesday, 23rd June

I go and see my favourite doctor about my back. There are no magic solutions.

The door opens at my first swipe. It is becoming boring. I shall stop talking about it - unless it goes wrong. I think I've made my point.

Chris Smith gets on to Ivor. He can't manage NESCO (I think) without Melvyn Bragg who gets on to Ivor. He can't manage the House of Lords with NESCO - he wants to give the House of Lords a year for him to get to grips with it.

'It's refreshing,' says Ivor, 'to hear someone saying that. I told Chris Smith and Melvyn Bragg we'd do what we could to help.'

It doesn't sound to me as if Melvyn Bragg wants Ivor to help.

'Our problem is finding things for our back-benchers to do ... after about a year they realise all they are is lobby fodder. And most of the time that is exactly what they are.'

The Team is being 'very protective'. The Tories have asked for a debate on reform of the Lords, in July. The Team is not keen: 'What possible reason have they got for it except to embarrass you around the time of a reshuffle?'

They'll have the debate after the shuffle.

Ivor had lunch with the *Financial Times* who was full of political gossip about who's in and who's out in shuffles. He said Derry was 'a disaster waiting to happen.'

Ivor and the FT agreed that Blair had never been tested. He's never faced adversity. He's never lost anything. He's taken risks (Clause 4) but nothing that's gone wrong.

'As I said to Peter Mandelson at the time of the leadership election, I'd support Blair but I would prefer Brown. I think there's more steel there.'

I told him today's tale of New Deal.

'That's not what we're told,' he says, 'we're told it's working.'

'It's not working in Lambeth.'

I wrote my ALS Annual Report today. My remaining task is to produce a booklet of literacy worksheets for our New Dealers. It is not encouraging to be asked to do something that you believe nobody will ever look at.

Friday, 19th June

The mouse poison is undisturbed.

I do not go to work. I don't have anything to do if I go. I write this.

Saturday, 20th June

We get new saucepans for the first time since 1974. And we watch the mice.

Sunday, 21st June

William is at the Science Museum with Sara, Florence and Harry (who was the new baby) and Ivor is getting into the *Sunday Times* in the backyard.

'Look at this!' He is most interested to read that Hague has no intention of supporting the hereditary peers and the Tories are putting together a proposal for a reformed House of Lords.

'Cranborne will be furious!' say I.

'If there's any truth in it ... I might write him a little letter,' says Ivor.

'He'll deny it.'

'In that case we'll have his letter,' contradicting his party's policy.

Remaining in the backyard, among the mice, Ivor has a germ of an idea: he could start questioning the Tory peers' method of finding themselves a leader.

'What is it?'

'He's appointed.'

'By Hague?'

'Yes.'

Ivor was elected in opposition by the other Labour peers.

Monday, 22nd June

The door opens at my first swipe.

Write out my timetable for next year—time taken: five minutes.

Ivor returns from the Tugs of War. Every year there are tugs of war between

Wednesday, 24th June

Jones The Pictures rings from the house. They have no electricity. My capacity to do much about it is limited by being in London.

William and I go to the dentist. Then I take William to school, then I come home to sort the laundry before going to Lambeth College. Jones The Pictures rings. They still have no electricity.

I get to work to find Bob-My-Boss relieved—he has been told 'they' are not tinkering with the Study Centre after all.

I get home to find a mouse that has eaten the poison. Unfortunately it is taking a long time to die and because I am tuned to be careful with rodents (we have gerbils and a hamster) I fail to do the kindest thing.

Ring Jones The Pictures. The electricity is back. I can hear sheep down the telephone and feel housesick. The sheep have been allowed in to mow the field and Jones The Books is attempting to contain diarrhoea round the house with a bucket of water and a scrubbing brush. That should keep him busy.

Ivor saw Robin Cook about the UN, Chevening and the Sudan. Captain Husband was helpful when Cook got married—shielding him from the press. But Robin Cook does not think much of the accountant—he got a bill for £1,000 for staff overtime.

'You shouldn't pay that!' said Ivor.

'I didn't think I should,' said Robin Cook.

For every £100 worth of aid that goes to the Sudan, £90 of it is going on transport. Helicopters have to be hired from Kenya. It's the only way to get the food in.

Thursday, 25th June

Get to Lambeth College to find Bob-My-Boss apoplectic. He has read that 'they' are tinkering with the Study Centre after all. 'They' have pinned up a 'Description of Works' while nobody was looking. I am apoplectic to read 'Remove and cart away existing carpet floor covering' which went down less than two years ago and has hardly been trodden on since. Even Derry's carpet was older than that. Wonder if I can cart it away. We could do with it.

'They' ring Bob later and tell him the Study Centre has to be emptied by the end of next week. Apoplexy rubs shoulders with amazement.

Ivor is early to put on a Black Tie for a dinner.

'Well ... we saw Blair about the reform of the Lords. There's a distinct chilling of the feet. He doesn't want the row. He's a short-term person. He won't take a long-term view. It may well not be in the Queen's Speech.'

'That puts you in an impossible position.'

'I'd have to resign. Your diary would make some money and I would get my wig out. I've done it before. About five times.'

William offers Ivor bubble-gum.

'I told Blair I thought I could still get a deal—but it would have to be on Two Thirds elected, One Third nominated terms. He said, "We'd have to think about that." He told me to flush the Tories out. Flush them out! I can't negotiate with them if I haven't got a mandate. He said, "Look at that mess you got into when you made that speech." I said I didn't think it was a mess. I thought it went down rather well. He doesn't like what I'm telling him ... he doesn't hear what he doesn't like.'

'If you resigned over this,' I reckon, 'you'd have practically the whole of the Labour Party—the Government—on your side.'

'It'd be a big row—I'd take it to Cabinet.'

And Ivor disappears to his dinner. While he's away I think this through.

I do not believe Blair will back out of the manifesto commitment. He may not like doing it but that is not the same as not doing it. And the Labour Party would not be on his side.

The last time Ivor was in the middle of such fraught crossroads of negotiation was in 1976 when he chaired the Geneva Conference on Rhodesia. He had the white Rhodesian factions, the black Rhodesian factions, a US secretary of state who got swept off into US elections ... the only faction that wanted a settlement enough to get one was the British Government. Another 30,000 people were killed before there was the will for a settlement and Zimbabwe came into being.

If these negotiations fall apart no lives are at risk.

When Ivor returns around midnight I give him the conclusion of my think-through. I tell him I think perhaps he was a bit hysterical.

He tells me that he was introduced at dinner as the man who had been addressing the Tory peers earlier in the day 'like a cat playing with a lot of very frightened mice'.

'If only they knew!' says Ivor.

He also says that The Team still think the thing can be rescued and they are putting together a piece of paper to Blair ('Again!' say I) to suggest announcing an all-in-one reform in the Queen's Speech: a Royal Commission at the same time as putting the hereditary peers on hold for the duration.

'I suppose I'll plod on. Try and see this through,' he said.

'Blair wants you to magic a solution out of a hat—like a rabbit,' say I. 'I'm sure you're right about his cold feet. But not about what he's going to do about them.' I plunge around in metaphors when I express my think-outs.

Tell Ivor I was interested to read in yesterday's *Times* that Downing Street insists on seeing every piece of policy paper, goes through it, fiddles with it and creates a last minute panic.

'That could just be right,' says Ivor.

Friday, 26th June

As it is Friday and I have more to do at home than at work I stay at home. I am sorting toys (I spend quite a lot of my life sorting toys) when Ivor rings - shall I go over to lunch?

I go.

All is quiet. Charles Williams is having a cigar with his port overlooking the river. Jane Williams is better.

I come back. I continue sorting toys. Whatever I do, their number increases in a tidal wave of wooden, plastic, paper, metal, perspex ... bits. They crunch under the feet. Occasionally somebody skids on something (marbles!) ... the dog suffered acutely walking on Lego. Then there was the time Ivor trod on the machine gun ... Ivor survived. Action Man besets us with a houseful of bits all by himself: his accoutrements include daggers, gloves, swimming flippers, masks, space gear, belts ...

Ivor gets back from the end of his working week. Damien rings at once: he has heard that the Tory Reform Group are bringing out a think-pamphlet recommending the end of the hereditary peers and a one third nominated, two thirds elected chamber.

No wonder Cranborne has, I'm told, being going around 'like a bear with a sore head' - rather than 'a rat in a trap'.

I quiz Ivor on where he thinks this government's cracks will first appear. It depends on Tony Blair's relations with Gordon Brown and those policy advisers ...

Saturday, 27th June

I drove to Gwen's new home near Cambridge. She has decided she cannot manage on her own and has sold her house and moved herself into a nursing home. She has two rooms which she is filling with her own furniture and possessions.

Sunday, 28th June

We are putting roast chicken on the table when Damien rings: watch television at once: the Tories' plans to reform the Lords. Cranborne's head must be getting sorer.

Monday, 29th June

Bob has been given two days to pack up the Study Centre. He has one hundred yellow plastic crates to pack it into. I pack up my two drawers into half a shelf of 'my' cupboard by 'my' desk in 'my' staffroom upstairs and throw away trees' worth of paper. Bob is told the Study Centre works will be finished by 24th August.

I reminisce: it is the third time I have done this in four years. In 1994 I packed myself up in Vauxhall and went to Norwood, leaving a cupboard and a desk in Vauxhall and taking two filing cabinets and a cupboard with me. In 1995 I took a year's unpaid leave and packed everything away wherever it was. In 1996 I was not wanted in Norwood so I abandoned everything there and retreated to Vauxhall ... here I am packing again in 1998.

At least I'm down to half a shelf.

I put together my workbook for New Dealers. That takes an hour.

The centre of Ivor's day has been drafting a letter to Blair about reform of the Lords. The papers are interested in the division among the Tories.

A semi-detached Tory peer came in to tell Ivor he would like to join the Labour Party. His main problem is his wife. It would help, he tells Ivor, if Blair could have them to 'one of his dinners' so she can see that he is a Real Person. Ivor explains that he has never been to 'one of his dinners' himself. So the semi-detached Tory peer is another who believes that Ivor (and Blair too) spends his evenings in political eating and drinking sessions from which they are excluded. The reality for Ivor, and I would guess for Blair, is they spend every evening they can tucked up with their families—especially if they have children at home. Their political eating and drinking sessions are the official/working dinners they cannot avoid ... heads of state ... of EU ...

Far better to break your bread among children who are bored by politics, complain about politics and want you to focus on the politics of their playground, their classroom, their squabbles, their bedtime ...

England is playing Argentina tomorrow. The Lords have a three-line-whip tomorrow. Emily Blatch is breathing fire over university fees.

'Won't you have trouble with everyone wanting to watch the football?'

'Yes - everyone except Emily Blatch.'

Ivor's outer office was riveted to Germany playing Mexico.

'Who are the enthusiasts?'

'Chris ... Simon ... Of course Damien is not interested in football at all ... they were making a terrific noise supporting Mexico ... then it all went quiet.'

'Did Germany win?'

'Yes ... I've got a big new television in my office ... I suppose they can watch it there tomorrow.'

Tuesday, 30th June

One or two of Bob's 100 yellow plastic crates have been packed. I perch in a corner. Now that my Lambeth Life is packed on to half a shelf upstairs all I can do is my own thing.

Driving to fetch William from school I see the Evening Standard's head-line: 'BLAIR'S HOPE FOR THE ARTS'. Mine too.

Ivor has finished drafting his letter to Blair.

We eat in front of the beginning of England v Argentina. Then Ivor is hounded out of his house by Emily Blatch who cannot be watching the World Cup because she is forcing votes. The Labour peers are massed in front of a big screen in the Moses Room which they will leave when a division bell sounds. Ivor rings me during the penalty shoot-out and we watch it togeth-er over the phone.

England lose.

Wednesday, 1st July

Many more yellow plastic crates have been packed. I pack some too. We must have packed 70.

I go upstairs to check on my half shelf.

'Janet ...'

'Yes?'

My colleague keeps her back to me. She too is packing. She is being sent to Clapham.

'We've got to be out of here by Wednesday.'

'Er?'

'Everybody's coming over from Brixton.'

'But I'm not moving anywhere ... this is my cupboard ... with my things in it.'

'That cupboard's been allocated.'

'It's my cupboard! What about my desk?'

'It's been allocated.'

'Perhaps I'd better go and sit in the corridor.'

'I'm sorry to tell you all this ...' (I don't believe her) 'your name wasn't mentioned when the room was being allocated.'

My cupboard and my desk and their contents suddenly look too vulnerable to leave for a moment. I make four labels the size of paving stones:

THIS CUPBOARD (+ CONTENTS)
BELONGS TO JANET JONES
July 1998

I stick them on each visible surface of my cupboard. I make one label for my desk and stick it on.

I go and find my colleague's boss who has been doing all this allocating.

'Yes,' she says, 'you'll have to be out of there in 24 hours.'

'Where to? The corridor?' She shrugs.

I go back to my desk and pack its paltry contents into my cupboard. I return to my colleague's boss to tell her I've packed 'as much as I can' and I will try and find somewhere to move to. I am at my most obliging. I find Danny the Study Centre Supremo sitting with her at her desk. He is Bob's boss - and thereby mine too.

I tell him I've been given 24 hours to move and I would like somewhere to move to.

'She's not moving,' says Danny the Study Centre Supremo.

'Yes, she is.'

'No, she isn't.'

'Yes, she is—she's moving upstairs as you said at the meeting last week.'

'No, I didn't.'

'Yes, you did.'

'No, I didn't.'

'I,' I interrupt 'am the meat in the sandwich here. I'll take myself off and you can let me know what's happening.' I return to my cupboard, my desk and my colleague and I advise her that the situation is unclear—not to say acrimonious. I inform her that my cupboard and my desk will remain where they are until things become clearer and calmer. I resolve to check on them every day. I retreat to the Study Centre to mop my brow. About eighty yellow plastic crates are packed. The packing has stopped.

The packers are doing nothing.

It transpires Danny the Study Centre Supremo has been to see them (that must have been on his way to tell me not to move) to tell them that A Final Decision Has Yet To Be Made. There may be no building works after all. In which case we are to unpack our 80 yellow plastic crates. Unbelievable.

No wonder education is so expensive. All those hundreds of yellow plastic crates (my friend in Norwood has taken delivery of 500). All the time spent packing. And unpacking. And going nowhere.

Students keep trying to come into the Study Centre to work. We send them away. All the computers have been put in yellow plastic crates—jammed in upside down, side ways ... whatever whichway. Danny the Study Centre Supremo is having a meeting at 11 a.m. (that must have been the one that got off to such a bad start with me as the meat) at which A Final Decision will be taken.

We continue to sit around doing nothing. Learn that all the building works in the School of Construction have come to a halt because nobody can find the maps of the electricity supplies to the workshops. They are thought to have been thrown away when the Inner London Education Authority ceased to exist and the building ceased to belong to them.

Bob comes in. We tell him what is happening—or not happening. He laughs: 'Somebody else made that joke to me this morning!' Some seconds pass before he is persuaded that it is no joke.

'I shall be really angry if ...' That is strong language for Bob. Bob decides to 'put his head into' the meeting. He brings it out again without a decision.

We decide to go to the pub. It is called 'The Surprise'. Bob leaves a note on the Study Centre door saying where we have gone. Tensions are running so high he spells it wrong. Danny the Study Centre Supremo comes and finds us in 'The Surprise' two and a half hours after his meeting started. A Final Decision has not been made. The tenor of the meeting cannot have improved after I left it. There is a SMT (Senior Management Team) meeting at 2.p.m. A Final Decision will be taken there. Why have a meeting to take a decision if you do not have the authority to take a decision? Plus ca change, plus c'est la même chose.

SMT is The Throne, The Power, The Finance Director and two A.N. Others.

We finish our drinks and go home.

I write this.

I mutter the while.

Unbelievable.

You have to laugh.

It is so sad.

The waste...

Will I be packing or unpacking tomorrow? Moving or not moving? Or waiting for A Final Decision?

I regale Ivor with all this at the end of our day.

'Then,' he says, 'you will be interested to hear that David Blunkett's decided to put more money into FE rather than HE. '

'No!'

'He thinks he's an expert on FE.'

'He may be ... outside London. But in London ...'

'You can't tell him.'

'Perhaps I ought to see him.'

'He wouldn't believe you.'

'He can come along and count the crates if he wants to.' I think of the mahogany that is being thrown out ... the acres of nearly new carpet ... the hours spent in meetings that go nowhere ... And the students who are sent away, if they ever come.

Ivor recognises The Tale of the Cupboard. When he first got to the Lords he had half a coat peg.

Ivor has seen Derry about the letter to Blair. Derry does not approve—'but of course you can write to the Prime Minister if you like ...' 'then go swing ...' Ivor finishes the sentence. Ivor also saw Jonathan Powell about the reshuffle and the Lords.

'What shuffling?'

'I don't think much is necessary—just Simon Haskel who is excellent, excellent, but can't handle the despatch box.'

'So Jonathan Powell is beginning to realise you know something about the Lords?'

'He asked for another list of peers.'

'Will he take any notice of it?'

'He said he's "beginning to understand how Tony works—you put something to him and nothing happens", "It festers", I said, and he said "something different comes back that you don't recognise."'

Jonathan Powell also told Ivor: 'You shouldn't take what Tony said the other day too seriously.' About reform of the Lords.

'I told you,' I said, 'he doesn't want to do it but he knows he's got to.'

'And he wants me,' said Ivor, 'to deliver—he doesn't want a row.'

'Who can blame him? I'm sure he's simply passing on his own anxiety about the whole thing.'

The good news from Jonathan Powell is that John Prescott ('he is sensible') has decided he needs one less minister in the Commons and one more in the Lords. It is interesting that Jonathan Powell is 'beginning to learn' how Tony Blair works. I expect Tony Blair is beginning to learn how Tony Blair works too. Jonathan Powell, Alastair Campbell and Peter Mandelson are closest to him and, Ivor believes, those three get on among themselves—'which is good for Blair'. But there is endless jockeying for position among the 150 or so fiddlers who work in Downing Street.

The final amusement of the day is that some Tory peers have started a campaign to Preserve an Independent House of Lords. They are appealing for money. Even the Telegraph does not take it seriously and reports that Some Tory Peers have denied that it is a Campaign to Preserve the Hereditary Peers. Just like jam. Some jam jar.

Thursday, 2nd July

I get into Lambeth College early and sit among the yellow plastic crates in the Study Centre to write this. Bob comes in after an hour and takes the message on his mail box. A Final Decision: get packing.

Three of us pack. I do the labelling. By midday the 100 crates are full and everything, from the clock to the telephones, is labelled. We are waiting for more crates. We go to the Chinese restaurant and discuss Lambeth College and then Death.

Bob has learnt that there is no penalty clause in the contract with the builders for the building works ... he asked The Throne why not. The Throne said it would be too expensive.

The Government is continuing to lose votes in the Lords and the Government, (alias Ivor) is enraged that the Liberals are siding with the Tories and aiding the Government's defeats. He 'stormed' into Bill Rodgers and John Harris ('it wouldn't have happened if Roy Jenkins was still there')—'Sit down, Ivor.'

'No.'

'Calm down, Ivor.'

'No.'

'Have a drink, Ivor.'

'I'm not drinking tainted liquor.'

'But we're right, Ivor,' said Bill.

'You've been in politics long enough, Bill,' said Ivor, 'to know that that is not the point.'

I tell Ivor he had better get used to it because there are going to be plenty more Government defeats in the Lords and 'It's not worth having a heart attack over'.

'I'm not daft. It's a good idea to get angry sometimes.'

Friday, 3rd July

I go down to Norwood to its final party before it is abandoned. Nothing is happening. Nobody is there. Acres of brand-new carpet. A brand-new creche. Brand-new furniture. I meet one person on the stairs after half an hour. We chat. She has given up and is going for good. When I decide to go home a few more people are drifting in.

The Downing Street Policy Unit—the Fiddlers—have been fiddling with Ivor's letter to Blair. He's been letting them get on with it and will do what he wants afterwards.

Saturday, 4th July

William and I join our annual picnic of neighbours-with-children. It is in Dulwich.

Sunday, 5th July

William parties in Dulwich again and Ivor and I take ourselves to the Dulwich Picture Gallery. Then we sit in the sun and discuss the cracks that are showing quicker than expected—it was last Friday, the 26th, that Ivor foresaw Trouble with the Fiddlers. Today *The Observer* is 'exposing' a 'cash for access' scandal and naming one of Downing Street's fiddlers-in-chief as part of it. (The one of whom Ivor said he was not quite sure what he did when we saw him outside La Traviata.)

'It is all these unelected, unaccountable people' I say.

'Yes' says Ivor.

Damien rings about going on *Today* tomorrow.

Monday, 6th July

Ivor goes on *Today*, today—soon after the presenter has reported on the fiddler's plight. The presenter's professionalism must be strained as I believe he's quite fond of the fiddler—we've watched them watching fireworks together with their children. I've always had time for the fiddler too—from my neighbourly perspective he's an asset.

Ivor and Cranborne have a spat. I think Ivor is a bit of a sledgehammer to Cranborne's nut. But I do have my prejudices.

The spat is about fees in Scottish universities.

I get to Lambeth College and get a shock. The Study Centre has been stripped. Stripped bare. There is a light on in a far corner and a few loose sheets of paper lost on the floor ...

I go upstairs. My desk is buried under somebody else's files. My cupboard is lost in a crowd of yellow plastic crates.

Colleague tells me she's heard I'm being moved 'upstairs'. Further upstairs that would be. I tell her that I have not heard that.

'It's like wading through treacle,' says Lesley to Ivor of the difficulties they're having Getting Things Done.

'I've got Pat MacFadden at one end ... Derry Irvine at the other and the Prime Minister ...' says Ivor of the people who obstruct his work. That's within the Government. Pat MacFadden is Downing Street's policy adviser on the constitution—from Ivor's point of view he is Fiddler-in-Chief. And he wants a 100 per cent nominated chamber and anything Ivor suggests he finds fault with ...

The Tories are insisting on their debate on reform of the Lords and, Ivor suggested, they have it after the Government's green paper comes out in the autumn. No, said Blair—in other words there was fiddling in between Ivor and Blair. Ivor is told he has to focus on the wider picture. He has no idea what the wider picture is.

Tuesday, 7th July

The fiddler who talked still has a job—according to the news.

I go in to Lambeth College and check my cupboard upstairs.

'You're being moved upstairs.' My colleague who is sorry to tell me these things tells me again. I revisit my cupboard before I leave.

The Government is defeated again on university fees.

We have dinner in the Lords with Colleen and Merlyn Rees.

Merlyn asks about Cabinet meetings.

'They're a farce,' says Ivor. 'A farce. Nobody says anything.'

'Doesn't the Foreign Secretary say anything?'

'Not really .. Ann Taylor says a little piece about Commons' business. I say a little piece about Lords' business. Blair asks if anybody wants to say anything. Nobody does. Sometimes Blair says a little piece. It's all fixed up in advance. I'll give you an example: My Cabinet Committee decided to have the House of Lords' reform debate after the green paper. Then over the weekend the Prime Minister overturned the decision. Said we had to look at the whole picture. Whatever that is.'

'It's all changed,' said Merlyn. 'When did it change?' He absorbs this vision of a silent cabinet. 'None of them know how to do it. None of them have been there before.'

'And,' says Ivor, 'he's getting cold feet about reform of the Lords.'

'He can't do that,' says Colleen.

When we get home I ask Ivor what is the point of having ministers if they are not allowed to take decisions.

'Someone has to run the ministry. You have to have ministers. But it is President Blair.'

I think I am getting a cold.

Wednesday, 8th July

I have got a cold.

I go down to Clapham to the end of year ALS meeting.

'You can't go there!' says Security as I start towards the Study Centre (they have one in Clapham too).

'I've got a meeting.'

'It's all closed off through there.' There are builders and sand and evidence that building might be happening. I see someone I know and mention Danny the Study Centre Supremo.

'Danny?' 'You might catch Danny through there. He was in the boardroom.'

I go 'through there'. I find a lot of new furniture and only two yellow plastic crates. I see The Throne walking across his office. I see The Power talking in her office.

'Through there, is awash with Management.

Danny the Study Centre Supremo appears: 'Meeting? What meeting?'

Others appear from Vauxhall but none from anywhere else.

I go back to Vauxhall. I read the in-house magazine. There are so few New Deal students that Lambeth College has given up trying to provide for them outside what is provided for everybody else. I check on my cupboard. It is all forlorn.

Ivor finishes his day forlorn too. The Tories are not going to vote out the Government next time. The Liberals are. Ivor got on to Jonathan Powell who is getting on to Paddy Ashdown.

'Co-operation with the Liberals!' says Ivor. 'Like hell.'

Thursday, 9th July

My cold is getting richer.

I go to Lambeth College and find my upstairs staffroom. It is full of plants. I am encouraged.

I buy all sorts of cold cures on my way home. I watch people going home from the office opposite. Some are in shirt sleeves and T-shirts. Others are in winter coats. This elemental confusion does not help colds.

Peter Mandelson 'looked worse today than I have ever seen him. I asked him if *The Observer* had got more.'

'Heaps. Don't read it.' In a two hour meeting he spoke two sentences.

There is rising tension at the prospect of a constitutional crisis in the to and fro between the Lords and the Commons over the Education Bill. There could be no legislation to cover the paying of university fees this autumn. Jonathan Powell told Blair who told Paddy Ashdown (who is in France) who told Bill Rodgers who told Ivor: 'Blair lied to Ashdown!'

'?'

'He said there could be a constitutional crisis!'

'There could be.'

Friday, 10th July

William and I fly to Aberdeen.

Ivor sounds tense on the phone from London.

Sunday, 12th July

The Observer's 'heaps' are nine pages. I can't find anything I haven't found before.

Monday, 13th July

Wind and rain. William and I and my Oldest Friend's son carry flowers to the cross at the roadside where she died on March the 18th. We carry more to her grave.

Tuesday, 14th July

William and I fly south.

Ivor and Cranborne 'do a deal' to get the Education Bill through.

Friday's tension was because the Government was preparing to declare a state of emergency in Northern Ireland. To do that the Privy Council has to meet and that was arranged for Saturday at Windsor Castle.

Ivor mutters that there is a Government Reception for ministers and their spouses at 10 Downing Street tomorrow evening.

'The whole Government?'

'Yes.' (I learn later from Denis Carter that The Whole Government is 120 ministers.) 'I suppose it's just in time to say thank you before he sacks them. I hope he doesn't sack too many. Do you want to go?'

It may have been noticed that I do not usually want to go but if this is the one chance of my life to see inside Number 10 Downing Street I shall regret it if I miss it.

I say I would like to go. There is a pause.

I sometimes forget that it usually suits Ivor that I do not usually 'want to go'.

Wednesday, 15th July

Tony, replacing John, drives us up to Downing Street. I walk on pavement I have not walked on since about 1958 when my grandparents took me to see The Door. This time I go through the door into a big Georgian house which smells of its wooden panelling like any other Georgian house. There are stairs to the public rooms which are impersonal with chandeliers and portraits. I notice William Pitt, the Younger.

Male ministers have been allowed to bring unmarried daughters—as if to a Buckingham Palace garden party—which widens the variety of people.

There is orange juice and water and wine and bits: a prawn and a piece of green pepper; smoked salmon on rye bread; hard-boiled quails' eggs in pastry.

People stand around and talk to people they already know. They do not circulate. They have to be asked to move further into the room—to stop them huddling in the doorway. The tension is high. Who has got the job who wants? Who has got the job who does not want? Who is there for the last time before they lose their job? Who will be shuffled in? Who will be shuffled out?

Fear. Ambition. Tension. Aggression. Under a veneer of orange juice and chat.

Meet the Robin Cooks and enquire after Captain Husband.

'Have you met him?' I am asked.

'Oh no – but he rather haunts us. I wondered what he was like as a person.'

'He's very nice to your face ... and then goes away and writes horrible letters to the Private Office,' says Mrs Cook and Mr Cook regales his neighbour with the story of Captain Husband's House-for-Life on the Chevening Estate.

'You'll have to do something about it,' says the neighbour.

Robin Cook squares his chest. But he knows there are limits to what the Foreign Secretary can do.

There is the sound of a pair of hands clapping. The Prime Minister is standing on something. I can't see what it is.

'He wants to speak,' I say to Ivor.

'That's why we're all here,' says Ivor to me.

The Prime Minister is careful to direct what he says to Everybody and to Nobody.

'I'm sorry I'm late but I've been with the Queen.' He pauses. 'Don't worry. I'm not going yet.' Little laughter greets this. Too many people would love him to go if it gave them a chance. Anyway, laughter might not be the 'correct' reaction. 'This is my way of thanking you all for all the work that you have done over the past 12 ... 14 months ... I've been going round the departments ... the civil servants ... thanking people and we have made a difference ... one of the things I've learnt in Government is how long it takes from taking a decision to it taking effect ...' Ivor nods, 'The next two or three years are going to be hard. We are going to have some hard and difficult times ... The Public Spending Review ... the Opposition don't know how to oppose it ... but we can have public spending and enterprise ... and with them and with esprit de corps I am sure we can do well.' These do not sound like the words of a man who is about to sack everybody he is talking to. He stands down. There is some clapping. Nothing too enthusiastic. Some surliness - a manifestation of Feeling Awkward ... and some nodding. I notice Nick Brown, like Ivor, is a nodder. I also notice Cherie Blair with a fixed smile and eyes careful not to meet other eyes ... it is lonely when you are surrounded by people watching for a sign of a favour or spurning.

Then we left, passing Alastair Campbell on guard in the doorway armed with his mobile phone: a 21st century sentinel to a 21st-century leader.

There was a spare table at the third restaurant we tried to get into and we ate fish together.

Thursday, 16th July

Read David Blunkett is giving plenty to FE to fund thousands of student places. Where are those students? We can't find them in Lambeth.

CRP H of L met today. That is the official title of the loggerheaded

Committee. Lesley and Simon know it as Crap House of Lords.

'I got all I wanted out of my little committee today.'

'What was that? '

'Two detailed papers.'

'And? '

'A Royal Commission.'

'Does everybody on the committee agree with you now?'

'Oh, yes - it's just a question of when we remove the hereditaries and no Royal Commission will recommend keeping them so we might as well do that straightaway. A Royal Commission is the best way of getting at least a partly-elected chamber. As I have been saying for five ... seven years.'

So the Queen's Speech will remove the hereditaries and set up a Royal Commission. The Commission will report in 18 months to two years, in time for the next parliament. So the next election manifesto will carry The Royal Commission's reformed second chamber.

'Could you be asked to chair the Royal Commission?'

'No. I'm too committed.' Ivor has got his eye on Roy Jenkins to do that— 'if he's got time.'

'It'll be difficult for Blair to ignore your committee,' I realise.

'Yes. But he could have cold feet.'

Ivor is voting late again tonight. Denis Carter says they have to open the drinks cupboard in Ivor's office. Roy Hattersley is in the car park and sees the lights on and people moving about so he comes up to see what's going on.

'When did you last see him?' I ask.

'About three weeks ago. He knows what I think of him. He's very bitter. Especially with Kinnock.'

'Why?'

'When Kinnock resigned he did it all without consulting Hattersley.'

'People don't have friends in politics.'

'Not many.'

Ivor also spent some time talking to Helena Kennedy who had not voted with the Government on the Education Bill.

'But it was wrong,' she said.

'Of course it was wrong,' said Ivor, 'that's not the point. The voting was not about the issue. It was bigger than that. It was about relations between the Commons and the Lords. How many times can the Lords throw legislation back at the Commons?'

My cold is still with me.

Friday, 17th July

We are awake by five because today is the day William's class is taken to France. As we assemble by the coach at the roadside I learn that some children have been up all night with excitement. You don't go to France for the day very often, especially if you're eight years old.

We wave the coach off into a grey damp morning. We come home and make coffee and Ivor says that the ship could sink, the bow doors could stick, the coach could crash—but the chances are that none of those things will happen.

I go down to Lambeth College and work on this and check my cupboard.

I go into the Support Office as it is called, to look in my pigeonhole. Everybody has new pigeonholes. Except me. I have no pigeonhole at all. I go upstairs. My cupboard has gone. My desk has gone. I go further upstairs. My cupboard and my desk have not arrived. I sit among the plants and work. On my way out I spy, along a corridor, a lone desk and a lone cupboard. They are mine! I leave them there and wonder where they will be the next time I pass by.

At my own desk, at home, I read the John Donne that my Oldest Friend has left hanging on her kitchen wall in Aberdeenshire:

'No man is an island, entire of itself;
Every man is a piece of the continent, a part of the main.'

I sat at her kitchen table to copy it out and have brought it back with me because I was not sure I had it here. And if I haven't: I can't find it to check the punctuation and the lines.

She was killed four months ago tomorrow.

The traveller returns from France. Unlike many of his fellow travellers, he has not been sick.

Sunday, 19th July

The Observer has nearly given up on the fiddlers.

Ivor and I spend most of the day cutting over-growth out of our backyard. There are forsythia and jasmine killing everything else. The mound of pruned over-growth soon overtakes the backyard and I carry loads over the road to our dumping ground.

'Is anyone watching you?' asks Ivor, every now and then.

'I don't know, I'm too busy to notice,' I reply, with more irritation each time. End the day well scratched and with thorns in my thumb. Ivor remarks that if we are chased up about our Garden Waste when I have left London and he is plodding on at the Lords (they have to get Landmines through before the recess) he will say, 'My wife did say she took a few twigs over ...'

Monday, 20th July

Sun! It is hot for the first time since May. Our shorn backyard lets in more sun than got in before.

I do laundry and put it outside to dry for the first time this summer. I still have a cold. I go to Sports Day. I am instructed not to enter the mothers' race: 'I still haven't recovered from when you humiliated me two years ago.' (I came last.)

I notice that 'a few twigs' are making their presence felt at the roadside.

Ivor, when he comes in, has noticed 'a few twigs' too.

He is oppressed by the House of Lords. It is the worst time of year with too much legislation and too little time.

Planet 54, the newest of New Labour Peers, wants to make his maiden speech on the lowering of the homosexual age of consent but he has a Personal Interest and has not been a peer for much more than five minutes and Ivor has told Denis to stop him.

'He will make an arse of himself.'

Simon, whom Jonathan Powell wants in Downing Street is rumoured not to want to go. It is said the atmosphere is Not Good: relations between the civil servants and the fiddlers are Positively Bad—Richard Wilson may be managing OK but the rest of the civil service (among whom Simon would number) are in tricky positions and it is Not Nice. Ivor is not sorry that Simon is rumoured not to want to go.

Tuesday, 21st July

I get my hair cut. There is near-tropical rain. There is plenty of wet laundry hanging around our basement. And there is plenty of gossip in the papers about a cabinet reshuffle. The papers claim to know far more than cabinet ministers. Ivor has no idea if his two hours with Jonathan Powell (Simon Haskell is the only necessary move in the Lords) will have any effect. Though, as Ivor learnt in those two hours, Jonathan Powell has no idea if his time with Blair will have any effect either.

When I am picking William up from school I see the part-time-music-teacher-cum-accountant-cum-computer-buff and I ask him if Lambeth College is going to throw away its computers to the school.

'I can't believe it,' he says.

'They are?'

'We're getting sixty—and the servers for nothing and the cabling—we spent two hours looking at them last week—fifty pounds each—Lambeth College had told me they were giving them away—and they told me they are getting 345 new machines! ...'

I don't quite believe it either.

Ivor is in Swansea for the night. He's getting an honourary degree in the morning. I ring him up to say goodnight and can tell from his staccato grunts that the phone is in a public place. 'I've seen lots of people I know,' is his longest sentence. Ivor was having such trouble leaving the House of Lords and its precarious votes to get down to Swansea that Lesley tried to get him a helicopter. Downing Street was 'not keen'.

Wednesday, 22nd July

Go into Lambeth College for the last time this summer. My cupboard and desk remain in the corridor. I have no pigeonhole.

Ivor gets caught in The Age of Consent: The Lords don't want it and Ivor, who does want it, finds protestors milling near his car so he stays in his office and watches: 'They won't know that I'm one of those who voted in favour.'

We eat at 10.30 p.m.

SUMMER *1998*

Thursday, 23rd July

William and I drive down to the house. The tadpoles have become froglets. There is no bull in either field.

Friday, 24th July

Ivor rings: 'This place, (the Lords) is full of rumour, full of rumour.'

The heart of the rumour is that Everybody believes The Reshuffle is to be on Monday and Nobody knows who is going to be shuffled and Everybody is rumouring to Everybody and Nobody knows Anything.

'What's the evidence?' I ask.

'Well ... there is a piece in the FT ... Damien has talked to Milliband'

'What did Milliband say?'

'He made some equivocal remarks.'

'Then, he's not sure of anything either.'

'He is close to Blair.'

'But Blair's the only one who knows and he may not have decided anything yet ... and isn't Damien a bit of a flapper?'

'Yes.'

'And doesn't he lose his job if you lose yours?'

'Yes.'

'That's why he's in a mega-flap.' Unless he's superhuman.

'I may be out of a job on Monday.'

'We've had this conversation thousands of times before.'

'I've been sacked before.'

'Well the bow doors may stick, the coach may crash ...'

'Milliband told Damien I'm too much in favour of an elected House of Lords.'

'That's what Milliband thinks. I thought Blair chatted to Jenkins.'

'He does. Jenkins is even more in favour of elections than I am.'

'Then Jenkins would not approve of you being sacked.'

Ivor is called away from the phone for the third time while we are trying to talk to each other. He goes.

I think this through and can only see Panic and Jumble.

Ivor rings back and I go through what we know that is free from rumour:

1. Blair's words to the Government last week were not the words of a man about to sack the people he was talking to.
2. Blair does not like rows.
3. Blair knows the danger of making enemies.
4. Sacking people is one of the best ways of making enemies.
5. Blair decides things on his own.
6. There is no evidence that Anybody knows Anything.

The local news is not good: local farmers' incomes went down by an average of 79% last year, compared to a national average of 49%. When Ivor tried to cheer Denis as Lords' business wobbled by saying, 'Think of all your lovely, contented pigs!' Denis told him that pig prices were at their lowest for over 20 years.

When Ivor gets off the train from London he is more agitated: 'Denis is talking to Jonathan Powell.'

'What about?'

'If he wants to discuss a reshuffle in the Lords.'

'Isn't that just stirring thing up even more?'

'No. It's perfectly sensible. It's perfectly sensible for the Chief Whip in the Lords to talk to Powell about Lords' whips ... when we had that meeting with Powell, he said he'd get back to us about Lords' shuffles.'

'And he didn't.'

'No ... Charles Williams is convinced he's getting a job on Monday.'

'I hope he blames Blair and not you when he doesn't.'

'It's going to be a Bad Weekend.'

'As far as I can see Everybody is going to have a bad weekend—nobody knows anything—Peter Mandelson will have one of the worst weekends.'

'Yes, things haven't gone too well for him recently.'

We are going through the front door of the house when Denis rings. I answer the phone and he can hardly say his words: 'Denis! It's Janet!'—such is his state he turns himself into me. Denis has spoken to Jonathan Powell. Jonathan Powell tells Denis they are going to 'start with the cabinet and work down ... any shuffles are going to be transverse rather than in and out.'

'Whatever that means,' says Ivor to me.

'It means,' say I, 'that Blair is going to move people about within the Government rather than bring them in or kick them out, it also means that Powell probably doesn't know for sure either.'

'He must do.'

'I doubt it. Blair won't have decided yet.'

'He must have done.'

'I don't see why.'

By the end of the day we are not speaking to each other. In an attempt to fight Hysteria and Time-wasting (as I see it) I have Got Cross.

Much more seriously, our exchange was interspersed by the news that Security came to see Ivor today. Back in May, Ivor's Security Risk Rating rose from Light to Moderate, from 5 to 4. This was at the time of the Good Friday Agreement. If his rating was to move from 4 to 3 all sorts of things would have to happen: special locks, special windows, special curtains. In the meantime, Security would like to come and look at the house in August. That would be The End. We would have to leave. The problem is not the IRA. It is the splinter groups.

Ivor has been given videos which he and I are supposed to watch. This is difficult as we do not have a machine on which to watch them.

'Security seems to know you're not going to be sacked,' I try a little joke.

'They don't know anything about it.' Ivor does not find me amusing. 'But,' he says, 'you can get used to anything. Merlyn had policemen living in his drive for years.'

I do not find that encouraging.

Saturday, 25th July

1. 'If I'm sacked on Monday, I shall tell the Prime Minister what I think of the way he runs his Government.' Pause. 'On the other hand, I probably shan't.'

2. 'If I'm sacked on Monday, I shall write an introduction to your diary.'

3.   'If I'm sacked on Monday, I shall have to earn a living.'
4.   'If I'm sacked on Monday, I'll start The Campaign for The Democratic Lords. I'll speak in the reform debate in the spillover.'

I do not look forward to his happening every year and say so. 'It'll be worse next year,' says Ivor.

Later. 'Blair's only in favour of one thing: getting re-elected.'

'Isn't that partly what politics is all about?'

'It is. But a great deal is going to be sacrificed to that.'

And: 'Some of The Team have been talking of the Nightmare Scenario, from their point of view.'

'What's that?'

'That Peter Mandelson gets my job. Or Ann Taylor. Or Harriet Harman.'

'That'd be crazy..'

'The Lords is a very useful place to put people when you don't know what to do with them.'

'Yes ... but ... Peter Mandelson! That'd really upset the Lords.'

'He wouldn't touch it with a barge pole ...You can put anybody in my job.'

Also: 'Whatever else this is, it's an example of how not to do a reshuffle.'

Sunday, 26th July

7.45 p.m. Downing Street rings. Ivor goes mottled green.

'Hello? Hello? Jonathan. Yes 9.15 tomorrow, the House of Commons. I'll find it. That sounds ominous!'

'Er. No. Wait and see,' says Jonathan.

Turmoil. The last train went half an hour ago.

'I'll hire a car,' says Ivor.

You cannot hire a car without a driving licence. Ivor's driving licence is in London.

'There's a midnight train,' I discover. Who wants to sit up all night on a train?

'I'll take the car,' says Ivor.

'I'm not staying here without a car,' say I. 'I'll hire a car.'

My driving licence is not in London.

My Oldest Friend's family is coming tomorrow.

Ivor rings the local taxi. Yes. He can drive Ivor to London. Yes. Now.

We gobble some supper. The local taxi comes over the hill.

Ivor leaves in the rain and in the taxi.

I suppose Blair wants to discuss ministers in the Lords.

Monday, 27th July

I walk in from shopping to a ringing telephone.

'Out,' says Ivor.

'Out?' say I.

'Out.'

'I'm surprised. I am surprised.' I am surprised.

'He had me in. Richard Wilson was there. He said: 'Sit down. There's no easy way to do this. I want a change.'

'Why?'

'I want somebody else.'

'Who?'

'I have to speak to the person concerned.'

And I stood up: 'As you will, Prime Minister.' And I walked out. It was rather pathetic really. I had my piece of paper on Lords' ministers with me ... when I first arrived Jonathan Powell and Alastair Campbell were sitting at their desks ... wouldn't look at me ... nothing ... so I thought something was up ... It'll be all right if it's Gareth. There'll be problems if it's Margaret. She's not liked. Respected, but not liked.'

'Jim'll be embarrassed,' say I.

'He will.'

'I don't think he liked you,' say I. 'I think it's as simple as that.'

'Yes. And I was too much in favour of reform.'

The sun is out. Water shines in the grass. We play French cricket.

I ring back later.

'They're putting it out that I stood down,' says Ivor.

'Oh.' I say .

'Oh, indeed. The coffee room is in revolt.'

'They'll come round?'

'Of course.'

'Though there'll be some trouble,' say I.

'There will. Though I don't want to ferment it.'

Jones The Business rings. Jones The Books rings. My step-daughter rings.

We find a loose pig. It heads for the road. We worry. It heads for the open spaces. We worry less. Our Local Conservative appears: 'Oh, that's Roamer: She's the tame one. Ivor's out.'

',Yes.'

'Perhaps he'll become a Tory.'

'That's one thing I don't think he'll ever do.'

My Oldest Friend's family arrive. After some while I tell her widower: 'Ivor was sacked this morning.'

How small. A grain of sand on their beach.

Tuesday, 28th July

Jim has written to Ivor and finds him to say what he has written: 'Of course I'm pleased about Margaret. But I didn't see the need for it. Not at all. Not necessary.'

Damien wants to back the Campaign for a Democratic Lords.

'I was summoned to see the Lord Chancellor,' says Ivor.

'What did he say?'

'He wanted me to know how surprised he was. How he'd not said anything about me to Tony. It was nothing to do with him.'

'Do you believe him?'

'No. At least he's got rid of the embarrassment of me.'

'You know too much about him.'

'Yes' Ivor goes on: 'then he asked me if there was anything he could do. I said there was. He was surprised. I told him I'd like to be a recorder. He said he'd make enquires. He made a lot of notes. I expect he'll come back and say it's too difficult.'

Ivor gives an interview to the *New Statesman* in which he says he's afraid the Government will drop the second stage of Lords' reform and not have elections.

He gives an interview to *The Times* on condition it comes out after the *New Statesman*.

Damien is talking to the *New Statesman, The Times* and *Today*.

Thursday, 30th July

'The politics of this is going rather well. I'm rather pleased. The Prime Minister was on the Today show and John Humphreys referred him to my piece in the *New Statesman* ...'

"Oh no!" said Blair. There would be a second stage and a partly elected chamber. So I've flushed him out in three days! We've got it on record. I'm giving another *Times* interview today in which I'll say I'm delighted to have it confirmed, for the first time, from the top of Government, that there'll be a partly-elected second chamber!'

'They can't have realised this was likely to happen,' I realise.

'No. They hadn't thought it through at all. Not at all. We'll see how Alastair Campbell puts a spin on that.'

'Do you think Blair knew what he was saying?'

'No. I don't. He hadn't thought about it.' And 'It'll be interesting to see the Green Paper I was working on for the autumn.'

'See how it's changed?'

'Yes. Simon's already been asking for all the official papers back. Damien's been saying he won't work for Margaret Jay.'

William has learnt how to weigh pigs.

I get *The Times* and understand Ivor's success. He has the main story (in the early editions) and the Government has been put over a barrel: it'll either have to go along with a partly elected second chamber or be seen to do a U-turn.

Ivor met Clare Short in the corridor. She hugged him: 'He's gone mad!'

She hugged him again. He met Gordon Brown: 'I thought you were good.'

He has to go and see the Queen to say goodbye. She has been reading the minutes of the loggerhead committee. They discuss them.

'She was nice to me. She's good at it. She's done it a lot of times.'

Turn my mind to getting another dog.

Friday, 31st July

My car - which has been sitting waiting in London for Ivor to drive it down here - is not working. Ivor helps it to the garage and is told It Is The Carburettor. It may be working by lunchtime.

It is raining.

Ivor rings. He is waiting for the car. He has not forgotten the gerbils. *The Times* has a 'straight-forward' piece on page two informing us Blair has informed us that there will be a two-stage Lords' reform leading to a partly-elected second chamber.

'He may not have meant to say it,' says Ivor, 'but *The Times* is telling us he has.' And so the fiddlers, perverters and twisters between Ivor and the Prime Minister have been circumvented.

Another irony takes the stage. In the losing of his job Ivor gets nearer fulfilling the heart of what he thinks mattered in it.

It may yet be the beginning of the end of New Labour as New Lords cross Old Commons.

Ivor's Head of Chambers rings: 'We're all blaming Derry ... Ivor did all the work before the election … Derry went on earning … we don't understand it … Ivor was by far the most experienced member of the Government.'

'That,' I say, 'may have been his problem.'

'We've got lots of work for him.' says the Head of Chambers.

'Thank you,' say I.

Ivor arrives with the gerbils through rain and darkness.

'You know,' he says, 'as I was leaving Damien said, 'That was a good week!'

Saturday, 1st August

We spend part of the day trying to hang a swing that ends the day drooping from one rope.

'Typical Richard-Jones Construction,' says Ivor.

William is offered the chance of bringing on the runts from two litters. We puzzle out how to house piglets.

Monday, 3rd August

Margaret Jay called Damien in and sacked him. Damien reckons she'd had a message from Downing Street saying they are Not Pleased. Downing Street does not like the Prime Minister being Flushed Out in three days. Damien is delighted.

'It was a good week!' he says.

Thursday, 6th August

There is Bad Feeling here. Ivor is getting more letters than the rest of us. William resents his role as Beast of Burden as he ferries them up the track. It is not, as he points out, as if Ivor was writing more letters than the rest of us.

Friday, 7th August

Ask Ivor if he would read this. 'Over the weekend,' he says.

Tuesday, 11th August

We catch a helicopter to the Scilly Isles.

Wednesday, 12th August

Ivor sees a woman on the Scilly Isles and thinks, 'Doesn't she look like Lesley?' And the woman crosses the road and talks to a man and Ivor thinks 'Doesn't he look like Simon?'

They are Lesley and Simon!

'How's the office?!' asks Ivor.

'Don't ask!' says Lesley.

'Oh, go on—it can't be that bad!' says Ivor.

'It will get better,' says Lesley.

Thursday, 13th August

Back on the mainland at the heliport, we find the car. And in the dust on the back window:

HELLO IVOR! L+S

Friday, 14th August

Ivor has not opened this.

Sunday, 15th August

A bomb kills 28 people in Omagh.

Wednesday, 19th August

A sow is farrowing at the farm. William rings to say he may be late home.

Thursday, 20th August

Our Local Conservative's granddaughter was born at 2.45 a.m.

Ivor reads most of this.

The *World at One* uses Ivor on the UN.

Monday, 24th August

The Study Centre was supposed to be finished by today.

The Government announces its plan to put New Dealers in classrooms as assistants. This has all the ingredients needed to inflame all the problems ... putting the people for whom life has not gone well to care for the next generation.

Tuesday, 25th August

Ring Bob-My-Boss. The Study Centre is as it was. He's been assured it will be finished by Thursday. I will ring Bob again at the end of the week. I have no intention of us all going back to London in order for me to stand around in a building site.

Parliament is being re-called later next week to sharpen anti-terrorism legislation.

'Left to myself,' says Ivor, 'I'm not sure I'd go along with all this'. Merlyn rings and they discuss it.

'Merlyn's never been in favour of internment. It doesn't work.'

Wednesday, 27th August
It would have been my Oldest Friend's birthday.

Thursday, 28th August
Get back to *The Everywhere Chair*.

There are finches in the japonica.